MYTH & MEANING

Head of Zeus. Fourth century B.C.

MYTH & MEANING

James G. Head

Linda MacLea

McDougal, Littell & Company

Evanston, Illinois

JAMES G. HEAD is Vice Principal at Maplewood Vocational School, Scarborough, Ontario. He was formerly Chairman of the English Department at Sir Wilfrid Laurier Collegiate, Scarborough, and has been an Associate Teacher and Lecturer for the Faculty of Education, University of Toronto. He is the author of many reports and articles on education, both theory and practice, and has conducted workshops in mythology and in mass media across North America.

LINDA MACLEA has studied under Northrop Frye and has been a Senior Teacher of English at Sir Wilfrid Laurier Collegiate, Scarborough, Ontario, and an Associate Teacher for the Faculty of Education, University of Toronto. She now teaches English in Athens, Greece. She has spent many summers in Greece pursuing her main interest— mythology.

Editorial Direction: **JOY LITTELL**

Research: **JANET ELLIOTT, SARAH SWARTZ**

Design: **WILLIAM A. SEABRIGHT, PAMELA KIMBALL**

Maps and drawings: **MAURICE SNELGROVE**

Acknowledgments: See page 253.

ISBN: 0–88343–299–4

Contents

To the Reader

This book will come as a pleasant surprise: it respects your intelligence. As a matter of fact, it assumes that you are not only interested in good stories about our ancient past but also that you realize there must be more to them than just strange tales of fantastic people.

Myths are not mere short stories. They are a unique form of literature which often serves a variety of functions. Myths must be explored on their own ground, at their own level. *Myth & Meaning* creates a basic framework for this exploration.

Myth & Meaning does not attempt to be inclusive—it cannot be. It demands that you extend yourself by reading other material or by further pursuing problems that interest you. It asks you to explore ideas and concepts —to test your powers of logic and imagination and to come up with answers that satisfy the conditions of your analysis. The book assumes, therefore, that you will look for parallel situations with which you are familiar and will see in them similar situations (or questions) that affect your own life.

Myth & Meaning provides a new understanding of mythology while at the same time offering a bit of comic relief. No subject is so serious or sacred that it cannot be laughed at. And on that note we will end, for we know that once you get into this fascinating subject of mythology, you will enjoy . . . .

Jim Head

Linda MacLea

Part 1

ΕΝΑΙΑ

GREEK MYTHOLOGY

Conception

Throughout history, the religion of each cultural or social group included an explanation of how the world was created, how people came into being, and just what their relationship to their creator was. In the Norse myth, the world was created from the body of a god; the Iroquois Indians believed that the earth was created through the labor of several animals. In Norse mythology, men and women originated from trees and were brought to life by the gods; the Chinook Indians believed people were created by a coyote who then taught them the art of farming.

In return for this gift of life, the human race owed respect to its creating spirits or gods, and each society developed rituals of worship in order to ensure the creator's continued goodwill. The influence of these gods was great: everyday existence and the laws of the society were governed by them. By praying and offering appropriate gifts, humans believed that good fortune would follow. Conversely, if misfortune struck, it was a sign that humans had insulted the gods or were in some way out of favor with them.

Because the creation myth has existed in every culture, we must conclude that it springs from a basic human need. Just as a child needs answers to satisfy his unquenchable curiosity, so early people needed something beyond themselves to explain a confusing universe and their presence in it.

The need of each society to produce a creation myth is obvious; the question which now concerns us is why the actual accounts are so very different. For instance, there is quite a difference between the Norse myths about gods and their relationship to humankind and the Greek myths on the same subject. It seems to be clear that the kinds of accounts that any particular society created are a reflection of that society's way of life. The kinds of stories told will give us tremendous insight into the people who created them. Since our study in this section is of Greek mythology, we are going to discover a great deal about how the Greek mind worked and also about life in ancient Greece. This should be of particular interest to us because so much of our Western culture stems from our Greek heritage.

Preceding page: Athena and Poseidon. Detail from Greek vase painting, Ca. 540 B.C.

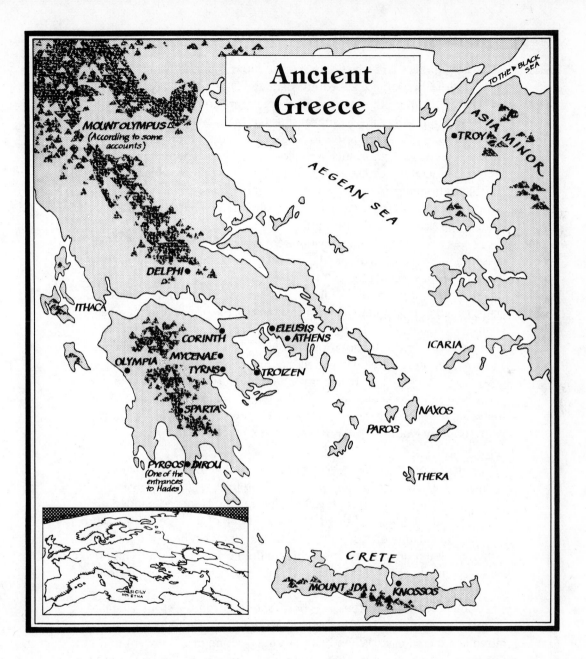

Ancient Greece

MOUNT OLYMPUS
(According to some accounts)

TO THE ► BLACK SEA

ASIA MINOR

● TROY

AEGEAN SEA

DELPHI ●

ITHACA

● ELEUSIS
● ATHENS

● CORINTH

ICARIA

OLYMPIA ●
MYCENAE ●
TYRINS ●
● TROIZEN

NAXOS

PAROS

SPARTA

THERA

PYRGOS ● DIROU
(One of the entrances to Hades)

SICILY
MT. ETNA

CRETE

MOUNT IDA △
● KNOSSOS

3

The Creation of the World

In the beginning, there was Chaos. Everything was in confusion and darkness. Out of Chaos, there appeared Night and Depth (Erebus).

From the union of these two elements came Eros, which was Love and the most significant figure to appear thus far. Many words come from this name. Erotic is one and it refers to sexual love in our modern sense. But the Greeks did not see Eros in such a single-minded way. To them Eros represented a principle of *order*. They believed that it was Eros which was capable of bringing an ordered universe out of Chaos. In its role as a principle of order, Eros performed the first marriage by bringing together Uranus, the sky, and Gaea, the earth.

Gaea and Uranus had many different types of offspring. When discussing a marriage of such grand dimensions as that between the earth and the sky, we must accept the extraordinary. Gaea gave birth to monsters called the Hundred-handed Children. She also produced huge, one-eyed giants called Cyclops. Perhaps her most famous offspring were the twelve Titans, who were huge giants, and in whose image human beings were later created. Uranus did not prove to be an ideal father. He was jealous and afraid of his children. He feared that his children might try to usurp his power and attempted to solve this problem by burying them alive in the earth. Naturally, Gaea was very unhappy with this and plotted with Cronus, the youngest of the Titans, to overthrow Uranus. Cronus, with his mother's help, seriously wounded Uranus with a long, curved knife, and became supreme ruler.

Once in power, Cronus began to worry that he too might be overthrown as he had overthrown his father. Therefore, as a safety measure, he released only the Titans from the earth, leaving the Hundred-handed Children and the Cyclops buried. He married one of his sisters, Rhea, and together they had twelve children. But mindful of what he had done to his father, he determined that none of his children would ever usurp his power. He therefore ate each child as it was born. Rhea determined to save one child.

When her last son, Zeus, was born, she fed Cronus a stone wrapped up in a cloth and sent Zeus in secret to Mount Ida in Crete where he was raised in a sacred cave. When Zeus became a young man, he went to his father's court disguised as a page and fed him an emetic. This caused Cronus

4

to regurgitate all of his eleven children—fully grown. Naturally, the children were only too willing to aid Zeus against their father, and a war developed.

Zeus and his forces established their headquarters on a high mountain called Mount Olympus. His main allies were his brothers, Poseidon and Hades, and two Titans, Prometheus and Epimetheus. Zeus also released the Cyclops on condition that they would aid him. After ten hard years of fighting, when it seemed first one side would win and then the other, Zeus was finally victorious.

Zeus divided the world among himself and his two brothers. Zeus became god of the sky and the upper world, Poseidon became god of the sea, and Hades became god of the underworld. Other brothers and sisters received favors as well. Although Zeus was generous to his allies, he was merciless towards his enemies. Atlas, a Titan who had fought for his brother Cronus, was forced to hold up the world for all eternity. Atlas was not the last person to discover that going against the will of Zeus would result in horrible punishment.

Now that you are familiar with the Greek creation myth, consider some of its implications.

We have seen that the Hundred-handed Children and the Cyclops were buried alive in the earth. On first reading, the monstrous form of these offspring and their fate may seem childish and laughable. But consider: this account is one of the earliest of the Greek stories and is an attempt to *explain* the earth. What sorts of natural occurrences do you think the movement or anger of these children could explain?

There is an interesting footnote to the story of Cronus. We have a modern English word that comes directly from his name—chronology, the science of computing time. In Greek, *Chronos* means time. Therefore, it would seem that Cronus is Time or that he brought into the world the idea of Time as opposed to Infinity. It is interesting to note that our figure of Father Time, as he is depicted at the end of every year, carries a sickle (a curved knife). Many people are aware of this figure, but very few realize that the idea originated from the Greek creation myth.

Since these myths were made up by a society which had only its own experience to draw on, the resulting stories reveal something about that society. By examining the way in which Cronus and, later, Zeus took power, what conclusions can you draw about life in the ruling classes in Greece at the time?

We must also deal with the problem of whether the Greeks actually saw these gods as enlarged humans or as abstract ideas. If one looks at the myth closely, it becomes obvious that the gods became more "human" as the story progressed. It was easier to see Zeus as a human-like figure than Gaea, even though Gaea was often given human motives. Perhaps we must accept the fact that it is just natural for a human when discussing the earth and sky—clearly non-human forms—to humanize them. After all, human reason is the means by which we comprehend.

6

Genealogy of the Greek Gods

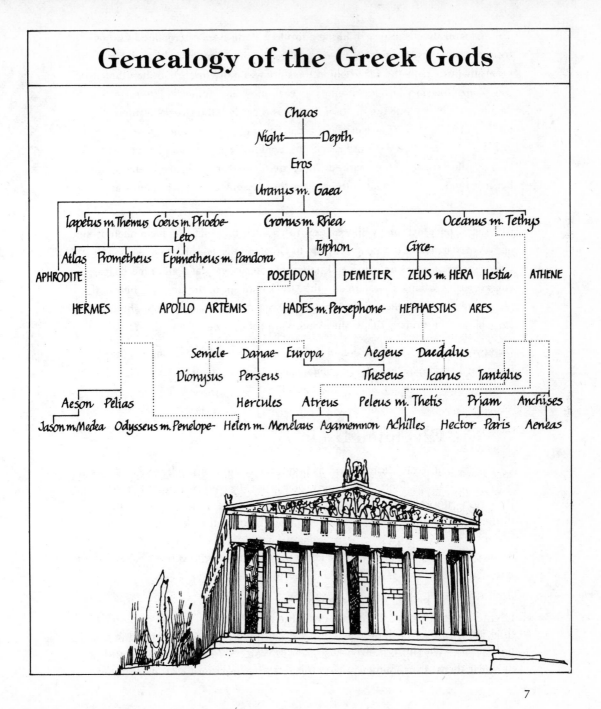

Chaos

Night —— Depth

Eros

Uranus m. Gaea

Iapetus m. Themis   Coeus m. Phoebe   Cronus m. Rhea   Oceanus m. Tethys

Leto

Atlas   Prometheus   Epimetheus m. Pandora   Typhon   Circe

APHRODITE   POSEIDON   DEMETER   ZEUS m. HERA   Hestia   ATHENE

HERMES   APOLLO   ARTEMIS   HADES m. Persephone   HEPHAESTUS   ARES

Semele   Danae   Europa   Aegeus   Daedalus

Dionysus   Perseus   Theseus   Icarus   Tantalus

Aeson   Pelias   Hercules   Atreus   Peleus m. Thetis   Priam   Anchises

Jason m. Medea   Odysseus m. Penelope   Helen m. Menelaus   Agamemnon   Achilles   Hector   Paris   Aeneas

7

This humanization is also seen in the effort to put the story of creation into the form of marriages. Marriage was something that the Greeks could understand. It seems that originally the *idea* behind the story was more important than the effort to visualize the story in human terms; an example is the domestic life of Gaea and Uranus. But by the time the myth of Zeus was recorded, the Greeks wanted more human-looking gods. They were larger than life, but they had enough human qualities to which people could relate. It is well to remember that the gods could take on other shapes if they wished. There are many stories of such changes, but because human beings created the stories, they imagined the gods mainly as superhumans.

Although Greek mythology may be new to you, words which you have been using in everyday conversation relate directly to Greek myths. For instance, when you view a scene of utter confusion and state that you cannot stand all of the chaos, you are really making a reference to the Greek concept of the universe before the gods were created. If the people who named ocean liners had thought about the story of the unfortunate Titans, they would not have named a ship the *Titanic*.

Using your knowledge of the creation myth, account for the meanings of the following: *geography, geophysics, geology, erotic, atlas, olympic.*

The Olympian Gods

Our study of the creation myth has taken us to the point where Zeus was supreme ruler and living on Mount Olympus. His two brothers, Hades and Poseidon, helped him rule the world. Their areas of authority were the underworld and sea, respectively, while Zeus ruled the sky. There were nine other very important Olympian gods and goddesses who also had specific areas of control. These twelve Olympians directly affected the destiny of the world.

ZEUS   Zeus, because he had led the fight against Cronus, was the most powerful Olympian god. His major symbol was the eagle. When he was depicted in drawings or described, he was constantly linked in the Greek mind with this mighty bird. If you read the newspaper or watch television, you should not be surprised at this. Think of the symbol of the President of the United

States, for example. The presidential seal labels the eagle "President of the United States." Of course, we know this is not to be taken literally, but the association between that high office and the mighty powers of the bird is being stressed. Think of all the comments about the President and the American people that this association with the eagle makes.

The Romans used the eagle as a symbol of their power and might. The fact that the Greeks chose this bird to symbolize their chief god should tell you how powerful and frightening they considered him to be. An eagle suggests not only power, freedom, and strength, but also cruelty and sudden death to its prey. And Zeus too was capable of cruelty and harsh vengeance.

The other object constantly associated with Zeus, which suggests his more harsh and vindictive side, is the thunderbolt. He was often portrayed carrying his own thunderbolt, made by the Cyclops, ready to be hurled at any god or mortal who was foolish enough to arouse his anger. We see remnants of this symbol in our society in comic strips like B.C. and in remarks people make such as "I was thunderstruck at the news." If you remember that Zeus was the sky god, it should not be difficult to figure out how the Greeks came to associate Zeus' anger with thunderbolts and under what particular weather conditions they knew that he was somehow angry.

The Nazi party in Germany adopted the eagle as its symbol. Why?

What does America's national symbol, the eagle, tell the world about us?

Zeus was notorious for his many adventures in love. Look up the ingenious methods he used to seduce the following women: Danae, Leda, Callisto, and Europa.

POSEIDON

There are not as many stories told about Poseidon in Greek mythology as there are about Zeus or Hades, but that does not mean he was unimportant. If you take a look at a map of Greece, it will become obvious why the Greeks built many temples to Poseidon and were careful never to offend him. His symbols were the horse and the trident, a spear with three prongs. He had total mastery of the sea and all of the sea creatures.

Odysseus found out at his own cost that it did not pay to offend this god. After the Trojan War, Odysseus was foolish enough to dishonor Poseidon. For this folly, Poseidon made the seas so rough and the naval disasters so numerous that it took Odysseus eleven years and help from some of the other more sympathetic Olympian gods to get home.

Where do you see the trident today representing the sea?

Two famous horses were associated with Poseidon: Arion and Pegasus. Compare Poseidon's involvement with their birth with some of Zeus' amorous affairs.

HADES

Hades is a fascinating figure in Greek mythology. His domain was the underworld where the dead spent eternity. The Greeks did not have a Christian concept of Heaven and Hell. Everyone who died went to an area in Hades. Some suffered terrible punishments for their evil deeds on earth, but others suffered no pain except the terrible knowledge that life was denied them and that they would exist as shadows forever. All in all, it was not a very happy place and even Hades tried to alleviate his boredom, as we shall see in the future story of Persephone. Hades' symbol was a dark cloak which made him invisible. He was associated through this symbol of the cloak with the power of darkness. The name of the underworld was the same as that of its ruler.

Pegasus, from a
Corinthian coin,
325-308 B.C.

Why do you suppose the criminal element in a society is called the underworld or that crooked business deals are called "shady deals?"

What other words can you think of that can be associated with Hades and the Greek underworld?

Account for the fact that Hades was so often associated with either the color black or invisibility.

10

No mention of Hera has been made so far, but she was a very important goddess. She was Zeus' sister and his wife. Hera's character is best suggested by the symbol that the Greeks had for her, the peacock. Have you heard the expression "proud as a peacock"? Like the peacock, who struts and shows its feathers, Hera, too, was proud of her beauty and spent a great deal of time trying to ensure that her husband thought she was the ultimate beauty. She constantly tried to destroy any maiden whom Zeus admired. There are many stories about Hera punishing Zeus' loves and of Zeus inventing ingenious ways to avoid detection. Zeus was the original hen-pecked or, more correctly, peacock-pecked husband. Many mortals were to suffer as a result of Zeus' and Hera's domestic quarrels, since Hera had a great deal of power herself.

To find out more about Hera's vindictive personality and pride, look up the stories of how she punished, or tried to punish, three of Zeus' mortal lovers: Io, Semele, and Alcmene.

Hera competed in the first beauty contest, a contest which was to result in the Trojan War. The prize was a golden apple and, naturally, she applied all her wiles in an effort to win acclaim as the most beautiful woman. Read accounts of the cause of the Trojan War to find out what happened.

Demeter was another sister of Zeus. She was very important to the Greeks because she was the goddess of grain and of all other crops. Her symbol was a sheaf of wheat. The fact that the Greeks worshipped Demeter as much as they did should tell you something about a very important aspect of Greek endeavor—agriculture. The Greek countryside is harsh and mountainous in many places. Growing crops was a difficult task in the best of times and failure meant death. Since it was believed that if the crops did not grow the goddess was displeased or unhappy, people were always careful to offer Demeter sacrifices of the most choice grains, honey, and sometimes, animals.

Even though society has become industrialized and it may seem to many city people that vegetables grow in cellophane, Americans still incorporate a very important ritual into each calendar year in order to thank their God for having

provided crops. **Look up the story of the origin of Thanksgiving and see what connections you can make between it and the Greeks' worship of Demeter.**

ATHENE

Athene was the daughter of Zeus. There are various theories about who her mother was, but it was not Hera. The account of her birth is very strange. In order to protect her from Hera's wrath, Zeus took the unborn child from the mother and placed her in his body. The story goes on to say that Athene was born from Zeus' forehead.

Again we see that, taken literally, these stories seem foolish, but taken symbolically they make sense. Athene was the goddess of wisdom. She was esteemed by the Olympian gods and by mortals to such a great degree that there are hardly any disrespectful stories about her. In this sense, she is unique among the Olympians.

What aspect of the Greek value system is revealed by the fact that Athene was so generally respected?

The great city of Athens named itself after this goddess. Look up the story of why the Athenians chose her as their patroness over Poseidon, who wanted the position. It's an interesting story and it tells us something about the Athenians' wisdom.

One of Athene's major symbols was an owl. Explain this.

APHRODITE

Aphrodite was the goddess of love. There are many accounts of her birth, the most famous being that she rose naked, and fully grown, from the sea. Another account suggests that she rose from the blood of Uranus after he was wounded by Cronus. In later accounts, Zeus claimed her as his own daughter, although Hera was not the mother.

Aphrodite was the most beautiful of the goddesses, another fact that did not endear her to Hera, and was patroness of all lovers. She represented sexual love and the principle of unity and peace. It is interesting to note that her symbol was a white dove. In our society, the white dove symbolizes unity and peace. The Greeks delighted in telling stories about Aphrodite, a fact which again tells us something about the Greek personality.

12

The Olympian Gods

GREEK NAME	DOMAIN	SYMBOLS
Zeus	father of gods and mortals; father of the sky; protector of family and strangers	thunderbolt, eagle, oak
Poseidon	lord of the sea	trident, dolphins, horses
Apollo	sun god; god of prophecy and music; god of healing and purification	chariot, lyre, laurel
Ares	god of war	armor, dogs, vultures
Hermes	herald of Zeus; conductor of the dead; protector of merchants	winged cap and sandals, caduceus
Hephaestus	god of fire; the smith	anvil, hammer
Hades	god of the underworld	cerberus, cypress dark cloak pg. 10
Hera	consort of Zeus; goddess of women and marriage	peacock, pomegranate
Athene	goddess of wisdom and war	breastplate and aegis, owl, olive
Demeter	goddess of agriculture	sheaf of wheat, poppy
Artemis	queen of the chase; goddess of woodland and wild creatures	hunting weapons, stag, crescent
Aphrodite	goddess of love and beauty	myrtle, dove

Aphrodite was the winner of the beauty contest mentioned previously. The judge of this contest was Paris, a mortal. What does the fact that he chose Aphrodite over both Hera and Athene suggest about the Greek attitude towards women?

We have some modern words which relate to this goddess. "Aphrodisiac" is one. Look this up and see if you can connect its meaning to what you know about Aphrodite.

APOLLO

Apollo, the son of Zeus and Leto, a mortal, had many areas of control. Many temples were built to him all over Greece and Asia Minor. Perhaps his most important function was his control of the sun. As a sun god, each day he drove the fiery chariot across the skies in order to light the world.

As a youth, he had learned to be a wonderful musician. In fact, he was so good with his lyre that he had only to play it for Zeus or anyone else who may have been angry with him and their anger would disappear. Because of his great skill, he became the patron god of musicians and all arts.

Apollo was famous for one more important facet of Greek life. He began the shrine at Delphi, which all noble Greeks consulted to foretell the future. Apollo's connection with this important shrine is a long and involved story. The following account is merely a summary.

As a child, Apollo wounded a sacred python which had been sent by jealous Hera to kill his mother. The python escaped to Delphi, where Gaea lived, and sought shelter in Mother Earth. Apollo came there and killed the python. To appease Gaea, he built a shrine in which a priestess sat over the chasm where the snake had been killed. By inhaling fumes from the chasm, she was able to prophesy future events. Since the prophecies could always be taken two ways, the priestess was never wrong! Apollo then soothed Zeus' anger by playing music for him. Zeus expiated the crime by holding games at Delphi once a year—the Pythian games.

Why do you think Apollo's position as sun god would make him so honored by the Greeks?

It was mentioned that Apollo was the patron of the arts. Greek art is still considered the best in the world by many experts. The Greeks loved beauty and proportion. Artists would often dedicate their work to Apollo or pray to him for artistic help.

When someone achieves excellence in any field today, we often say that his reward is his "laurel." The greatest poets in England, chosen to write for the nation, are called "Poet Laureates." This is interesting because a branch of the laurel tree was always associated with Apollo in his role as patron of the arts. Roman generals were crowned with the laurel after victory. What association were they hoping their people would make?

The stories about the Delphic oracle are numerous and entertaining. Read up on this aspect of Apollo's function yourself. Be sure to look for illustrations of Delphi. It is a beautiful site and even today it seems that there is something sacred in the very air which surrounds it.

ARTEMIS   Artemis was Apollo's twin sister. She was the goddess of the hunt and of virgins. Because of this last duty, she was in many ways a counterpart to Aphrodite. All young maidens prayed to her. Her most important symbol was the bow and arrow because of her love of the hunt. Hunters would all pray to her as well.

There are many accounts of men falling in love with Artemis, but she refused all of them. Look up the story of Artemis and Orion. This story was just as popular in ancient Greece as modern stories of ill-fated love are today.

Twelve Olympians, from an early fifth-century relief. Left to right: Demeter, Hermes, Aphrodite, Ares, Persephone, Hades, Hera, Poseidon, Athene, Zeus, Artemis, Apollo.

HEPHAESTUS   Hephaestus was the son of Hera and Zeus. Perhaps this god explains why Zeus chose to have most of his other children by other women. Hephaestus was a cripple and the butt of many cruel jokes among the gods. One of the more famous jokes was the fact that the gods married Aphrodite to him. This is Olympian malice at its worst. Aphrodite despised her husband and ridiculed him at every opportunity.

Hephaestus did have one talent, though, for which the gods paid him homage. He was the artisan of the gods. He could fashion beautiful armor and jewelry in his huge, fiery forge. When the gods needed his talent, they were willing to overlook his bad temper and his infirmity.

Some of Hephaestus' inventions were works of pure genius. Investigate the properties and uses of the following: the invisible net and Ares; the crown of Ariadne; the fatal necklace of Harmonia; the shield of Zeus.

HERMES   Hermes was the messenger of the gods and was indispensable to them because of their constant commerce with each other and later with mortals. His symbols are well-known to modern society. Anyone who has looked at a florist's window is aware that Hermes had wings on his shoes and helmet.

A more unusual symbol of Hermes was the caduceus, a sword with two snakes wound around it. There are many opinions as to what this means. It is thought that Hermes was probably borrowed by the Greek people from Eastern religions and put on Olympus. It seems his origin was earlier than the main Olympian gods and the caduceus is a remnant of this earlier prominence. The sword is said to represent power and magic, and the two snakes, wisdom. In the earlier religions power and wisdom were thus shown to be closely associated. But by the time the Greek religion was established, Hermes had been demoted to a messenger.

Explain the presence of wings on Hermes' feet and helmet.

Why do you think the medical profession today uses the caduceus as its symbol?

ARES   Son of Zeus and Hera, Ares was the god of war. As such, his favorite animals were the vulture and dog, who followed him on his many wanderings. It is

16

significant that although all ancient cultures had a god of war, for the Greeks he was not a favorite figure. Even the Olympians did not like him.

There are few myths involving Ares in any great detail, although he is a constant companion of Aphrodite and weaves in and out of fights and wars, as does his sister Eris (discord). His sons were Deimus (terror) and Phobos (fear), and he was the father of the fierce female fighters, the Amazons.

The Greeks constantly wished to humiliate Ares. The two stories for which he is most famous (being trapped in a net by Hephaestus, and his many shameful defeats during the Trojan War) show the Greeks' lack of respect for this unpredictable personality.

Many words come from *Phobos*. Look up the meaning of the following: *acrophobia*, *claustrophobia*, *cynophobia*, *nyctophobia*. What others do you know?

Although the Greeks were often involved in battle, they and the Olympians did not respect Ares. What does this tell us about the ancient Greeks?

Look up the story of Adonis to discover Ares' role in his death.

This completes the naming of the twelve most important Olympians. A word of caution is in order. The Greek religion did not appear in its totality all at once. The hierarchy of gods we have been discussing was the gods who were accepted and revered at the height of Greek civilization. But the stories about gods and goddesses took a long time to evolve. Even at that, there are many different and even conflicting versions.

There are two main reasons for this. One, the stories were not written down at first. These myths were part of an oral tradition handed down by the great poets of the ages. Like any stories told verbally, variations are inevitable and even desirable. A bard in any given area of Greece, telling the story to the nobles of his state, would often include new details which would appeal to the local audience. The fact that several areas in Greece claimed to harbor the "real" entrance to Hades, for instance, is one example of this. So the myths circulated for many generations before the advent of great writers such as Homer, Hesiod, Pindar, Apollonius of Rhodes, and Apollodorus.

The second point is a little more complicated. The Greek people were a combination of many tribes and each of these tribes had distinctly separate cultures and gods. As Greece became more unified, the gods slowly merged into the Olympian hierarchy. This process took a long time, and consequently there are remnants of older beliefs and stories. (See the section on Hermes.)

Dionysus

All religions undergo a continual process of change, often incorporating older beliefs or including newer ideas as society changes. Even after the Olympians were established, new gods or demigods were incorporated into the religion. Dionysus is one such god. He was said to be the son of Zeus, but clearly he was a much older creation than Zeus. He was the god of wine. The fact that the Greeks would insist on his presence indicates how much they appreciated wine. Dionysus was also a fertility god. People prayed to him when they wanted children, and sometimes even if they

Dionysus (center) with Satyr and Maenad, followers of Dionysus.

wanted crops to grow. This all leads back to the idea that fertility and growth were very important to the Greeks. Dionysus, in time, became as important as Demeter.

The Creation of Mortals

Unlike the story in the Old Testament, in Greek mythology human beings were not created by the most powerful deity. Instead, Zeus gave the duty of creating all of earth's creatures to a Titan, Epimetheus. Epimetheus means "scatterbrained," or, to be even more accurate, "afterthought." True to his name, Epimetheus acted on impulse, without thinking ahead.

Epimetheus

He created creatures out of clay and then breathed life into them and gave them whatever powers they needed in order to survive. But Epimetheus' own powers were not infinite. When he was given the task, he was given a limited number of powers to distribute. For the most part, he did an admirable job. To the panther, he gave speed; to the lion, strength; to the elephant, size, and so on. But it seemed that his urge to create exceeded his supply of powers. Epimetheus decided to create an animal which would be in the image of the gods. But what a pathetic creature this was in comparison to the other animals. This creature had no powers for survival in a world full of far more powerful animals, nor was he immortal like the gods.

Without an advantage over other animals, mortals could not survive. Epimetheus was simply not the person to solve this problem and if it had been left to him, they would have had a very short history. Fortunately, Epimetheus' brother, Prometheus, meaning "forethought," kept watch over his rather impulsive brother. When he saw his brother's creation, he wanted to save it because it resembled the gods.

Prometheus

After some thought, Prometheus decided that these poorly endowed creatures needed the gift of fire, that only this gift would enable them to compete in the world. But Zeus guarded the sacred fire, and would not give such a wonderful power away. Therefore, Prometheus stole the sacred fire from Mount Olympus and gave it to mortals.

When Zeus discovered the theft, he was furious and chained Prometheus to a rock. Every day an eagle ate his liver, and every night it grew back so that the torture could be repeated. This was Prometheus' reward for his gift to mortals.

As you have probably already gathered, a story in which two characters are named Forethought and Afterthought is not to be taken entirely literally. This story has hidden meaning and explains quite a lot about mortals and their powers. What do you think fire represents?

What connection does intelligence have to fire? Quite a lot, if you use your imagination. First of all, consider all the words that relate to light which are used for someone who is clever. What visual picture always occurs over the comic strip character when he gets a bright (ignore that hint) idea? Consider why the association between light and intelligence is a natural one for all societies to make. In fact, this association is found in the Bible. See *Genesis*, Chapter One.) We even update the reference to take in modern inventions. This can be seen in phrases such as "Now, you're cooking with gas."

Zeus was angry that mortals had this power because he realized its worth. Since the fire was sacred and belonged to the gods, this fire or "intellect" could raise human beings to almost the heights of the gods. You might be interested in another universal concept here, the idea of the gods being "above." Perhaps this is why intelligence is referred to as the "higher" power and why one "looks up" to a person of superior intellect.

It is obvious that Zeus,.at first, did not want mortals. But he did see the advantage of having someone intelligent enough to worship him properly. His only concern now was to make sure that mortals could never gain enough power to overthrow him (that old problem for rulers). Zeus set out immediately on a scheme to make sure that human beings, in spite of their intelligence, would never be a serious threat to him. His secret weapon was the creation of Woman.

Zeus ordered Hephaestus to make a beautiful woman, one so beautiful that no man could resist her. He named his new creation Pandora, which means "all gifts." (*That* name has all sorts of associations which we will leave you to ponder.) In order to be sure that his plan worked, he married her to Epimetheus. There was a condition. Zeus gave Pandora a sealed chest as a wedding gift. It was beautifully decorated, but under no circumstances was she to open it. Of course, Zeus knew that this would be impossible for the woman, since curiosity had been built into her character. He also knew that Epimetheus would not watch over her as well as he should.

So, one day, the inevitable happened. Pandora was alone; she could not resist knowing the contents of the box a moment longer and opened it.

Immediately, all of the evils which now exist in the world came pouring out—disease, poverty, greed, lust, and death. Pandora was horrified and hurriedly closed the chest. But it was too late. Forevermore, the intelligence of mortals would be hampered by physical hardships and evil thoughts. Although, in their better moments, human beings might aspire to the position of the gods, they would always be pulled back by their perilous mortality.

The fact that the Greeks saw a woman as the cause of all the evil in the world raises an interesting question. What does this story tell you about the Greek attitude toward women?

It is impossible to avoid a comparison between the story of Pandora and the story in the Bible of the fall of mortals from the Garden of Eden. Read that account and discuss the similarities. Why do you think the similarities exist?

Women have resented the story of Pandora (and of Eve) for a long time. Even in the twentieth century, the notion of women being the weaker sex persists. You might like to debate this issue and think about how this basic attitude has hampered women's fight for equality throughout history.

In many accounts Pandora closed the lid just in time to keep one of Zeus' questionable gifts locked inside. That last gift was Hope. Why do you think this last item remained? What comment on the Greeks' relationship to the gods might that part of the story explain?

Together, the accounts of Prometheus, Epimetheus, and Pandora tell not only how mortals were created but also why they were the way they were. Through these myths we are presented with a concept of mortals who, because of their intelligence, were superior to all other forms of life, and yet who were capable of greed, selfishness, and cruelty beyond anything else seen in nature. Mortals, in effect, had a duality in their personality. They were a mixture of both good and evil. This seems a very pessimistic view, but we must not forget that according to the myth, Hope still rested within human grasp. When we look at this assessment of human beings, we suspect that they really have not changed very much in the last two or

three thousand years. Test this concept of humankind by comparing the Greek view with your own feelings on the subject. Consider the history of humankind if you wish.

Life

All humans realize that there are many phenomena in life which we do not understand. An explanation of our own origin and personality is our first concern. We have seen in the previous section how the Greek myths dealt with this. But there are other aspects of everyday existence which also needed explaining. Human beings were creators—toolmakers and artisans— creating order out of essentially shapeless and disordered materials. It is understandable why, when regarding an ordered universe where everything followed an obvious pattern, they should decide that it was a creation of some higher form of life, that nothing was accidental, and that they were part of some grand design. They looked at nature and saw that it too had life. They tried to explain the laws of nature in a way that was consistent with their understanding of the universe and to understand their role as mortals in the scheme of the cosmos. Just as important, they had to come to terms with their role as moral beings in the framework of an ordered society. By looking at some of the Greek myths which deal with nature and morality, we will see the Greek attempt to answer the questions posed by existence.

The Natural World

When Uranus had been wounded by Cronus, twenty-four giants were born from the drops of blood that ran down his side. After Cronus was de-throned, these giants rebelled against Zeus but were finally defeated in a fierce and bloody battle. Gaea was enraged by the atrocities against her

Typhon
children, and produced a new offspring, the monster Typhon. There are many descriptions of this creature. Some say that from his shoulders sprang a hundred serpents' heads full of fire and brimstone and that he had a voice terrible as a raging storm. Others describe him as a fierce creature with serpent's coils.

Receiving his instructions from Gaea, Typhon charged up Olympus to do battle with Zeus. Zeus replied with his thunderbolts and chased the monster to the borders of Syria. The combat was so fierce that the universe shook when the two attacked each other in bloody battle. Finally, Typhon got the upper hand and managed to grab Zeus' curved knife and cut out the sinews from his wrists and feet so that he could not move. After imprisoning Zeus in his cave, Typhon went off to visit the Three Fates to replenish his strength. They were in league with Zeus, however, and fed Typhon food which weakened him.

Meanwhile, Hermes rescued Zeus and replaced his sinews. Zeus then returned to the battle and pursued Typhon to Sicily where he finally hurled Mount Aetna at him, pinning him to the ground forever. Typhon still tells us he is around when he belches fire or screams in anger at his imprisonment.

This myth is interesting because it reveals some very important "scientific" attitudes. We are told that Typhon is produced by Gaea. Why is this logical?

Explain why the conflict between Zeus and Typhon could not result in death for either.

What word in modern English comes from Typhon?

There are several accounts of creatures and other matter being created from the blood and flesh of Cronus. Look up these accounts and, in each case, try to explain why the myth exists.

There are many other myths which attempt to explain natural occurrences. Look up the following: Charybdis and Scylla, and the Sirens.

In this myth of Typhon, mention is made of the Three Fates (the Moirai). These three sisters were a carry-over from the pre-Olympian gods and were the offspring of Night and Erebus. Look up the function of Clotho, Lachesis, and Atropos.

PERSEPHONE AND DEMETER

Persephone was the beautiful daughter of Demeter, goddess of all that springs from the soil—vegetables, fruit, and grains. Hades had long been in love with Persephone, but Demeter opposed the match because she did not want her daughter to live in the land of the dead. Hades took his suit to

Hades and Persephone in the Underworld.
Interior of a Greek cup.

Zeus. Zeus did not wish to offend his sister Demeter by granting Hades his wish, but he was even less happy about refusing his powerful brother. He therefore merely winked at Hades who immediately chose to consider this as Zeus' consent and returned to Hades to plot his next move.

One day while out gathering flowers, Persephone spied a bloom of amazing size and beauty. As she wandered from the path to pluck it, there was a mighty roar and the earth parted. Out of the great chasm came Hades in a flashing chariot drawn by powerful black horses. Grabbing the terrified girl he placed her in his chariot and fled down the black crevice as the earth closed over them. Demeter heard her cry and rushed to the scene but the fields were empty.

For nine days and nights, Demeter roamed the earth searching for her daughter. On the tenth day, she came to Eleusis, the city where her mysteries were later celebrated, and was entertained by King Celeus and his wife. Moreover, their son, who had been herding his sheep at the time of the abduction, was able to tell her the full story. At once she realized that Hades must have acted with Zeus' knowledge. Demeter was so enraged that she refused to return to Olympus and instead wandered the earth forbidding it to give forth its fruit. Soon all humankind was starving and in danger of extinction.

Only one action was left to the wily Zeus. He admitted to Demeter that Hades had Persephone, and said that her daughter could be restored to her only if the girl had not eaten any of the food of the dead. Unfortunately, Persephone had eaten seven red pomegranate seeds. A compromise had to be reached. Hades agreed that Persephone could return to Demeter for five months of the year, but for seven months, one for each seed eaten, she must return to him. Demeter was so delighted to have her back that she released the earth and it was productive and bright and green. But when Persephone returned to Hades the land mourned her loss and was barren and grey.

This is one of the central Greek myths and is obviously an attempt by an agricultural society to explain the seasonal pattern of growth. In the spring and summer months, the worship of Demeter was an extremely important aspect of Greek life. In the winter, crops did not grow and animals were not born. This myth explains a scientific fact which no god or goddess could alter.

In some accounts of the myth, Persephone ate only five pomegranate seeds. In which part of Greece do you suppose this version originated?

Look at the part Zeus plays in this story. What conclusions can you draw about his character?

The Greek concern for the fertility of the soil can be seen from the type of offerings which the Greeks made to the gods. In some areas it even involved human sacrifice. There are accounts where young men were killed in the prime of their lives and their rich blood drained into the earth to renew it. These very secret rituals were called mysteries, not only because the worshippers were sworn to secrecy, but because the life force that allowed the crops to grow again was a mysterious process that could not be fully explained. This ritual killing may sound strange to us, but the same motive may be seen in the Christian account of Christ's death. His blood too was shed in order that others might live.

For a fascinating account of human sacrifice in ancient Greece, read Mary Renault's *The King Must Die*.

There are many variations of Demeter's wanderings while searching for Persephone. One such story deals with how Achilles, a great hero of the Trojan War, achieved almost complete invulnerability. Read about this aspect of the Demeter myth.

ANIMISM The Greek concept of nature differed quite sharply from our own modern outlook. The Greeks believed in a life force called animism: to them, *all* of nature was alive. There were spirits in everything. Spirits in the woods, in the streams, and even in the mighty ocean existed along with the great Olympians. Those that inhabited the water were called nymphs, naiads, and sprites and were generally feminine; those that inhabited the forests were often part beast, such as the satyrs and centaurs, and were masculine. The many myths about these creatures showed the Greek love for and profound identification with nature.

PAN AND SYRINX One myth which illustrates the ancient Greeks' relationship to nature is the story of Pan. Pan was a god of the woods and forests, and, as his name suggests (Pan means "all" or "every"), was a spirit that was in *all* nature.

26

For this reason he was part man and part animal, having the ears, horns, tail, and hind legs of a goat. One day while Pan was dancing through a sunlit glen he spotted a beautiful maiden with whom he instantly fell in love. Unfortunately, the girl did not find him as attractive and ran from him at once. But Pan could easily follow her and was determined to make this girl love him. The girl came to an impassable stream and, seeing that she could not escape, prayed to the gods to help her. This they did, and she was instantly turned into a bunch of reeds.

Pan was perplexed but, still determined to have her, he cut the reeds and made the first musical instrument—a shepherd's pipe. The name of the maiden was Syrinx, the Greek word for "pipe." Even today, the sad sounds of these "pipes of Pan" may still be heard by shepherds in the mountains.

As a science myth, this explains the existence of reeds and the beginning of music. There are other myths in which people have been metamorphosed (changed shape) into an object in nature. Read the myth of Daphne and Apollo; discuss the primitive science involved.

Explain the origin and meaning of the following words: *Pan, panic, pantheism, panasonic, metamorphosis, animal, syringe.*

ECHO AND NARCISSUS Echo was a beautiful nymph whom Zeus had employed to keep Hera occupied with gossip while Zeus crept away on one of his romantic escapades. Hera eventually discovered this trick and in punishment decreed that Echo would never speak again except to repeat the very same sounds she had already heard. While Echo was wandering through the woods she spied the handsome youth Narcissus and fell deeply in love with him. Since she could not talk, however, she was unable to communicate her strong love for him.

One day Narcissus called out, "Is anyone here?"

"Here," replied Echo, from the woods nearby.

Then, when Narcissus saw no one, he cried again, "Come."

And Echo could only answer, "Come."

Narcissus replied, "Why do you avoid me?"

And Echo answered with the same question. Not knowing what to do, Narcissus said, "Let us come out here." Happily, Echo repeated the words and stepped out into the sunshine. But Narcissus, who was a self-centered, conceited youth, felt he was too handsome for any girl, and quickly rejected her. From then on, Echo gradually pined away out of love for the beautiful youth, refusing to eat and hiding in the dark woods. Finally, only her voice remained, which still exists today.

Narcissus, realizing that girls liked him, and not desiring to be married, did the same thing to many beautiful young girls until at last the gods decided to punish him. Artemis, goddess of the forest, arranged for him to find a clear, silver pool from which he could drink. Looking down as he stooped to drink, he chanced to see his own reflection. Thinking it must be someone else, he desired to touch the person who was so beautiful and then discovered, to his dismay, that it was an image of himself. Try as he may, he could not stop admiring his face. At last, he too pined away and died, whereupon a flower which bears his name sprang up in his memory.

"You think you're the only one around with an identity crisis?"

There are many types of narcissi. One type common in Greece is purple and white. Since it was made from the body of Narcissus, what do you think the purple and white represent?

Knowing what you do about the myth, where do you think the Narcissus grows best?

Why would the words *narcissistic* and *narcotic* both come from this youth's name?

The story of Echo and Narcissus is a "science" myth to explain not only the echo but the presence of the flower. There is a moral involved in the story as well, and this brings us to the second part of the Greeks' concept of the world around them: how people should live in a society where their baser instincts threaten to bring them to destruction. Just as the myth of Narcissus tells us that we should not be egotistic, there are many other myths which tell us how we should live.

The Moral World

MIDAS When the centaurs inhabited the earth, a famous king by the name of Midas ruled a mountainous region of Greece. One day, one of these creatures was found near Midas' palace, quite helpless. The king, being a kindly man, took him in and looked after him for a number of days. In reward for this kindness, Midas was taken to the god Dionysus, who granted him any wish he desired to make. Not thinking, Midas asked that everything he touched be turned to gold. The wish was granted. Midas touched a branch and instantly it became gold. He was so delighted he ran home to tell the wonderful news. He touched a fountain; it glistened gold. He patted his dog and to his dismay and alarm it turned into a gold statue. He sat down for dinner and his knife and fork became gold. Then his food turned into the shining metal and his wine became liquid gold.

Alarmed, he got up and accidentally touched his daughter. Suddenly, to his horror, she turned to gold. Running back to Dionysus, he pleaded for help. Dionysus told Midas to wash three times in a mountain stream to remove the magic and to wash away his greedy desires. After he had done this, Midas was able to enjoy the simple pleasures of life again—his garden, his pets, his food, and his family.

If we look at the myth again, we can see there are a number of good rules that would be useful to anyone. This story is also a "science" myth. Can you explain why the river and gold are associated?

Every society has its share of fools, and the ancient world was no exception. In many ways, Midas was the mortal counterpart of Epimetheus in that he was not so much evil or greedy as lacking in forethought. Look up the other famous story about how Midas got ass's ears. This last story is not only a morality tale but also a "science" myth.

Stories about how instant riches have ruined lives have been told down to the present times. The story of the fisherman and his three wishes is one; *The Pearl*, by John Steinbeck, is another. How can you account for the popularity and persistence of this type of story?

You should not have any trouble now explaining the phrase "The Midas Touch."

DAEDALUS AND ICARUS Daedalus was a skilled craftsman who excelled in all he made, be it in science or in art. It was said that he descended from the great god Hephaestus. On one of his journeys, he landed in Crete and was welcomed by the famous king Minos, for whom Daedalus designed a palace and the complex maze underneath it called the labyrinth. At first, the king was pleased to have such a great craftsman at his court making wondrous new inventions. But one day Daedalus offended Minos by telling his daughter, the princess Ariadne, how to help the great hero Theseus escape from the labyrinth. When Theseus escaped, he took Ariadne with him and consequently Minos never forgave Daedalus.

Minos attempted to imprison Daedalus and his son Icarus in the maze. Though leaving the maze presented no difficulty for Daedalus, he did have to solve the problem of getting off the island. He carefully made two sets of wings out of feathers and finely molded wax so that he and Icarus could flee. Before their escape, Daedalus instructed his son not to fly too high lest the sun melt the wax nor to fly too low lest the waves tear the wings, but to fly a safe middle way. They then easily left the labyrinth and flew into the free Mediterranean air.

At first, Icarus followed closely behind his father. Soon they had left Crete, and the smaller islands of Naxos and Paros, far behind. Then, feeling the rapture of soaring through the air, Icarus began to fly higher and higher until the wax began to melt. Suddenly Daedalus realized that his son was not behind him. Looking about, he spied the drowned body floating on the waves below. Daedalus took Icarus to a nearby island and buried him. The island

and the sea around it are named in his honor. Finally, Daedalus went sadly on his way to escape the wrath of Minos who he knew would follow him.

Two morals for living are evident in this story. The obvious lesson is that one should take the advice of one's father, or, more broadly, one should listen to one's elders. The ancient Greeks took this lesson very seriously. They held their elders in great respect. Compare this attitude toward age with that in our culture.

The other moral, although not as obvious as the first, is just as revealing about the Greek moral outlook. Daedalus told his son to fly "the safe middle way." The ancient Greeks did not believe in extremes in daily living. Everything was to be done in moderation. Many ancient Greek buildings have emblazoned on them: NOTHING IN EXCESS. Consider this idea. To what extent do we adhere to it in the twentieth century? Is it a good idea?

Why is it logical that the poets recounting this story would make Daedalus a relative of Hephaestus?

Look up some of the other stories surrounding Daedalus and find out about some of his inventions.

The name Theseus, the great King of Athens, emerges in the story of Daedalus. The story of Theseus and how he slew the Minotaur is one of the most fascinating tales about the Greek heroes and their deeds. Read the account of the "real" secret of Minos' labyrinth for yourselves. One good source for this is the exciting *The King Must Die* by Mary Renault.

Once a religion or a mythology is established and adhered to in any society, a new element is introduced. In order to ensure that the people in that society adhere to the religion, certain penalties are established within the religion if a person does not. For example, in the Christian religion, people who do not follow the Ten Commandments set down by God through Moses in *Exodus* are doomed to everlasting punishment in Hell. Another famous Old Testament story tells of God's punishment of the ancient people who would not worship him. He sent the flood and spared only Noah. Greek mythology contains such a story as well, and its similarity to the story of Noah's flood is really quite amazing.

DEUCALION AND PYRRHA
After Zeus had been in control on Olympus for some time, he looked down to earth and saw that people were no longer worshipping him as they should. In fact, they had become lawless and evil, neglecting even sacrifices to the gods. According to some accounts, Zeus actually disguised himself as a person and wandered the earth seeking the hospitality of the people. It had always been a custom in Greece that one must honor a guest, but Zeus was treated cruelly wherever he went, except in one house. When he came to the house of a poor old man, Deucalion, and his wife Pyrrha, he was immediately welcomed and given what little they had. Since Deucalion had never neglected to sacrifice and pray to the gods, Zeus determined that he would destroy all people on the earth and spare only this pious couple.

As a result of this decision, a terrible flood was sent. Deucalion and his wife were saved because Zeus had previously instructed them to build a raft. After the flood had abated, Deucalion and his wife found themselves alone in the world. They were very old, and so the problem of repopulating the earth with a new race of people had to be solved by the gods. As Pyrrha and Deucalion were praying to them, Zeus said, "Veil your heads and cast behind you the bones of your mother." They considered for some time what this message meant. Finally Pyrrha arrived at the solution. She realized that by "mother," Zeus had meant Gaea, the earth mother. Surely the bones of the mother were rocks. Therefore, both Pyrrha and Deucalion gathered stones and threw them over their shoulders. All of Pyrrha's stones became women and all of Deucalion's stones became men. Thus, the earth was repopulated by a newer, more pious, race of men and women.

Perhaps the presence of many flood stories in different mythologies can be accounted for by an actual flood which occurred in the fifteenth century B.C. in the Mediterranean area. However, what is more significant is the fact that the flood was seen by ancient people as a god's punishment for people's evil doing. Compare the story of Noah's flood to Deucalion's flood. Is the idea still with us today that terrible natural disasters are a form of a god's punishment for not observing the proper forms of religious behavior?

FATALISM   From these stories about the ancient Greek concept of morality, we have seen that the Greeks valued forethought, moderation, and piety towards the gods. However, one area of morality that we have not yet probed is this: to what extent were the Greeks responsible for their own actions and to what extent were they controlled by the gods? This is a central question in any culture. In our society, we have a tendency to see ourselves as responsible for our own actions. We are "free" to choose the direction which our lives will take and are responsible for our successes and our failures. If people see themselves as ruling their own lives by free choice, they believe that they are capable of "self-determination." But there are certain problems with this view. Do children born in a ghetto or children from a broken home have the same freedom of choice as to which direction their lives will take as does a child with a happy home life and wealthy parents? If you think so, then you obviously believe in self-determination and your view is very optimistic because you feel that anyone can better himself regardless of outside forces or situations.

But if you consider the facts about the ancient Greek way of life, you will realize that the Greeks did not really see themselves as having much self-determination concerning their own destiny. They were fatalists. With the twelve Olympians ever present and ever watchful, the Greeks felt themselves more acted upon than acting. They felt a constant awareness of the power and influences which surrounded them. One of the most powerful examples of this outlook can be seen in the myth of the Moirai.

THE MOIRAI   A Titaness by the name of Themis (which means "law" or "justice" in Greek) was depicted in drawings as always sitting at Zeus' right hand and holding a balance. Very early in the history of the creation, she gave birth to three sisters, the Moirai, or the Three Fates as they are better known: Clotho (the Spinner), Lachesis (the Apportioner, the one who measures the length), and Atropos (the Inflexible, the one who is determined and will not change). These three were in charge of birth and the newborn; the thread they spun was the destiny of each individual. Wherever Lachesis marked the thread, Atropos cut it and that life lived and died within that measured time. And so, mortals had only a certain time in this life in order to achieve their goals, a time predetermined by these three goddesses.

Where do you see Themis depicted in modern times?

Using the above myth as a guide, explain the meaning of the following words: *cloth*, *atrophy*, **and** *fatalist*.

We can see that, to a certain extent, the length of human life was related to justice, but not necessarily a "justice" that was obvious to people. The Greeks did not always understand the reasoning of their gods and in fact considered that their gods were as often motivated by selfishness and greed as by goodness. This attitude reflects a sense of fatalism about people's lives and a sense of uncertainty. In a world where fate and accident constantly upset their plans, the ancient Greeks realized that all they could do was hope for the best and try to please the gods whose decision regarding their lives was final.

Considering the events of the twentieth century, to what extent do you agree with this concept of fatalism?

Nowhere can we see the direct influence of the gods in determining the direction of people's lives better than in Homer's account of the Trojan War. We can examine this influence in the cause of the war as well as in the battle itself.

The cause of the Trojan War did not originate among the mortals at all; it began during a wedding feast on Mount Olympus. All of the gods and goddesses were invited except Eris, the goddess of quarrels. Angry at being excluded, she devised an ingenious plan to promote discord at the festivities. She arrived unexpectedly and placed on the table a golden apple engraved with the words: "For the most beautiful." Immediately Hera, Aphrodite, and Athene turned to Zeus and demanded the prize. Understandably, Zeus wanted no part of the contest and stated that the goddesses should seek the judgment of Paris, a mortal considered to be most just.

Paris

Paris was a shepherd near Troy, but he was really the son of Priam, king of Troy. At his birth, Priam had received a prophecy that this child would destroy the city, so he had left him on a hillside to die of exposure. But a prophecy cannot be altered, and Paris was discovered and raised by a kindly shepherd. It was to Paris that the three goddesses came, each one trying to convince him, by promises of gifts, that he should choose her. Athene offered wisdom and victory in battle. Hera offered to make him the greatest ruler of Asia. But Aphrodite's offer proved the most attractive, for she offered him the most beautiful mortal in the world for his wife. Paris was unable to resist such a prize and awarded the apple to Aphrodite.

Before seeking his reward, Paris first went back to Troy where he was recognized by Priam because he still had several of the ornaments which had been left on the hillside with him so many years before. It was after being made Prince that he discovered that his future bride was to be Helen, Queen of Sparta. There was one problem, however. She was already married to King Menelaus, brother of Agamemnon, high king of Greece.

Helen

Paris pretended to make a friendly visit to Menelaus' palace. Helen, placed in a trance by Aphrodite, immediately fell in love and left with him for Troy, taking along most of the palace treasury. The Greeks demanded Helen's return; Priam refused, and so the Trojan War began.

It is important to notice that at one point, Paris did have a choice. He could choose wisdom, or power, or love. He chose love. Do you think he made the right choice?

Obviously, no matter what choice Paris made, he could not avoid his fate. First, there was the prophecy that he would destroy Troy. A prophecy could never be averted; this was fatalism at its most powerful. Secondly, no matter what choice he made, he would offend two powerful goddesses. The entire war could be said to be the work of Eris and then of Aphrodite, Hera, and Athene. Or, if we look deeper into the cause, we could blame the war on Zeus who, by his refusal to make the judgment himself, brought to the ancient peoples one of the longest and most destructive wars in their history, a war in which the Olympians continued to take sides and to interfere in the battles of the mortals.

The war continued for ten years, during which time Aphrodite constantly plotted on behalf of her favorites, the Trojans. On the other hand, Athene and Hera plotted just as craftily on behalf of the Greeks. In many cases, these goddesses were actually the direct cause of deaths; at times they, themselves, suffered wounds. Zeus tended to favor the Trojans unless Hera insisted, as she did at times, that he side with her. Thus, we have an epic battle being fought, apparently by mortals, but in reality, among the gods. Finally the Greeks, aided by Power and Wisdom, won over the forces of Love, and Troy was destroyed. However, the great heroes on both sides suffered terrible deaths, and it would seem that the only real winners of the Trojan War were the immortal Olympians.

Homer's account of the Trojan War in *The Iliad* is fascinating in itself and a great source of information on Greek mythology. Read one of the fine translations of this epic or, if that seems too ambitious, try Robert Graves' short, but excellent, account of this conflict in *The Siege and Fall of Troy*.

According to historians and archeologists, the Trojan War actually did take place. In fact, Heinrich Schliemann, by following the directions in *The Iliad*, found the site of Troy in Asia Minor. However, it is unlikely that anyone in the twentieth century would be as willing to attribute its causes and events to the Olympians as were the ancient Greeks. The fact that the Greeks placed so much responsibility for the war on the gods of *their* creation rather than on themselves is a telling insight into their concept of a mortal's place in the scheme of destiny. We must go back and remind ourselves that the gods and the myths were created by people in order to understand their place in the universe—to explain the human personality and the mystery of existence. We see from this overall discussion of morality that they did believe in goodness, moderation, and piety, but that deep down, they felt an underlying fear that they were really in the power of harsh and changeable forces which, at any time, could frustrate or destroy them. The best that they could do was to hope and pray.

This attitude toward life, and the role of human beings in it, was recorded three thousand years ago. To what extent has it become outdated in the modern world?

Death

In our Western society, which is basically a Christian culture, the idea of life after death is very well developed. If people have led good lives and have believed in God, then their reward is Heaven and life everlasting. Conversely, if people have been evil and have denied God, their punishment is eternal suffering in Hell. Death is not regarded as the end of existence, but the beginning.

The ancient Greeks had no such idea about death. For them, death meant that the body became a faint and unhappy shadow, wandering in the regions of Hades. In the earliest accounts, Hades was described as being under the earth, but there was no belief that people were either rewarded or punished there for acts in life. Hades was simply a gloomy place where the dead resided—gloomy because they knew that life and its joys were denied them.

Hades, himself, had none of the evil associations of Satan. He merely ruled the kingdom of the dead, following the orders of the Fates, and saw that no one escaped. He did not pass judgments himself, nor did he seem to take any enjoyment in the unhappiness of his residents. Very few stories were told of Hades. He remained as mysterious in the Greek mind as his kingdom.

Given this depressing and gloomy view of "life" in Hades, what value do you think the Greeks placed on life in this world, in spite of its harshness? Would a Christian agree?

The Geography of Hades

The geography of Hades changes slightly from account to account. There are two reasons for this. One, the Greek idea of "life" after death was not a cheerful one and, consequently, it is discussed at times in a very vague manner. The Greeks never referred to people as dead. They were always "the departed ones." But natural reluctance is not as significant as the second reason, that the landscape of Hades changed over the years. At first it was a one-dimensional area "somewhere" under the earth. As time passed, the ancient myths created levels to accommodate good and bad people. It was almost as if the Greeks found the original idea of Hades so unattractive that they were constantly trying to make it more bearable. Some geographical features, however, do remain constant.

Just what area of the underground Hades occupied is never too clear. Many Greek communities claimed (and still claim) that the gates to Hades were near their communities. Two of the more famous "gates" are near Sparta and near Pyrgos Dirou. As you might suspect, the gates were huge caves leading down into the earth. Today at Pyrgos Dirou, visitors can still enter a huge underground cavern, complete with stalactites and stalagmites, which is the mouth of a large underground river.

Before actually entering Hades, the dead had to cross five rivers. They were, in order: the Styx (hated), the Acheron (woeful), the Lethe (forgetful), the Phegethon (fiery), and the Cocytus (wailing). The actual significance of the names and the order of the rivers is not clear, but the emotional feeling about the passage into Hades is certainly obvious enough. In order to cross **Charon** the rivers, a boatman was needed. The figure of Charon supplied this need. He was an old man who demanded payment for the crossings. For this reason, coins were always placed on the eyes or in the mouth of the dead so that the boatman could be paid.

Once the rivers were crossed, the dead entered Hades itself. The gate **Cerberus** to Hades was guarded by a huge three-headed dog named Cerberus. It was his duty to see that only the dead entered Hades and that no one escaped. His three heads were of great value since two could sleep while one remained on guard. Once they passed this "watchdog," the dead entered the dark, foreboding gloom of Hades itself.

38

You should be able to figure out the meaning of two modern words from this account: *cerebral* and *lethargic*.

In what countries in modern times do we encounter the idea of putting money on the eyes of the dead?

There are many accounts of heroes attempting to enter Hades and thus having to subdue Cerberus. Read how Heracles managed to do this.

The Regions of Hades

As mentioned before, Hades was originally just an area of undifferentiated gloom and darkness. But as time passed, the Greeks began to describe it as having distinct areas. First there was Tartarus, which was the deepest part of Hades. People whom the gods disliked were sent there after death to suffer terrible punishments. Then, the idea of a place for people whom the gods favored was developed. This place was called the Elysian Fields, the one area where the dead retained their bodies. They were not gloomy shades, but immortal as the gods were immortal. An even later development was the idea that Tartarus and the Elysian Fields were not just for those chosen by the gods, but for evil and good people respectively. We can actually see, in this historical development of the accounts of the under-world, the rise of ethical or moral ideas on the part of the Greeks. Slowly the underworld became a place for rewards and punishments. It is im-portant to note, however, that the majority of the dead still went to that ill-defined middle area. Tartarus and the Elysian Fields were for special cases. Interestingly, it was not Hades who determined where the dead were to be sent. Instead it was Zeus or one of the three judges of Hades. These last were shades who had been famous for good judgment during their lives on earth. Their names were Minos, Rhadamanthys, and Aiakos.

The Elysian Fields, or the Isles of the Blessed as they were sometimes called, were eventually seen as being above ground. Why do you think the place for good people would be seen as a high place and a place for evil people would be seen as the lowest area of Hades?

Two people who went to the Elysian Fields were Heracles and Achilles. Look up accounts of their lives and see if you can determine why they were numbered among the lucky immortals.

Some of the punishments given out in Tartarus were terrible but fascinating. Read the accounts of the punishments of the following: Ixion, Sisyphus, Tityus, the Danaids, and Tantalus.

Everyone at some time has daydreamed and envisioned what life would be like if he or she were immortal. Escaping death has always had a fascination for mortals, and countless stories have been told about meetings with the person known as Death or about attempts to cheat him of his prize. The following love story is one of the most famous.

ORPHEUS
AND
EURYDICE

Orpheus was born to the Muse Calliope and therefore inherited a great talent for music. Aided by the gift of a lyre from Apollo, who taught him how to play it, Orpheus soon became the most famous musician of all Greece. So great was his power that when he played he could actually charm wild beasts and even get inanimate objects such as rocks and trees to follow him in a dance. On one of his travels through the countryside he met the lovely nymph Eurydice and fell in love with her. Soon, after winning her heart with his music, he married her and for a short time they lived happily together. But one day she was bitten by a poisonous snake and died.

Orpheus, grieved over his loss and in a desperate mood, decided to do the impossible. He would go to his love and with his music win her back from the god of the underworld. He descended into the dark regions of Hades and then, one by one, charmed the inhabitants of that nether world: Charon, Cerberus, and even the three judges of the dead. With his lyre he reached Hades and so charmed him and his queen that Hades consented to release Eurydice on one condition—that he not look back at her as long as they were in the shadows of the abode of the dead. Overjoyed, Orpheus led his wife towards life, and though he longed to look at her again, he resisted until he was at the entrance to the dark cave that separated Hades from earth. Then he looked back, but Eurydice, being slower, was still in Hades. He caught a fleeting glimpse of her, and she was recalled to Hades' kingdom.

Having lost his beautiful wife a second time, Orpheus felt that life no longer had meaning. He wandered the earth refusing to have anything to do with another woman. This cost him his life.

When chancing to stumble upon some worshippers of Dionysus, wild females called Maenads, Orpheus ignored their requests to join in their revels and they, in a drunken frenzy, set upon him and ripped him apart, knocking his lyre into a river and severing his head, which they also threw in. The gods, saddened by the loss of his music, placed his lyre in the sky where it became the constellation of Lyra. His limbs were buried at the foot of Mount Olympus where, it is said, the birds sing more sweetly than in any other place in Greece.

Discuss the meaning of the following words from the myth: *calliope* **(the instrument),** *music*, *Orpheum* **(the name of many theatres).**

What other stories do you know about attempts to cheat Death? Why is it no one ever wins? What would happen if Death took a holiday?

At this point you are on your own. No doubt you have already encountered many myths not included in this study. Our purpose has not been to be comprehensive so much as to offer a way in which to examine the myths by dividing our discussion into the basic areas of Conception, Life, and Death.

We have attempted to offer three things: a basic knowledge of the pantheon of gods, some of the best-known myths, and a framework for further study. We hope that at this point you will feel confident to pursue your own reading in Greek mythology and to draw your own conclusions about this fascinating area of our cultural past.

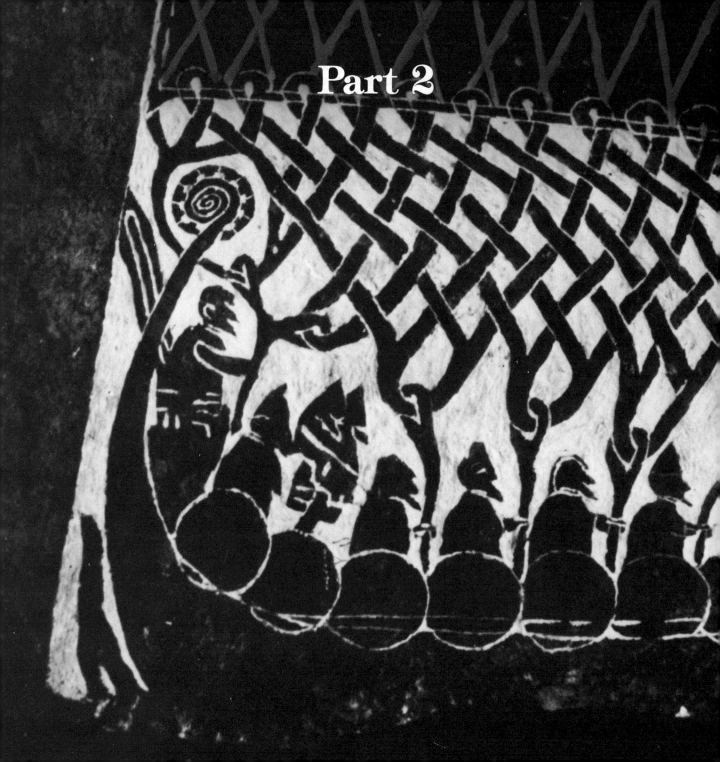

Part 2

COMPARATIVE
MYTHOLOGY

No book of this size could ever do justice to as broad a topic as comparative mythology; nor does it have to. After a close reading of Part One, the reader can see that there is a useful method of approaching mythology that can be applied to any cultural body of myth. All cultures are primarily concerned with the three fundamental areas of existence: Conception, Life, and Death. Consequently, Part Two takes four very different cultural groups and applies the same approach to their mythologies, while providing for further study and exploration of other mythologies.

One could ask why we have chosen Norse, Indian, Eskimo, and Chinese mythology when there is such a wealth of mythological material from Rome, Africa, Egypt, and other countries. Part of the reason is contained above: we are providing a method of approach that works for any mythology, and it is hoped that students of myth will feel free to investigate those cultures that specifically interest them.

Roman mythology, though culturally relevant to us, is largely a rewriting of the Greek myths with significant name changes. As much as we would have liked to investigate the myths that are specifically Roman, we felt that a comparative study should look at similarities between more varied mythologies.

Norse, Indian, and Eskimo mythologies have been sadly neglected in other mythology texts—and for obvious reasons. It is very difficult to obtain material about these myths. Most of the Norse tales come from two fragmentary sources, and often require scholars to help fit together large gaps that are missing in the narrative. Eskimo mythology is even harder to decipher. The Eskimo tribes had a profound disdain for the white race and often considered it beneath their dignity to answer truthfully questions about their culture. They were proud of the fact that the white people could not survive in the hostile environment that the Eskimo had lived in for hundreds of years. Thus, when talking about their origins or an afterlife, it is difficult to know what the Eskimo *really* thought.

We feel that it would be valuable to investigate those mythologies which are closely related to us, but for which information is not easily accessible. Indian and Eskimo mythology is of national interest to us, being the mythologies of our North American continent.

Norse mythology should be of interest to all English-speaking people. After all, the study of the origin of our language begins with Old English, which is closely entwined with the Norse, Scandinavian, and Germanic

44

Preceding page: Detail from stone with designs found on the Island of Gotland, Sweden. The votive barque is similar to those sometimes found in ancient places of worship.

peoples. In this sense, a study of Norse mythology provides an understanding of our own cultural beginnings.

Chinese mythology is the basis for a culture and a world view very different from our own. In this shrinking world, joined by satellite television and instant communication, the East has finally met the West. It is now more important than ever that we understand the thoughts and culture of our neighbors to the East.

Norse Mythology

A reading in Norse mythology is an entry into a new and different realm, and for that reason the Western world has always taken an interest in it. The strange cults and tongue-twisting names are a rich part of the Norse culture and have their origin in Iceland. Some of that Icelandic tradition is still with us. The days of the week (Tiwsday, Wodensday, Thorsday, and Freyasday) are named after their gods, and a few other mythic concepts such as Hel, Valhalla, and the Valkyries are well known. And yet, these myths have not affected the mainstream of our culture in the way that the Greek myths have; they have always remained intriguingly on the edge of our cultural consciousness.

The Norse myths are part of a larger cultural tradition which influenced beliefs in northwestern Europe over a very long period of time. First there was the Bronze Age, which covered the time period from 1600 to 450 B.C. in Northern Europe. Very little is known about the beliefs of this period since nothing was written down, but it would appear that many of the later religious practices of the Norse dated from this time.

Then came the Migration Period from about the third century A.D. to the sixth century A.D. when all of Europe was in a transition period after the collapse of the Roman Empire. It was during this period that the Germanic and Celtic tribes moved from Russia and other eastern areas into the North and West. They brought with them their own religious practices and, after a time, many of their rituals became similar. This is not too surprising since all of the tribes were essentially warlike and led the same sort of life. Therefore their gods would likely have had similarities as well.

45

The last great period was the Viking era in the ninth and tenth centuries. Long after Germany and England had been Christianized, the Vikings in Scandinavia and Iceland remained loyal to the old gods and the old way of life. It is from this last period that most of the stories probably achieved their final form.

Luckily, a few writers collected the myths of that time. These writings are called *Eddas* and were compiled in Iceland. The *Poetic Edda* is a collection of old Norse verse from the tenth and eleventh centuries; the *Prose Edda* is a collection of myths and tales written by Snorri Sturluson in around 1200 A.D. Sturluson collected these tales because he realized that few people in his time remembered the myths.

But even with the *Eddas,* we do not have a complete picture of the religion. The *Eddas* contradict each other in places, indicating that the authors used several traditions in gathering their material; this is inevitable when one is dealing with an oral tradition. Very few of the myths are complete, and we are faced with many fragmentary tales. To round out their knowledge of this period, mythographers have been forced to read contemporary histories of the period, such as the works of the Roman Tacitus, to glean cultural information from such sources as the great Anglo-Saxon epic *Beowulf,* and to rely heavily on some of the archeological discoveries made in the last century. Much more than Greek mythology, Norse mythology is something like a giant jigsaw puzzle, with pieces still missing.

The astounding archeological finds in the nineteenth and twentieth centuries have greatly increased interest in Norse mythology. Weapons, and even bodies in a remarkable state of preservation, have been found buried in peat bogs. In fact, at Sutton Hoo, England, an entire Viking ship burial and its treasures were discovered. With a little research, you should be able to gather information about these artifacts and what they reveal about the Vikings. One excellent book which has illustrations of these finds is H. R. Ellis Davidson's *Scandinavian Mythology*, Tudor Publishing Company, New York.

One of the parts of the puzzle you may be able to supply is that of the difference between the Norse and the Greek myths. Most of the stories connected with the

Greeks had to do with humans or the gods' involvement with humans. This is not true for the Norse; almost all of their stories have to do with the gods. In your reading of the following stories keep this in mind and see if you can suggest a reason for this by the end of the section.

Impression of a ship from the Viking Age.

Prow of a Viking ship, unearthed in 1904 from a burial mound in Öseberg, Norway.

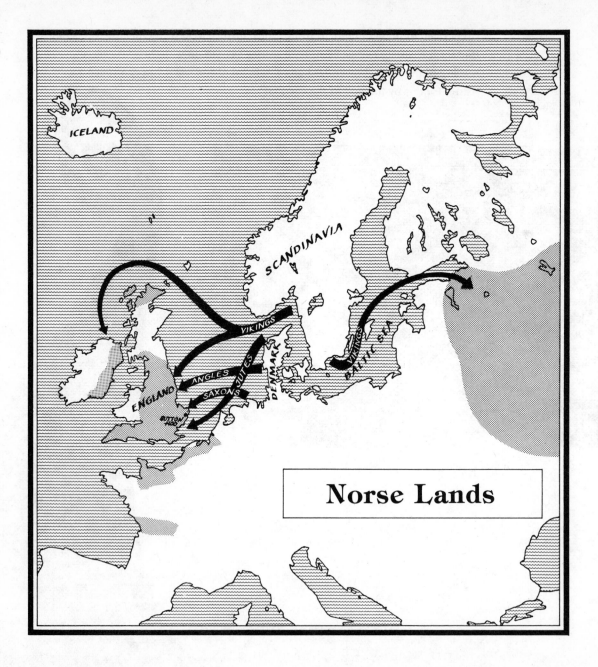

ICELAND

SCANDINAVIA

VIKINGS

VIKINGS

BALTIC SEA

ANGLES

JUTES

DENMARK

SAXONS

ENGLAND

SUTTON HOO

Norse Lands

Conception

The Creation of the Gods

Before creation took place, there existed two great areas: Niflheim, a northern waste of ice and fog, and Muspellheim, a southern region of brightness and flame. Between them stood a gaping pit called Ginnungagap. From this central region, where warmth and cold met, the first creature, Ymir, was eventually formed; so too was a great hornless cow, Audhumla. The cow fed on the salty brine of Ginnungagap and produced milk for Ymir to drink. As Ymir grew, a male and female were produced from each of his armpits, and a family of Trolls from his legs. These Trolls produced the Frost Giants called Jotars that soon multiplied, producing many fair and ugly offspring. The cow too helped in creation, for as it was licking the ice-blocks around Ginnungagap, it uncovered a creature called Buri.

Buri married one of the more beautiful of the Jotars and had a son, Bor. It was Bor's three giant sons, Odin (meaning spirit), Vili (meaning wild), and Ve (meaning holiness) who founded a special family of gods—the race of Aesir, a fierce race which looked for a way to unleash their new powers. But, before they could do this, they had to get rid of the one powerful figure who might oppose them: Ymir.

Finding their chance one day, they slew Ymir and pushed his bleeding body into Ginnungagap. The blood from his mighty wounds soon filled up the region, drowning all of the original Frost Giants except one, Bergelmir. Bergelmir escaped, eventually repopulated the icy wilderness, and vowed to avenge the deaths of his fallen brothers. It was from this incident that the bitter enmity between the Frost Giants and Odin's followers began.

The Creation of the World

Eventually the Aesir decided to raise up Ymir's body, and from it formed the world. His blood became the sea and lakes; his flesh formed the earth; and from his bones, the mountains were made. Bones that were already broken became the rocks and pebbles.

Not stopping there, the Aesir made the dome of the sky from his skull, placing a dwarf in each corner of the earth to hold it high. Around the earth, they created a wall from his eyebrows and called it Midgard. This, they said, would protect their next important creation, people, from the Frost Giants who roamed the cold regions of Niflheim.

The Creation of Human Beings

One day while Odin and two of his court, Hoenir and Lodur, were out looking at the results of creation, they came upon two trees beside the cold sea: the ash and the elm (some accounts say the alder). Wanting to populate the earth with beings who would respect and worship them, they conceived a plan. Odin breathed his spirit into the tall and hardy trees. No sooner had he done this than they came alive as man and woman. Hoenir gave them the gift of understanding, and Lodur gave them their outward form and the five senses. This first man and woman were given the earth as their home.

Below the earth, the gods created the Dwarfs, small twisted creatures with strange names, who had great skills in forging metals and working with the precious gold and silver so dear to the Aesir and, hence, to human beings ever since.

Above the earth, to keep the man and woman warm, the Aesir created the sun and the moon, and two children to drive them across the sky in their chariots. The sun was driven by a beautiful maiden, and the moon by a fair-haired boy. The giants, lovers of the dark and cold regions of Niflheim, were enraged by this beautiful, warm creation of the Aesir and sent two of their number, disguised as wolves, to destroy the charioteers of the new light. Thus the sun and moon had to be driven across the sky quickly, for the day when one of the wolves could catch the sun or moon would be the day when the gods and all of creation would come to an end. This would be the great day of doom, or "Ragnarok."

The World Tree

Amid all of this creative activity stood the giant ash tree Yggdrasil. No one knew where it came from or how it grew, but its very presence in the world was the sustaining force of the universe. As long as it lived, the gods, the world, and human beings would live. Its branches stretched up to the heavens and into the realm of the earth. Three great roots supported its mighty trunks: one passed into the realm of the Aesir, another into the land of the Niflheim, and a third wound its way among the land of the dead.

Beneath its root in Niflheim was the spring of Mimir, from which came the clear waters of understanding and insight. It was said that Odin himself had given up one of his eyes just to be able to drink from its precious waters.

The Norns Beneath the tree was the sacred spring of Fate called the Well of Urd, looked after by the three Norns, females named Urd (Fate), Verdandi (Being),

The three Norns, from a pen drawing by Arthur Rackham.

and Skuld (Necessity). Sometimes, these three women were called Past, Present and Future. Their duty, besides controlling the destinies of humans, was to water Yggdrasil from the Well of Urd and to anoint its bark with white clay in order to preserve it from the ravages of wild forest creatures. Although water fell from its branches and nourished all of the earth, the tree was in constant danger and needed protection.

On the topmost branch of Yggdrasil perched a giant eagle which shook his wings from time to time, causing all of the leaves in the world to blow. On his beak sat a hawk whose duty it was to scan the four corners of the world for enemies. Together, the eagle and the hawk guarded Yggdrasil. Their eternal duty was to protect the tree from the giant serpent which lay at its roots.

This giant serpent was constantly entwined about the base of Yggdrasil and, by gnawing at its base, tried to topple it. Hence the serpent was at war with the eagle. This conflict was kept alive by a malicious squirrel which ran from one to the other carrying insults; hence, eternal strife reigned in the universe.

All of this time goats and deer nibbled on the tender branches of Yggdrasil, while birds and insects bored into its bark. Were it not for the Norns who took care of the tree, it would have died and with its death would come Ragnarok, the destruction that everyone fought to prevent.

Who is Ymir's counterpart in Greek mythology? Why do you think that both the Greeks and the Norse would have the belief that the earth was created from the body of a giant?

As in the Greek myth, the world begins with a male figure but almost immediately a male and female are produced. From then on, creation in the realm of the gods and on earth is a result of marriages. What does the fact that the original deity in creation is male tell you about the outlook of each culture? Why would it be logical for societies to then see succession and procreation in terms of marriage?

In Norse mythology there are two separate approaches to the creation of humans. In one account, Ymir is responsible; in another, Odin is the creating force. This is true also for the Greeks and, if we were to examine a number of cultures, we would find this a regular phenomenon. Part of the answer can be accounted for by the different oral sources available. However, other reasons could be suggested with a little reflection.

In Norse mythology humans are made from trees, whereas in the Greek story humans are made from clay. Can you account for this difference in materials?

The most implacable enemies of humans and the Aesir gods were the Frost Giants. You should not find it difficult after consulting a map of the Scandinavian countries to explain why.

The world of the Norse does not contain the order and symmetry of the Greek world. Even the gods have enemies; the sun and moon are constantly threatened, and the World Tree, Yggdrasil, needs constant attention in order to overcome the attacks of insects, forest creatures, and the serpent. This is a world that is constantly in danger of annihilation by Ragnarok. What does this tell you about their culture, environment, and everyday existence?

The Different Worlds of the Norse

Unlike the Greek world which was divided into three distinct areas—earth, Hades, and Olympus—the Norse myths mention a variety of regions.

First there were Muspellheim, the land of brightness and flame, and Niflheim, the land of cold and darkness which later contained Hel, a region of gloom. Out of the meeting of these two regions (Ginnungagap) came all of creation.

But when the Frost Giants were born, they inhabited a new region of ice and frost called Jotunheim and they became known as Jotars.

Protected from Jotunheim was Earth, realm of mortals; it was surrounded by Midgard. This area had been created by Odin when he made the human race.

There was a region under Earth as well. It was the land of the Dwarfs or Gnomes who mined the earth for precious metals. This land was called Darkalfheim.

Elsewhere, there was the land of the Elves, a sunny place called Alfheim.

The most important area was Asgard, home of the Aesir gods. It was also protected from the Jotars by a huge wall and the rainbow bridge Bifrost. No Frost Giant could cross this bridge because it was made of fire, their mortal enemy. Asgard had been created by Odin and his brothers. There gold and silver were in abundance, even for the fences that bordered the paths.

The tallest building in Asgard was Odin's palace, at the very top of which rested his throne. From this throne, Odin could see over the entire world, and even into what was happening in the underground world of the Dwarfs. No one else could sit on Odin's throne except his wife Frigg. Thus, she too knew the secrets of the universe along with her husband. In some accounts, there was a region above this where all the good people went— the golden palace of Gimli.

In Asgard, all of the gods feasted daily on pork, which never was depleted because, as they ate it, the part eaten was miraculously replaced. They also drank quantities of mead, which ran from the udder of the goat Heidrun, who, in turn, was nourished from the branches of Yggdrasil.

Asgard also housed part of another group of gods who have not been mentioned yet, the Vanir. The Vanir originally lived in Vanaheim and did not figure in any of the creation stories, but they became prominent in the pantheon of gods and some came to live in Asgard. The Aesir were basically warlike gods. That is, they represented the warlike qualities so admired by the Vikings. But the Vanir gods, less famous in accounts of the Norse, represented a more obscure part of the Norse mentality, love and peace. At one time the Vanir and Aesir gods had been at war, but they realized that they had to live together. It is perhaps significant that, although some Vanir did enter Asgard, Odin was still their chief. Both the Aesir and Vanir gods were worshiped by humans.

It is impossible to place any of these areas geographically. All that we do know is that the World Tree, Yggdrasil, passed through all areas and was the life force that held them all together.

The Pantheon of Gods

ODIN Odin was the supreme ruler. He was god of battle, inspiration, and death. On his shoulders perched two black ravens who flew off in opposite directions each morning and circled the world, arriving back each evening to report their observations. Their names were Munin (Memory) and Hugin (Thought). At Odin's feet sat two great wolves, symbols of his power. Odin also had a huge eight-legged horse, Sleipnir, which was capable of jumping

Memorial stone with runic letters.

even the barriers of Hel. Other gods often borrowed Sleipnir for special journeys.

Odin was a worthy leader. Not only had he sacrificed one of his eyes to gain wisdom and insight for people, but he also had allowed himself to be hanged on Yggdrasil for nine days and nine nights in order to obtain the secret of the Runes. The Runes were letters having magical properties that only the initiated could understand. Odin had had himself impaled upon the tree by his own huge battle spear and, on the ninth day, the Runic letters had shaped themselves on the leaves of the tree and revealed their meaning to him. Thus he learned not only the art of writing, for Runes were an alphabet, but also the art of magic. Because of this, Odin was able to inspire his poets, priests, and even his warriors with this mystic insight.

Originally, there were three chief gods: Odin, Vili, and Ve. We never hear much of these other two after creation and, hence, Odin becomes supreme. What theories could you give to account for this phenomenon?

Odin's Anglo-Saxon name is Woden. On what day of the week do you think he was worshipped?

Why do you think the ravens who reported to Odin would be called Memory and Thought?

Odin's role as the god of inspiration needs some explanation. To "inspire" is literally to breathe life into something, just as Odin had breathed life into mortals. To be inspired, then, is literally to have the god, and all of the powers associated with the god, flow through you. Inspiration can manifest itself in two ways. First there is the creative inspiration of the poets. In this case, poets feel inspired by some insight or knowledge which is somehow greater than themselves and must communicate it. Then there is the destructive form in which people literally become "possessed" by the god and are unable to control their own actions. Odin, as god of battle, often "inspired" his warriors to almost superhuman feats of bravery.

Among the Norse, there was a certain elite group of warriors, called Berserks, who were sacred to Odin. They cultivated the receiving of this divine inspiration by a combination of drinking mead and praying to the god. When they felt the god enter their beings, they rushed into battle in a state of divine frenzy, heedless of all

56

dangers. Naturally, they were always the most ferocious warriors on the field. Why would the Norse have fostered the idea that these Berserks were to be honored and revered?

Can you think of any other culture that had a similar type of warrior?

Does the magical association with letters suggest the power of writing in an illiterate culture, or is there another explanation?

Odin's sacrifice on the World Tree would seem to have a Christian parallel, but, according to scholars, the sacrifice of Odin predates the coming of Christian mis-- sionaries. It is one of those curious coincidences that so often occur when one is studying mythology and must be accounted for in some other way. What explana- tion would you give?

What does the fact that Odin is the highest deity in the Norse pantheon of gods tell you about the values of that culture?

FRIGG   As the wife of Odin and the only other one allowed to sit on his throne, Frigg knew the future of gods and humans and was a constant help to her husband. She was often depicted spinning yarn on a golden distaff and spindle. If a mortal woman worked very industriously at spinning during the day, Frigg would leave some of her own yarn for her as she slept. This was a marvelous gift, for it was never used up no matter how much was needed.

Frigg was the goddess most prayed to by women, especially at the time of childbirth. She was even able at times to trick Odin in order to answer a woman's prayer against the edicts of her husband.

Can you remember a fairy tale that involves spinning? Describe it and relate the story to what you know about Frigg.

THOR   Thor was the son of Odin and Earth. He was the strongest of the gods and was constantly called upon to do battle with the Frost Giants of Jotunheim. To help him he had three magical weapons: the hammer "Mjolnir" which burned red hot, could shatter even locks, and always returned to its master's hand; an iron glove to catch the hammer when it returned; and a belt of

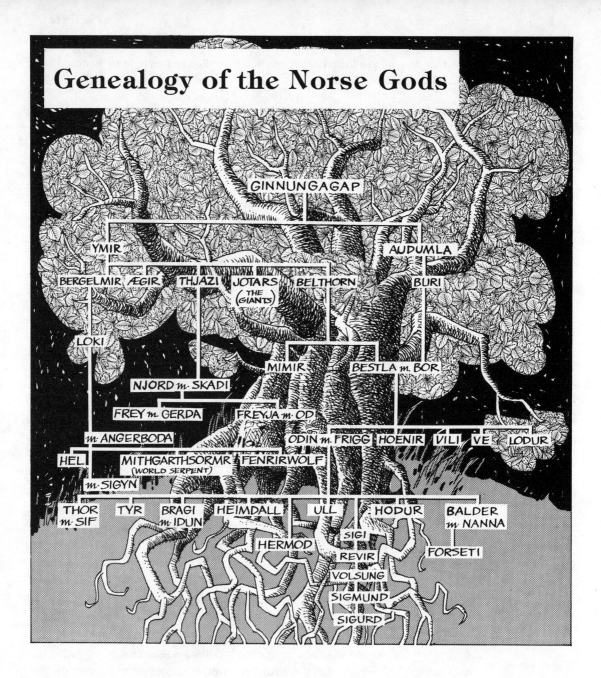

Genealogy of the Norse Gods

power that doubled his strength when tightened. Although Thor was usually good natured, he was famous for his sudden fits of temper. As the god of Thunder, he made a striking figure with his flaming red beard.

Thor had a huge chariot drawn by two goats to take him across the sky. Whenever he was hungry, he would slaughter these animals, being careful never to break their bones as he ate their flesh. Because their bones were intact, the two goats would always reappear whole the next day and the cycle would repeat itself.

More stories are told about Thor than any other Norse god, especially stories which concern his exploits of strength and his ingenuity in the use of his weapons.

The main symbol attached to Thor was the oak tree. It was sacred to his worship. Why do you think this tree was chosen?

What natural phenomenon would Thor's "Mjolnir" explain?

Why was Thor's beard red?

LOKI Loki is one of the most interesting Norse gods. He has no counterpart in Greek mythology. Originally Loki was a Frost Giant, but he found favor with Odin because of his nimble mind and smooth tongue. For this reason he was allowed in Asgard. This god could change his shape at will, and often did so—sometimes to help the gods, but more often to play tricks on them. It would seem that Loki always retained some of his Frost Giant heritage because he often caused mischief among the Aesir, as if he were trying to avenge his people and keep up a constant strife in Asgard. Sometimes, however, he fitted into the role of trickster—a figure which appears in all cultures.

Once, while in the shape of a horse, he was reputed to have given birth to Sleipnir, Odin's eight-legged steed. This would have no doubt endeared him to the supreme god. This horse was not the only one of Loki's creations. His first wife, the giant Angurboda, had given birth to the wolf Fenrir, to the world Serpent which constantly threatened Yggdrasil, and to Hel, the female ruler of the land of the dead. All of these offspring had been born before Loki was accepted into Asgard and their negative nature suggests that he was not a totally desirable figure to have among the gods. When he came to Asgard, Loki left Angurboda and married the fair Sigyn, a gift of Odin.

59

Because of his cunning and magical tricks, Loki was a central figure in many of the myths. He was involved in the creation of Asgard and Ragnarok, the beginning and the end of the world.

To see why Loki was valued by the gods, read the account of his participation in the building of the walls of Asgard.

Look up the story of Loki and the theft of Sif's hair. Sif was Thor's wife. Thor was so angry about this practical joke that Loki was sent to the underground world of the Dwarfs to replace it. He returned with many great treasures for the gods of Asgard and, thus, found favor with them again.

HEIMDALL One of Odin's sons was Heimdall, the watchman of Asgard. He was born from nine sisters, maidens of Jotar. He was always pictured by the World Tree, guarding Bifrost, so that no harm could come to Asgard. Heimdall was given this task by Odin because he could see great distances and because his hearing was so acute that he could hear the wool growing on the backs of sheep.

Whenever danger threatened, he was instructed to blow his great horn called Gjallarhorn. One blast from this horn could be heard around the world.

NJORD Before time, the Aesir and Vanir gods were at war with one another. Eventually a truce was called and the two groups exchanged hostages to show their good faith and to help keep the peace. The Vanirs sent Njord, the god of the North Winds and the sea, to Asgard. As you can easily understand, Njord was worshiped more by the coastal and island people than anyone else. The ship was most often associated with him as a symbol. Since the Viking ship represented trade and was also used for royal burials, Njord was often linked with wealth and the dead. His two offspring, Frey and Freyja, however, were even more important than he was.

FREY Frey was a god of fertility. He gave to humans the gifts of rain and sunshine and was responsible for their rich harvests. Because of his role as a bountiful providing god, Frey was also considered to be the god of peace and prosperity and was thus a great favorite of the common folk. His sword was said to gleam as brightly as the sun, and he had a horse that could leap through mighty fires. His place was not in Asgard but in Alfheim, the pleasant land of the Elves.

The Aesir gods gave him many gifts. One gift was the ship Skidbladnir, which could fly over land and sea while holding all of the gods, but could fold into a tiny pouch when not in use. Another gift was a huge boar with golden bristles which could fly across the sky and light up the world below. This boar became a very popular symbol among Viking warriors. They felt that it placed them under Frey's protection.

Frey's twin sister was the fairest of the goddesses. Her name was Freyja and she was the goddess of love. Her husband Od had disappeared in battle, and often Freyja would search for him in her chariot drawn by cats. As she searched, she would cry tears of pure gold. At times Freyja would assume the shape of a falcon, to carry out her search.

Freyja's home was in a huge palace in Asgard, where she often entertained the gods. Her hall also housed half of the princely and noble warriors who had fallen in battle on earth. This was Odin's tribute to Freyja, for he kept the other half himself in Valhalla, his special place for the courageous dead.

A symbol often associated with the goddess of love was her necklace Brisingamen, her most cherished possession. Its real significance is unknown

FREYJA

61

to us today. There is one day of the week which reminds us of this goddess. Traditionally, it is on this day that it is considered lucky to be married.

TYR   Tyr was the god of battle, sometimes giving victory to those he favored rather than to the best fighters. He was the bravest god and had lost his right hand proving it.

It happened this way. When the wolf Fenrir was first born to Loki's wife, all of the Asgard gods felt that no good would come of it if this huge creature were allowed to grow unchallenged. Odin had already placed Fenrir on an island, but he grew so huge that it was decided that he needed to be chained there as well.

Fenrir broke all of the chains that the gods placed on him and even taunted the gods, telling them to find something strong enough to hold him. Odin responded to the challenge by having a thin chain made by the dwarfs from the roots of mountains, from the sound of a cat, and the breath of fish. When it was finished, it seemed thin and weak but it was unbreakable. It only remained for someone to put it on the wolf.

Fenrir suspected magic may have been used, although the gods swore that this was not so. As proof of their good faith, Fenrir demanded that a hostage place a hand in his mouth as the new and strange chain was placed about him. Only Tyr was brave enough to volunteer. When Fenrir discovered that the chain was unbreakable, all of the gods laughed at the trick; that is, all but Tyr, for the wolf had bitten off his hand.

BRAGI   Bragi was the god of poetry and of words. His wife was Idun, the keeper of the apples of youth. Although Bragi is mentioned often in the *Eddas*, his role, like that of so many of the Norse gods, is not entirely clear. It would seem that he shared some of the powers of Odin in his capacity as the god of inspiration.

One duty that Bragi had was to meet all of the heroes as they entered Valhalla, Odin's special place for heroes. This role of Bragi as a welcomer of heroes was stressed by the Norse nobles in their funeral ceremonies for dead warriors.

Like Odin, Bragi was usually depicted with a long beard and in full warrior dress.

62

Balder is most famous for the story involving the mistletoe. (See the section on Death, page 75). He was a sun god and one of Odin's offspring, while his wife Nanna was goddess of the moon. They had a son Forseti, who later was said to have given a law code to the Frisians, a Viking tribe.

When Odin first laid eyes on Loki's daughter Hel, she was so pale and ghost-like that he sent her to be ruler of the land of the dead. This was a kingdom close to the cold wastes of Niflheim and was soon called Hel, after the goddess.

All of those who had died of sickness or old age came to her vast hall which was made up of walls of winding serpents. On the roof of the hall perched a pitch-black rooster. The doorstep of Hel was called Pitfall; Hel's knife was called Hunger, and her table Starvation.

The Valkyries are probably the best known of the Norse deities. These were maidens, daughters of the gods, whom Odin sent to the battlefield. Their duty was to choose the Norse nobles who were worthy to be slain and to bring them back to Odin's hall of slain heroes, Valhalla.

Whenever a warrior felt the touch of one of these maidens in battle, he knew he was fated to die. The fallen hero would be claimed by a Valkyrie, placed on her horse, and taken to Valhalla. If he was particularly brave, Odin himself would offer the warrior mead. From that time on, the warrior would feast, drink, and fight in his new world, where to be a great hero was supreme.

Other Immortals

Giants and elves as characterized in a children's book.

Along with the gods were a whole series of demigods.

The Elves lived in Alfheim. Mostly they helped people, but they would also play tricks on them. Thus, many of life's unexplainable happenings could be accounted for by their actions.

The Dwarfs were skilled craftsmen who lived under the surface of the earth and to whom all of the jewels and metals belonged. They were depicted as deformed and tiny creatures who had an unnatural lust for human women and children. Often, but not always, their acts were malicious.

Trolls were a type of Dwarf, but had no saving graces. They were said to commit only evil deeds. Trolls lived in Jotunheim and were closely allied to the Frost Giants.

The Frost Giants or Jotars lived in Jotunheim and were not gods unless, like Loki, Odin accepted them into Asgard. These giants were the principal enemies of the Aesir and Vanir gods, and constantly tried to overthrow them.

As this study of the Norse pantheon of gods indicates, we are dealing with a very diverse group of immortals. There is not the coherence or simplicity here that is evident in the study of Greek myths. Nonetheless, some very valuable conclusions can be drawn from this survey of the major deities.

A number of deities have been omitted from the pantheon but, because they occur in many stories from time to time, it is worth looking up the following: Skadi, Ull, Mimir, Aegir.

What does the presence of Loki, Heimdall, and Ragnarok within Asgard, and the Frost Giants outside of Asgard, tell you about the Norse vision of life?

One of Loki's famous "tricks" involved the stealing of Freyja's necklace. You will enjoy reading this story because it shows the Norse mind at work. It accounts for why Heimdall and Loki became mortal enemies.

Sometimes more than one god or goddess was in control of a certain part of nature. For instance, Skadi and Ull were both goddesses of the mountains, skiing, and hunting. Examine the functions of Njord, Aegir, and Ran. What does the fact that there are three of them tell you about Viking geography?

The god of war was important in all of the northern European religions. In Norse mythology, Odin took this role. In Anglo-Saxon areas, he was worshipped as Woden, and in some Germanic tribes as Wodan or Wotan. But because of the importance of battle in this culture, many deities shared this function with Odin. Thor is one, and Tyr is another. Tyr was called Tiu and Tiw in Germany and was elevated to the same importance as Wotan. Tuesday comes from his name. Bragi also has associations with warriors, and some writers suggest that Bragi was not a separate god at all, but another name for Odin, since Bragi meant "leader" in the

Norse language. Scholars are not sure of this. But what does become crystal clear is that a warrior god reigned supreme in northern Europe, whatever his name. For an interesting account of Thor and one of his famous battles, read the story of Thor's encounter with the giant Hrungnir. An interesting side note to this story is that it is one of the few Norse tales that involves humans.

The demigods such as Elves, Dwarfs, Trolls, and Giants have long been popular in our society in the form of fairy tales. Using your own knowledge of these childhood stories as a guide, would you say that these figures still have the same function?

Life

The Natural World

Not as many myths explaining natural phenomena have come down to us from the *Eddas* as from Greek sources. Considering our studies of other mythologies, we would suspect that there are many, but that they were not recorded or, if they were, they have been lost to us.

However, there are stories which explain some aspects of the natural world and human beings, even if specific stories of how plants received their names or constellations their forms are few and far between. The following stories are quite revealing about the way in which the Norse people saw the world around them and their own natures.

FREY AND GERDA The earth was abundantly green, the harvest was plentiful, and people were happy with Frey, the god of fertility and harvests. But one day, Frey did a foolish thing and brought unhappiness upon himself. He overstepped the bounds of his authority by going up and sitting on Odin's throne in spite of the rule that no one but Odin and Frigg could do this. From this high seat, Frey was able to see out over the entire world.

While admiring the view, Frey spied a Jotar maiden named Gerda and instantly fell in love with her. After that, even as he walked through the glittering hall of Asgard, his thoughts kept coming back to images of Gerda, her radiant white arms and her golden hair. So intense became his desire for her that he could not eat or sleep. Gradually he pined away until his face became pale and gaunt and, as Frey faded, so did the earth.

Odin became alarmed at the barrenness of the land and at how his children were suffering from hunger because of Frey's love. He called on someone to volunteer to brave the perils of Jotunheim for Frey so that Gerda should know of his passion. Skirnir, a loyal servant of Frey, offered to help. Taking his master's horse which could jump through fire, and his shining sword, he set out to woo the Jotar maid. Across the fiery bridge Bifrost he sped, and through the darkness until he reached the land of Jotunheim.

At the house of Gerda, Skirnir was treated with the respect always accorded to wanderers, whether friend or foe. But as he announced why he had come on such a perilous journey, he was met with derision and laughter. Neither the gold nor the jewels that Skirnir brought could persuade Gerda to marry a Vanir god and leave her people.

The resourceful servant was forced to persuade her in some other way. He drew out the magic sword of Frey before the astonished girl and carved one of the mystical Runic letters before her. He began to cast a spell, warning Gerda that she would be transformed into an old hag, cursed even by the Jotars, unless she consented to marry Frey.

Gerda cried out in terror at this. She said that if Skirnir would scratch out the evil Rune and erase the spell, she would meet this Frey at the sacred grove of Barri in nine nights' time and marry him. Pleased, Skirnir agreed to this condition and returned to Asgard to tell his master.

Frey was both happy and sad. He did not want to wait the nine nights for his bride, but wait he did—and the earth waited too for Frey's blessing. Finally she came. So happy was Frey that the color came back into his cheeks and happiness returned to his soul. With this, his blessings returned to the earth, the crops began to grow, sunshine returned, and the gentle rains watered the barren land once more.

What elements of the Norse way of life come through in the telling of the story?

What natural phenomenon is the myth trying to explain?

The Runes were a Germanic development of Greek and Roman alphabets and came to be used not only in writing but as decorative inscriptions. These inscriptions, mostly on wood figures and wands, were said to have magical qualities. For that reason, words themselves took on a mystical significance. The Norse had a tendency

to name even inanimate objects, as the myths recorded here show. It was as if by naming an object, the speaker had power over it. Make a list of the objects named in these myths, and any others you read, in order to substantiate this.

KVASIR At one time, inspiration was not one of the powers of Odin. How he became the god of this quality is an involved and interesting tale.

When the Vanir and Aesir gods had been at war, they both realized that no one would emerge victorious and eventually called a truce. To make the truce official, both factions sat in a circle around a large bowl and each member spat into it. The saliva began to ferment and out of the fermentation was created Kvasir, a wise being who possessed all knowledge and could answer any questions.

According to one tradition, Kvasir was then sacrificed by two Dwarfs who let his blood drain into three huge vessels, mixed with honey and allowed to stand. Thus a rich mead or honey wine was formed. Whoever drank of this liquor would receive the gift of poetic inspiration and be able to utter words of wisdom. Hence poetry was often called "Kvasir's Blood" or "Ship of the Dwarfs" by the Norse.

At first the Dwarfs were the keepers of this brew, but they lost it because of a malicious deed, the killing of the Frost Giant Gilling and his wife. The Giants' son Suttung avenged his parents by fastening the Dwarfs to a rock towards which the tide rolled in. As they saw their death approaching, the Dwarfs begged for mercy and offered Suttung the mead.

Odin was most unhappy that such an important power should be in the hands of a Frost Giant and devised a plan to obtain the mead for himself. He constructed a whetstone of such quality that it would sharpen any weapon to perfection. He then offered this to the servants of Baugi, Suttung's brother. As Odin had foreseen, the giant's servants fought over the prize and killed each other off, leaving Baugi without any help. Odin then offered himself as a servant to Baugi providing that he obtain for him one drink of his brother's mead.

But after Odin had performed the required service, Suttung reneged. He wanted to keep this mead for himself. Thus it happened that Odin, with the unlikely ally Baugi, plotted a way to steal it. With Baugi's help, Odin drilled into the mountain where Suttung lived, changed into a serpent, and crawled into his dwelling. There he lay for three nights with Suttung's

67

daughter and had little difficulty in persuading her to give him three drinks of the mead, one for each night that he spent with her.

But as she brought him to where the three vessels were, he emptied their entire contents in three great gulps and, changing into an eagle, flew back to Asgard. There he spat out the mead into a bowl. From that time on, poetry and inspiration were the gift of Odin and the Aesir gods.

From what you know of the gifts of inspiration, why do you think Odin was so anxious to be the bearer of this gift?

It is quite true that saliva was and is used as a fermenting agent in primitive societies. Even "Kvasir" in early Germanic comes from the root word meaning "strong beer." What does this suggest about one means of acquiring Odin's gift?

In another version, Kvasir is an Asgard god whose actual being is sought after because he is the source of wisdom. This figure of Kvasir, very much alive, appears in a later story, "The Punishment of Loki." How could you account for these two versions and the close involvement of this figure with Odin?

The Moral World

The Norse were an extremely wise and practical race. Like any community, they realized that they could not exist without a certain number of basic attitudes and traditions to hold them together. When such attitudes and traditions are tacitly understood by the whole community as being necessary for living peacefully together, they are called *morals*. From the following tales and wise sayings, then, we may deduce the moral world of the Norse.

THOR AND UTGARD-LOKI

Thor was not always as powerful as he thought. Once, on a visit to Jotunheim, he was defeated by forces beyond his control.

Thor and Loki were traveling in the land of the Giants along with two mortals, Thjalfi and Roskva, who were serving Thor in penance for having harmed one of his goats. Upon coming to a large deserted hall, they all entered and soon fell asleep. This sleep was shortly interrupted by a terrifying roar. Try as they could, they were unable to discover where the sound was located.

However, when dawn came and they were able to see into the distance, they spied a huge Giant snoring on a distant hill. As they drew near, the Giant awoke and greeted them. His name was Skrymir (Big Fellow) and no one wished to argue when he suggested that they travel together. Before the journey began, Skrymir reached over and picked up the hall that the four had been sleeping in; it turned out to be one of the gloves he had set aside before he went to sleep. After this amazing revelation, they were a little concerned when Skrymir offered to carry their packs for them, and even more so when he disappeared into the distance, promising to meet them later in the day.

This reconstructed hall from approximately 1000 A.D. is similar to the "halls" of the Viking Age.

That night, Thor's group was able to catch up with Skrymir only when the Giant stopped under a tree for another nap. Thor was famished and tried to untie the Giant's bag containing their provisions. But try as he might, he could not unleash the strap. Thoroughly frustrated, Thor struck the Giant a blow with his great hammer. But instead of suffering a terrible wound, the Giant merely opened his eyes and asked if a leaf had fallen on his head.

Dismayed, all four decided to sleep without having eaten. Once again, however, Skrymir's snores awoke them. Furious at this and still feeling the pangs of hunger, Thor struck the Giant on the head with another mighty blow from Mjolnir, a blow that this time was calculated to kill even the World Serpent. But again, the Giant just opened one eye and asked if an acorn had fallen on his head.

When morning came, the Giant still slept, so Thor in desperation hit him so hard that his hammer was embedded in his skull. At this the Giant did awaken and suggested that a bird must have dropped something on him. The Giant then warned them that soon they would arrive at the hall of Utgard where the other Giants like himself resided and that they should be very cautious. With that, he rose and strode out of sight.

Just as the Giant had predicted, Thor, Loki, Thjalfi, and Roskva arrived at Utgard, a hall so huge that they were able to squeeze through the bars of the grill in the gate and enter. Once inside, they met the king, Utgard-Loki, who treated them with disdain. He haughtily challenged the visitors to a series of contests.

First there was an eating contest in which the usually insatiable Loki was defeated by a Giant called Logi. The Giant won by eating all of the bones of the animals as well. Then Thjalfi was defeated in a race by a youth calle Hugi, who was so swift that he not only reached the finish line, but was also able to come back and meet Thjalfi who was still running the course.

Next, Thor himself was put to the test. Thor's first trial was to drink the contents of a horned goblet, but after three tries, Thor was bloated and still the liquid had gone down only a few inches. Then he was asked to lift Utgard-Loki's cat from the floor. This seemed a simple task. Grasping the cat around the middle, Thor exerted all of his strength, but try as he might, he could manage to lift only one paw off the ground. The king then called in his aging old nurse to wrestle with Thor. To his dismay and chagrin, she easily wrestled him to the ground and would have killed him as he lay helpless had not Utgard-Loki stopped the contest.

A great feast was then prepared for the vanquished mortals and the gods, Thor and Loki. After that, the mystified guests were shown to magnificent bedrooms where they spent the night. It was not until morning that Utgard-Loki called them to his hall and revealed to them the ways in which they had been beaten.

Magic had been used to change the appearance of things: Skrymir was none other than Utgard-Loki himself, and the three blows from Thor's hammer had not fallen on him but on a mountain that he had conjured to come between himself and the blow. The evidence of the real power of these blows was in the three enormous holes in the side of the mountain. The strap holding the god's provisions could not be opened by Thor because it had been forged of iron bands. Logi was in reality Fire, which consumes more than any man; Hugi was Thought, which races faster than the swiftest feet. The horn that had been given to Thor had had its tip in the ocean and Thor had managed to drink it down to the level of an ebb-tide before he could do no more. The cat was in reality the greatest enemy of the gods, the World Serpent, and that Thor had lifted even one paw had amazed the Giants present. Thor's wrestling opponent was Elli or Old Age, who ultimately overcomes everyone.

With this last pronouncement, Utgard-Loki, his court, and his hall entirely disappeared, leaving the four to continue their journey and contemplate the mysteries of the world.

Although this tale does not offer actual guidelines for living, it does offer a lesson about life itself. What can you deduce about the Norse attitudes or insights about the world?

This story is an interesting example of how different the Norse world was from that of the Greeks. Not only are mortals involved in a contest to help the gods, but the gods themselves are also defeated. How would you account for this fact? What does it tell about the Norse world?

Often attitudes are reflected in the wise sayings of a culture. This type of wisdom in its simplistic approach to life is well worth examining, particularly as a contrast to our complex and restless society. Each culture has its own proverbs. Edith Hamilton's book *Mythology* contains a very good section on the Norse wisdom literature.

Moral Sayings of the Norse

The foolish man lies awake all night
Thinking of his many problems;
When the morning comes he is worn out
And his trouble is just as it was.

All creatures die, including man;
But one thing never dies:
The renown of the noble dead.

To one, tell your thoughts
But be wary of two;
All know what is known to three.

Brave men can live well anywhere;
A coward fears everything.

The path to a good friend's house
Is straight
Though he is far away.

No one is so good
that he has no faults;
No one is so wicked
that he is completely worthless.

GEIRROD AND AGNAR

One autumn, as Odin sat on his sacred seat overlooking Earth, he noticed two young brothers, Geirrod and Agnar, of whom he was particularly fond. He summoned his wife Frigg and made plans to visit the earth to bestow his blessing on both boys. Disguising themselves as an old peasant couple, they went down to an isolated island. There they prepared a rude hut to welcome the children, for Odin had caused a violent storm to arise while the boys were out fishing together.

Eventually, the waves washed their tiny ship up on the island. The boys took to the kindly couple. Geirrod, because of his strength and warlike nature, was attracted to Odin; Agnar, who was of a gentler spirit, was attracted to Frigg.

Through the friendly autumn, Odin taught Geirrod the skills of hunting and shooting the bow, the ability to handle weapons, and how to use his strength and bravery skillfully. Agnar, who was younger, listened to Frigg as she spun at home and told stories of bravery and deeds of valor. Together they would go gathering herbs while Frigg taught Agnar all the names of the birds and plants and the wonders of the world, and how they could be used for good or ill depending on the heart of the individual.

As the autumn turned to winter and then to spring, the children grew in wisdom and maturity. Finally, the time came for Odin and Frigg to return to Asgard. Odin placed the two boys on a ship and sent it back to their father. However, when it landed, Geirrod, who was stronger and who had grown resentful of Agnar, jumped into the sea and pushed the boat back, knowing Agnar would drift helplessly. Eventually the boat was washed up in the land of the Giants where Agnar was taken in and raised as a hapless orphan.

Geirrod returned home and was welcomed by his father. Sadly, his father listened to the lie Geirrod told of Agnar's drowning, but he rejoiced that he still had one son.

Time passed, and it was not until many years later that Odin and Frigg desired to know how their special charges had fared. Looking out, Odin proudly boasted that Geirrod was a strong ruler of his people, while Agnar was living obscurely, and in the hated land of the Giants. Frigg pointed out, however, that of the two, Agnar was the better person, and issued a challenge so that Odin might test his favorite. Odin responded by disguising himself again as a wanderer, and returned to the earth over the great bridge Bifrost.

While Odin was making his way to Geirrod's hall, Agnar, who had longed to return to his homeland, had just arrived—also in disguise—and hired himself as a lowly servant to the king, his brother. Frigg, in the meantime, had planted a word of warning in Geirrod's ear to beware of a stranger coming into his land to do him harm.

Thus, when Odin appeared before the king, Geirrod refused him the usual courtesies due a stranger and ordered Odin to be bound and placed between two huge fires. Although the heat was almost unbearable, Geirrod ordered that no one give Odin food or drink. Ashamed at this behavior, Agnar refused to obey and secretly gave Odin water to drink.

On the eighth day, as Geirrod came in to see his prisoner, he heard the stranger singing a strange song: the words described how angry the Aesir were at the evil of Geirrod and that on this day Odin himself would slay the foolish king. Geirrod drew his sword to kill the insolent prisoner. At that, the fires suddenly went out, the chains fell from the stranger, and Odin himself appeared in all of his terrible wrath. So taken aback was Geirrod that he stumbled and fell on his own sword and was run through.

Odin then raised Agnar to the level of kingship, telling the people how Agnar had secretly helped him and how he was of the royal line, being the brother of Geirrod himself. After that time, the brave and generous Agnar began a long, glorious rule under the benevolent eye of Odin and Frigg.

What element of the story reflects the barbarous qualities of Norse society?

What values did this story implant in the consciousness of the Norse?

Death

The following three tales and the consequent destruction of the gods present a comprehensive picture of the omnipresence of death and, conversely, the precariousness of life as seen by the Norse.

IDUN'S APPLES Once, when Odin, Loki, and Hoenir were walking on Earth, they came to a valley of oxen. In their hunger they slaughtered one of the beasts and prepared a huge fire on which they tried to roast it. For some reason, though, the fire would not burn properly.

Looking around, they saw a large eagle in a tree fanning his wings and staring at them. He offered to cook the oxen for the gods on the condition that they give him a portion of the roasted meat. This they agreed to. But when the meat was roasted to perfection, the eagle quickly grabbed the greatest portion and ate it. Loki, in a fit of anger, grabbed a stick and began to beat the huge bird.

Unfortunately for Loki, the eagle was stronger and grabbed the stick with Loki still hanging on to it. No matter how much Loki tried, he found that he could not let go of the stick, for the eagle was in reality Thjazi, a Jotar, and he had the power to force Loki to hang on. As Thjazi flew low over the land, Loki was bumped and jostled on every stone and pebble until he could take no more and cried to the eagle for mercy.

Thjazi stated that he would let him go only if he brought to him the Golden Apples of Idun, who was the wife of Bragi. Loki protested that this would be impossible since it was Idun's apples that kept all of the Asgard gods eternally youthful. Without them, the gods themselves would grow old and die. Thjazi insisted that this was the only prize he would accept and, since Loki did not wish to be punished further, he agreed to obtain them.

74

Loki then returned to Asgard to wait for the right opportunity. There came a time when many of the gods were absent on various adventures and Loki was able to employ his glib tongue to lure Idun outside of the protective walls of Asgard. Immediately she was encompassed by a black storm cloud and, under this veil, a huge black bird carried her off to the hall of Thjazi.

Without the apples of youth, the gods began to grow grey and wrinkled. Since Idun had last been seen in the company of Loki, Odin called Loki forward for an explanation. In his fear of Odin's anger, Loki confessed his part in the crime. The Aesir gods were furious and threatened Loki with eternal punishment. Again, he was forced to plead for mercy and promised to return the apples.

Loki borrowed the falcon shape of Freyja and flew to the Giant's hall. There he stealthily sought out the hapless Idun and told her of his plan. He changed her into a nut (some say a sparrow) and flew off with her. Because of the lightness of his burden, he gained enough of a lead to fly ahead of Thjazi, who had discovered the theft and was in pursuit.

The gods, who had been growing weaker each day, were watching for Loki from the walls of Asgard. When he came into view, they realized that Thjazi was close behind him and gaining. So they piled the walls of Asgard high with wood shavings. Just as Loki flew over the walls, they lit the fire. Thjazi had been so angry and was flying so fast that he did not realize what was happening. He could not stop in time and, as he passed over the fire, his wings were singed causing him to tumble ignominiously to the ground. There he was killed by the angry gods.

Quickly Idun was changed back to her youthful self and caused great rejoicing in Asgard as she produced her golden apples. The gods grew young and beautiful again, and Asgard was no longer a place of gloom and foreboding.

THE DEATH OF BALDER

As the twilight of the gods drew near, Odin felt a terrible foreboding. Even Balder, his handsome and goodnatured son, had changed his sunny countenance to that of a dark frown. When the other gods questioned Balder about his gloom, he admitted that he had been having dreams that foretold evil things and death in Asgard. Odin was troubled and determined to learn what these dreams meant, so he journeyed to the dread realm of Hel.

There, at a burial mound, he cast a sacred spell which he repeated three times. This would bring forth Volva, the prophetess of the dead. She appeared at the end of the third incantation and confirmed Odin's worst fears, that Balder would be killed by his blind twin brother Hodur and that a son, not yet born, would eventually avenge Balder's death.

Odin went back to Asgard with a heavy heart and tried to think of ways to forestall the death of his favorite. He had Frigg extract a promise from every living thing that it would not harm their son. All of creation gave this promise —all, that is, except the lowly mistletoe, for no one had thought it could do any harm.

The gods were delighted with what they thought was their foolproof plan to save Balder. He was now regarded as invincible, and it became a sport among them to throw spears or objects at Balder and to delight in the fact that nothing would harm him. All might have gone well, had it not been for the malice of Loki.

Loki was jealous of Balder. He disguised himself as an old woman and went to see Frigg to discover if she had forgotten anything when she had planned her son's invincibility. She admitted to this sympathetic "woman" that she had forgotten the mistletoe. This was all that Loki needed to know to put his plan into action.

Loki sought the blind Hodur and persuaded him to join in the game against Balder. At first Hodur declined, saying that this was no sport for a blind man, but Loki persisted and offered to guide his hand for him. Hodur at last agreed because it was not often that he had an opportunity to join in the fun of the Asgard Gods. Loki then placed the mistletoe in his hands; he threw it and it pierced the heart of Balder, who immediately fell dead.

A great lamentation went up in Asgard, and Frigg was so distraught that she begged someone to go to the kingdom of Hel to sue for Balder's release. Hermod, another son of Odin, was finally sent on this task by Odin, who gave him Sleipnir to ride on.

Meanwhile, preparations for the burial of Balder went on. He was laid out on his own ship Hringhorni, and Nanna, his wife, who had died of grief, was placed alongside him. Odin placed Balder's horse on the bier and also the magical ring Draupnir, one of the great treasures of the gods. The ship was then set on fire and pushed out to sea.

By this time, Hermod had reached the gates of Hel and had called its mistress forth. After much argument, she agreed that she would give up

Balder providing that he was mourned by every living creature. Hermod returned to Asgard in a joyful frame of mind, for who had ever hated Balder, the kindest and most beloved of the gods? Immediately, every living creature declared that he or she mourned for Balder—everyone except Loki, who had disguised himself as a giantess in the hope that his evil would go unrecognized. In the disguise, he had stated that he could not mourn Balder, for Balder had never performed any service for him. Thus Balder was doomed to live forever in the dark region of the dead.

LOKI'S PUNISHMENT

Loki realized that the gods would not forgive him for Balder's murder, once his part was detected, so he fled from Asgard. By a river, he built a hut with doors facing every direction. Then, as a further precaution, he changed himself into a salmon so that, if necessary, he could hide in the depths of the river. In order to elude the pursuit that he knew would come, he tried to imagine what methods the gods would use to catch him and figured out ways to avoid each possibility.

The thought that a new invention, a net, might catch him caused him some concern and so he made one in order to try to find a way to avoid its meshes. But as soon as he had it made, he saw the gods approach, led by Kvasir, and just had time to throw the net on the fire before jumping into the river. But he was worried because he had not yet devised a way to elude the net.

Kvasir entered the house first, saw the bits of net in the fire, and realized that Loki must be hiding in the water. Using Loki's own design, the gods built a net to catch him. After casting into the river several times, they caught him by the tail, forced him into his own shape, bound him with iron to a flat rock, and left him inside a cave. As a further punishment, a poisonous snake was hung over his head and left to drop its venom on his face.

Loki's faithful wife Sigyn came to him and tried to ease his suffering by catching the drops of venom in a bowl which she held over her husband's head. But each time, as the bowl filled, she had to turn and empty it. Loki's cries and struggles of pain as the drops of venom fell on his forehead caused the earth to shake and tremble.

But even as Loki suffered, he plotted his revenge. He would join the Giants on Ragnarok, the day of doom, and help them against the gods of Asgard.

Valhalla

In old Icelandic, "Val" means "the slain"; hence Valkyries means "the choosers of the slain" and Valhalla, "the hall of the slain." This hall was built by Odin to house those of noble birth who had given their lives fearlessly either in battle or in sacrifice. Thus, not only were men contained there, but also a few women who had chosen to follow their husbands into the afterlife. The case of Nanna and Balder shows that this must not have been uncommon and, in fact, probably shows that women had the option of dying with their warrior husbands in order to join them in death's kingdom.

The prime purpose of Valhalla was to preserve those brave mortals and to keep them in fighting form for Ragnarok, which Odin knew would come one day. The first hero to enter Valhalla was Sig, a son of Odin and a mortal woman; thereafter, many warriors filled the huge hall.

Valhalla had many doors for its occupants to pass out of on their way to the field of battle. Inside, the hall was emblazoned with shields and armor. Wolves and eagles haunted its floors and wandered among the huge tables laden with pork and mead. Each day the warriors would go out and fight bitter battles. When evening fell, all of their wounds would heal and broken limbs would miraculously be replaced in preparation for the feasting that went on each night. Odin always sat as host to these feasts. Thus, the lot of the brave warrior, even after death, was a noble one.

Ragnarok

The day of Ragnarok was foreshadowed by the chaos of the society of men and gods. It was preceded by a time of strife in which society was so evil that the bonds of kinship had become meaningless, and murder, incest, and intrigue had become the order of the day. Even the earth reacted and was bitter cold, for the wolves had finally caught up with the sun and moon and devoured them. The World Tree fell with a resounding crash and, with its destruction, Fenrir, the wolf, and his father Loki were freed. Fenrir bounded towards Asgard and Loki joined the Giants as they too set sail for Asgard in their magic ship, *Nagilfar*, made from the nails of the dead.

As soon as he saw the terrible horde approaching, Heimdall blew a great blast on Gjallarhorn and all those in Asgard rode forth for the final battle. Bifrost shattered under their weight as they rode to meet the Giants.

Thor fought with the World Serpent; Frey fought against a Giant, Surt. Tyr did battle with a hound from Hel called Garm, and Heimdall fought with Loki. But there were no victories. Thor killed the Serpent, but was destroyed himself by its poisonous breath. Odin was slain and eaten by Fenrir, but Odin's young son managed to slay the beast by tearing its jaws apart. Although Heimdall and Tyr destroyed their foes, they died in the process. Finally, only Surt remained, and in his fury he flung fire over the world and was himself destroyed in the resulting flood and holocaust. Thus, according to many, the world ends.

Perhaps the most startling feature of the Norse myths is that not only are the gods capable of dying, but that they *do* die. The Greeks certainly had no such idea, nor did the North American Indians. What does such a belief indicate about the Norse world view? Can you account for it?

Only brave warriors went to Valhalla. Those who died ignominiously went to the dread realm of Hel. Why would the Norse culture produce this myth?

There was a third dwelling place after death that is sometimes mentioned in Norse mythology. It was said to be in the highest region of the Norse world. It was called Gimli and was the place for the most virtuous. Is this consistent with their culture, or do you think it is a later addition influenced by Christianity?

In the beginning, Loki was a cunning but helpful figure in Asgard. But he gets progressively worse as Ragnarok approaches. Perhaps this was just his Frost Giant character emerging. Or perhaps Loki came to be identified more and more with the Christian Satan. Is it possible that Ragnarok itself is a description of the death of an old religion in order to accept the newer concept of Christianity? There is a story, recorded by Snorri Sturluson, which tends to support this idea. According to him, it was said that out of the destruction of the old world, a new and peaceful world would be born. Inside the World Tree, Yggdrasil, were two living creatures who would emerge after the destruction of Ragnarok and repopulate the land. A new sun and moon were to arise and a universe cleansed of suffering to begin. What aspects of the Christian religion do you think would be more attractive to a people weary of the rule of Norse gods?

Valkyrie bringing a dead warrior to Valhalla, from a painting by Konrad Dielitz.

Eskimo and Indian Mythologies

This section is intended as an introduction only. Although this is true of our studies in Greek and Norse mythologies as well, in the former two we have presented a fairly coherent picture of two total cultures. There are several reasons why a study of the mythology of our native populations cannot be as detailed or coherent.

The first and most obvious reason is the size, complexity, and variety of the communities or tribes. We may think of all Eskimos as being the same, but tribes had little contact with each other in the Arctic barrens, and there are local variations. The same applies to Indian cultures. There are several hundred tribes in North America and, although there are general similarities in outlook, many differences *do* exist. Hence, we have chosen only three sample groups to discuss.

There is a more significant reason for a less comprehensive study. Despite the fact that Indians and Eskimos were in North America first, we are more in tune with Greek and Norse myths. Our cultural heritage is European and we easily identify with these two cultures. We are entering new cultural territory when looking at Indian and Eskimo mythology. We must accept the fact that here we are foreigners learning a new cultural language.

The third reason for the less coherent form is that in the past we have made little attempt to understand the Indian and Eskimo cultures, and they have been reluctant to reveal their traditions. Consequently we are unable to record many of their myths; or if we have recorded them, we have changed them to fit into our own view of life. You will find various specific references to this fact as you read this unit. Many of the stories recorded here are found in only one or two books, and several accounts originate from oral recordings of elderly Indians and Eskimos. Therefore, there is the problem at all times of accuracy. Some of the stories you read here may seem stilted or fragmentary. We have tried to be as true to the accounts as possible, never adding details for narrative interest because that would be another reflection of our own cultural bias.

What is required here is the ability to see the stories within their own context, not to impose our values upon them. If you make this effort, the rewards will be high, for you will be affected by many beautiful and well expressed insights into life.

Eskimo Mythology

Conception

The Creation of the World

Unlike the other mythologies in this study, there are no widespread stories about the creation of the land or of the Eskimo people themselves. The Eskimos just seemed to believe that they had always existed, as had the Arctic environment which surrounded them. In a world where so little actually changed over hundreds of years, the idea of a "beginning" and a gradual development to a more progressive society was just not relevant. Since life did not change, the idea of the world beginning or ending would be a strange thought to these people.

However, there was a very important myth which could be called a creation story. At one time there were two great giants, a man and his wife. No one could say how they had come into being, but they lived in the manner of all Eskimos, by hunting and trapping. As time passed, a baby girl was born to them. This child grew at such a fantastic rate that it soon became obvious to her parents that they had brought a monster into the world. Her appetite for flesh was insatiable. She ate all that her parents could hunt and, to their horror, she even began to chew at their limbs while they were sleeping. The giants decided that they must destroy her, so they took her with them in their kayak far out to sea. There they began to cut off her greedy fingers and throw them into the waters. But as soon as her fingers entered the water they turned into sea creatures such as whales, seals, and fish. In their confusion at this magic occurrence, her parents threw the child into the sea as well and fled from the spot.

The child sank to the bottom and from there ruled all of the fish and sea creatures. Some called the female with mutilated fingers Sedna, while others called her the Old Woman of the Sea. It was to this deity's whims that the Eskimo would attribute either luck or disaster in hunting.

Why is it logical that, although the Eskimos have only one figure whom we could

81

recognize as having "goddess" status, they would choose the Old Woman of the Sea?

What does the character of Sedna suggest about the Eskimos' concept of life?

The Spirits

The Old Woman of the Sea

For the Eskimos, there was no pantheon of gods as in Greek and Norse mythology. The Old Woman of the Sea was the main deity. But this does not mean that she was the only "spirit" with whom the Eskimo felt in contact. On the contrary, the Eskimo's world was full of mystery, and all things had spirits. Each tribe or family group would have its own name for the spirits of caves, animals, birds, and all other aspects of the natural world. In this sense, we could compare the Eskimos' view of life to the animism of the early Greek religion. It seems to have been a fairly common idea among primitive people that all nature was alive or infested with spirits. It was not until a society became much more sophisticated that the idea of gods and goddesses living separate from mortals, usually in the sky, was introduced into mythologies. In Part One and in Norse mythology we are dealing with myths of a more complex society. In this section we go back to the earliest types of myths.

To the Eskimos, all the animals hunted had spirits which could be charmed and thus trapped into their nets or within range of their arrows. They had a respect and almost a reverence for their fellow creature, even though they might be stalking it for food. The flight of birds was seen as an omen of good or ill, and in some cases animals seemed to help the needy hunter. In the final analysis, though, the luck of the hunt was up to Sedna.

Another aspect of the spirit world was the appearance, in dreams, of the spirits of ancestors, who would advise where the hunting was best.

SHAMAN OR ANGAKOK

There were no temples built to the spirits as in the Greek myths. Certainly when the hunt was good, food was buried for the spirit or the dead ancestor who had offered aid, or for Sedna herself. But if someone should dig up this "food cache" later and it was still there, as it usually was, it was eaten by the finder. The spirits had been appeased.

There was a person in each social group who could communicate with the spirit world in a very direct way. He was the Shaman or Angakok. Unlike the other men in the village, the Shaman did not need to prove his worth by hunting, although he did this when necessary. His role was to visit the spirit world in a trance-like state either to ask favors or to receive information. There was no special time for this. He would simply beat on his drum when he felt a trance overcoming him, and all who were present in the village would enter his igloo or hut and sit in sympathy with his efforts. It was believed that this "sympathy" on the part of the tribe aided the Shaman. In his trance, the Shaman's spirit would be in contact with ancestors or animal spirits, and at times of need would even visit the Old Woman of the Sea. On these occasions, the Shaman would dance before Sedna and try to please her so that she would reveal where the good hunting grounds were or direct her creatures to present themselves to the Eskimos for food.

Throughout these visits to the spiritual world, the Shaman might be uttering incoherent cries or even speaking in a strange tongue. When he emerged from his trance he would interpret the messages to the people. In a great number of cases, his directions for achieving success in the hunt were very accurate.

Sea spirits and animal spirits
as characterized in Eskimo prints.

83

The Pleiades.

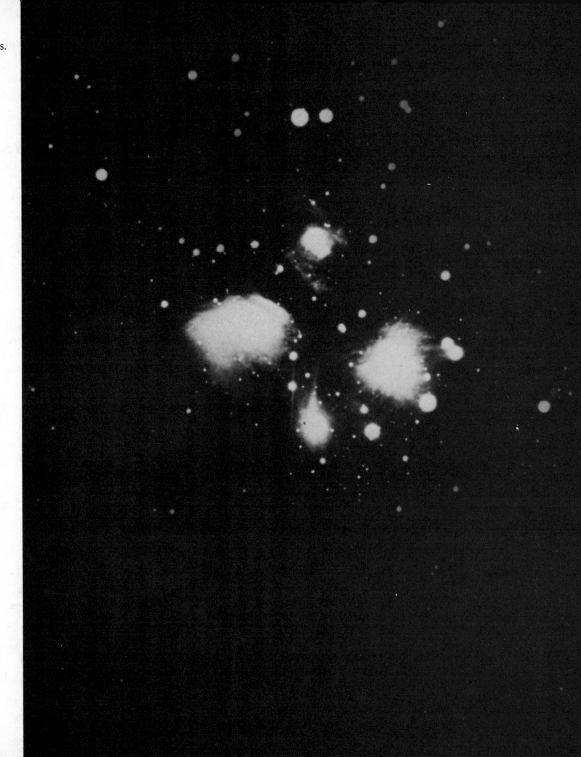

Another important role for the Shaman was that of the healer or medicine man. It was believed that if people were ill, they were possessed by evil spirits. This belief of possession was especially strong in the case of an obvious mental illness. The Shaman would be called to diagnose the illness and to determine how the evil spirit could be driven out. Sometimes the method was very practical. For example, it was believed that lancing a boil would release that particular evil spirit. Often the Shaman would declare that an illness was the result of a spirit's displeasure, and he would order the family to fast, or to abandon their home, or whatever else seemed necessary.

The Eskimos had many taboos that, if broken, would anger the spirits. For instance, if one died in one's own house, it was taboo for the family to remain there. They would have to build another house. Many times, the Shaman could attribute an illness to the fact that one of the taboos had been broken. Many of the taboos might seem foolish to us, but often they were practical. Abandoning the dead person's house might have prevented an epidemic if an illness were serious. The rulings of the Shaman also kept the tribe together as a social unit, operating under the same laws.

Can you offer any possible explanations as to why the Shaman's advice about good hunting would be so accurate?

Why would there be no temples to the spirits among the Eskimos?

The practice of offering a part of an animal to a deity is very common in mythologies. These offerings were often very practical in nature. Quite often, the gods were offered the entrails of the animal or some part that humans would not normally eat. In this way, the needs of the gods did not interfere with those of mortals. The Eskimo food cache was a good example of this. Often it was impossible for a hunter to carry all of the meat away; by burying it "for Sedna," he was assured of a supply of food when he passed that way again.

Look up *taboo* in an encyclopedia and find out as much as you can about taboos in primitive cultures. What taboos does our culture have that may have a practical origin?

Life

Nature and the Moral World

The presence of the sun and moon in the sky, as well as the configurations of the stars, gave rise to the most prevalent Eskimo myths. Because they saw all of nature as animate, they naturally attributed life to the heavenly bodies.

It was believed that the sun was a radiant woman who carried a light through the heavens, always followed by her brother, the moon. The moon was a hunter who had shining spotted dogs. Sometimes as the dogs went through the night sky, certain ones would fall to earth in a blaze of glory.

There were also many stories about how the constellations gained the forms they did. For instance, the Pleiades were formed when a bear was being hunted on earth by a very fast pack of dogs. They ran so fast that they ran up to the sky and became these stars. Other constellations were also animals related to the hunt.

Compare these stories of the formation of the constellations with what you know about the Greek stories. Why do you think that both cultures would invent and enjoy these myths?

Why would the major figures in the Eskimo myths of the constellations be animals, whereas the Greek figures were people?

THE CLOSED CAVE Because of the precarious existence in the harsh Arctic tundra, it was important that an Eskimo never offend the spirits of nature. There are many stories of the evil that resulted from such abuse. One such story concerns the wrath of the earth spirit against a group of Greenland hunters.

There was a cave, a huge cave by the sea, that the Eskimos of a certain tribe would use in winter for overnight shelter. It was particularly appreciated because the hunters who used it did not have to build igloos for the night when they were on a hunting expedition. It was the custom to show appreciation to the spirit of the cave by offering small gifts of food and by acting with propriety within the shelter. But it happened that some hunters refused to make an offering to the earth spirit because they said that the Old Woman of the Sea was more powerful.

Aroused to anger by this, the spirit of the earth plotted a fitting revenge. The next year, when the ice covered the sea and the Eskimos again wanted and needed the cave for shelter, they could not find it. At first the hunters thought they were in the wrong place. But soon it dawned on them that the cave had been mysteriously closed. It was full of pebbles. The men who had originally committed the impiety were not allowed to return. Though the others worked long and hard to remove the pebbles and reopen the cave, the cave was never again as big.

The punishment continued. One night when the hunters were camped there, one of their number had a strange fit. He said that he was overcome by a spirit and while in a trance traced a deep slit with his knife first up his left arm to the shoulder, then across the top of his body, and down his right arm. As soon as he came out of his trance, he died.

Proper funeral observances were made by his friends for five days, and care was taken to offend none of the spirits. After this incident, men could come in peace to the cave. Its spirit was appeased.

What natural occurrence could this myth be an attempt to explain?

For what moral purpose would the Eskimos recount this story?

Another legend which reveals a part of the Eskimo social structure, as well as the affinity between the Eskimo people and nature, is the story of the bewitched wife. This story, which came from an Eskimo tribe in northern Canada, was recorded by Diamond Jenness, well-known writer of Canadian Indian stories.

THE BEWITCHED WIFE

In one small village, an Eskimo husband treated his young wife very cruelly. He beat her and did not give her enough to eat. On one occasion when he left to hunt, the young wife resolved to run away. This was a very dangerous thing to do because she would starve if there was no hunter to care for her.

She wandered for days in the Arctic and finally, suffering from exposure and exhaustion, lay down to die. To her amazement she discovered that she was at the entrance to a grass and stone hut of some Eskimo hunter. The door had been so well camouflaged that she had not noticed it. She crawled inside and waited for the hunter to return and decide her fate.

Upon his return, the hunter at first was angry that anyone would invade his home, but when he saw that it was a woman, he fed her and told her that she could be his wife. He would look after her by hunting, and she would look after him by sewing and cooking. This worked out very well for both and they were happy. The hunter told her that she must never wander outside while he was gone, or talk to anyone, because her former husband might try to find her and get revenge. The young woman agreed to this.

But it was lonely being a hunter's wife and even after her two sons were born, she desired company. It happened that one day an old woman came to the hut and began to talk to her. The dutiful wife wanted to talk but ignored her. As soon as she departed, the old woman turned into the red fox that she was in reality. The red fox's aid had been enlisted by the former husband to punish his wife.

The next day, the red fox in disguise as the crone was even more pleasant. She offered to comb the long black hair of the girl so that it would be beautiful for her husband. This was a temptation impossible to resist, and the young wife accepted. As the old woman combed, the wife fell asleep and did not notice that the old one scratched the wife's head before she stole out and disappeared.

When the wife awoke, she had a terrible urge to run outside of the hut. When she did, she realized to her horror that horns were growing out of her head. As she ran further, she turned into a caribou and disappeared into the distance, leaving her two young children behind.

At night, the husband saw that her tracks turned into the tracks of a caribou and realized what had happened. He determined to find her. He left his young sons with bows and arrows and provisions and began to follow his wife.

After many days, he came upon a hut in which an old woman was telling her son the story of the Eskimo wife. He stepped in and asked the old woman where he might locate her. The old woman told him that she was the swiftest and slightest creature in the caribou herd. If he lassoed this caribou and carefully skinned it, the wife would emerge unharmed. The hunter thanked the woman and left. As he looked back at the hut he saw that the two "people" had turned back into the bears that they were.

He did as he was told, and his wife was restored to him. Joyfully they returned to their sons, who were glad to see them for they had had to defend their house against many wandering hunters.

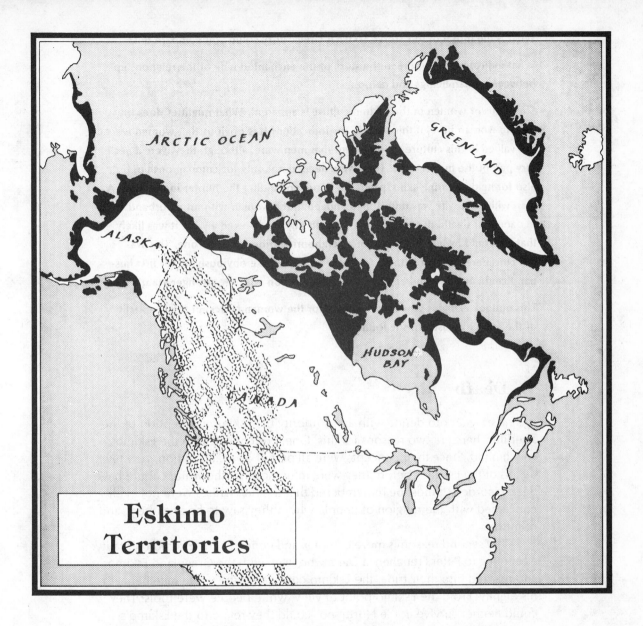

ARCTIC OCEAN

GREENLAND

ALASKA

HUDSON BAY

CANADA

Eskimo Territories

What is the moral of this story? To what Greek story could you compare this?

What indications are there in the story of the enchanted wife of the relationship between human beings and nature?

The status of women in the Eskimo culture is apparent. What qualities does the Eskimo woman have, if this story is any indication? It is obvious that women were not valued in this culture to the extent that men were, although they were a necessary part of the hunter's life. They were needed not only for companionship, but also for help in curing skins, preparing food, and aiding the hunter in the hunt. A man without a wife was unfortunate indeed, but a woman without a husband was in danger of death. If a man were strong enough and lacked a wife, it was likely that he would invade the house of a neighboring tribe and steal one. This was not considered a terrible thing for the woman because obviously, if her first husband could not fight to keep her, she was better off with the stronger man.

This outlook explains why it was so easy for the woman to accept the hospitality of the hunter whose hut she found.

Death

It is no easy task to define with any authority the Eskimo conception of the afterlife. There are two reasons for this. One, our contact with the Eskimos is very limited. Since their concepts were all part of an oral tradition, very few beliefs of the Eskimos before they were influenced by the white culture have been recorded. It must be remembered that the first whites were not at all concerned with the religion of people whom they saw to be "heathen" and primitive.

The second reason is more complex and concerns the Eskimo mentality. According to Peter Freuchen, a Dane who lived with the Greenland Eskimos and married into their tribe, the Eskimo considered the white race beneath his dignity. From the Eskimo point of view, white people were fools. They could neither survive in the North, nor could they relate to the Eskimo's concerns. The Eskimo regarded the white person's questions as absurd. Therefore, the tendency on the part of the Eskimo, who did not want trouble, was to agree with any suggestion white people made to them. If the white people suggested to the Eskimo that they believed in an afterlife similar to the Christian heaven or hell, the Eskimo would simply agree with them. What was the point of arguing with such fools? Naturally, the white people were gratified to find such a fertile field for converting the Eskimos to Christianity, and would never wonder why their leading questions were always answered in the affirmative.

From what we do know, it would appear that the Eskimo people did not fear death at all. Rather they saw it as inevitable. Their real concern was with the difficulties of life.

Many Eskimos simply saw death as an end; others saw it as a transition into a kind of spirit world under the ground. Often both beliefs were held at once, depending on the attitude of the person at a given time. The underworld was not defined like the Greek Hades, or even the Norse Hel, but there was the idea that the spirits of the old people could contact the living either through the Shaman or in dreams. The advice of the deceased was always benevolent. They told the living where the good hunting was.

Many Eskimos held a rather charming belief that the shining and shimmering lights of the Aurora Borealis were the souls of their dead ancestors dancing about a fire. The story of the Aurora Borealis being the souls of the dead gives us a picture of a compassionate and imaginative people, a picture that certainly does not conform to the white person's stereotype of the Eskimo.

It might be of interest to you to know that the Eskimos had stories about death that are akin to our fairy tales. If a winter was especially harsh, or famine plagued the land, the Eskimo mother and father were often forced to kill a young child. The first choice was always to kill the young female child, for in the Arctic she was the more useless in terms of survival. This seems hard and cruel, but this was a culture where necessity dictated morality. The Eskimos did not do this without anguish, and the following tale, commonly told, was perhaps a consolation.

The story went that when a young and beautiful female child was killed by her parents, she met a handsome prince in the spirit world who took her as his wife and gave her presents to keep her warm and well fed. Thus she lived happily ever after in the spirit world, and never knew hunger as her family on earth did.

The statement was made that the Eskimos did not fear death. Is this true of our culture? What is your own attitude toward death? Why?

Another story which proves that this culture accepted death as natural is told by Peter Freuchen in his excellent work, *Book of the Eskimos*. Suicide was not considered a sin; it was respected. If a man realized his uselessness, he not only wanted to quit life because he was no longer happy, but also because he knew that his life was a burden to the community. There are true accounts of the way in which the "suicides" were enacted. The old man's family would have a feast and everyone would come. There would be much merrymaking and eating. When the party was at its height, a young man, usually the son, would place a rope around the old man's neck. The old man would say goodbye to his friends, and all would have a hand in hoisting him to his death. Old women also would often opt for suicide, but apparently their preferred method was to be stabbed by a family member. Many in our own society would be horrified at this "cruelty." Consider our attitude toward old people. Which would you consider to be more humane? What are the alternatives?

Kenojuak/Luktak (Cape Dorset, 1960). *The Woman Who Lives in the Sun.*
In the Eskimo culture the sun is feminine.
This stone-cut portrays a joyful woman wearing the classic chin tattoo.

North American Indian Mythology

Before discussing North American Indian mythology, one common misconception must be done away with. We have a tendency to think of Indians as being one cultural group. This is a result of our own ignorance and prejudice over the years. In fact, it must be remembered that even the word "Indian" was applied by the Europeans who perversely refused to accept the fact that they had not found the route to the East and India. Now, of course, we (and the Indians) are stuck with the word, but we must put a different meaning to it. The word "Indian" was a way of referring to hundreds of cultural units which made up the native population of North America before the white race came. Even the word "native" in the last sentence has associations that are not flattering in our minds. Our language has played us and the Indians a perverse trick. Because of our own prejudices and ignorance, words which should only be descriptive have a prejudicial ring to them. We cannot change the words, but we can change our attitudes toward the words. One way to do this is to study these myths.

When we study Indian mythology, we see the common concerns of all humans emerging. We also see that each cultural group had a very different way of life, yet shared many of the same problems. We cannot possibly consider all the tribes, so we have arbitrarily chosen three diverse groups: the Indians of the Pacific Coast, the Haida in particular; the Indians of the Eastern Woodlands, the Iroquois in particular; and the Plains Indians. The first group were predominantly a hunting culture, the second were predominantly agricultural, and the third were a mixture of both.

The Indians of the Pacific Coast

Conception

Haida Creation Myth

Raven Before the world as we know it was created, there was a kingdom in the clouds called Cloud Land. This kingdom was ruled by Sha-lana, the Cloud King. He had many servants, including Raven. Raven was, by many accounts, a rather mischievous and clever creature, and he certainly did not like being a servant in Cloud Land. He also resented very much the fact that as he flew from place to place in Cloud Land, there was no spot for him to sit and rest on the great sea that lay below Sha-Lana's kingdom. So it happened that one day he decided to correct this situation by beating the water with his wings until the rocks were formed. These rocks then grew out over the sea to form dry land.

But what good is a kingdom of one's own without anyone there? So the lonely Raven decided to create humans out of clam shells. They were created in the form of two women. For a time all was well, but then the women began to complain bitterly that two women had been a mistake. So Raven listened to their entreaties and, with a deft throw of a limpit shell, changed one of the women into a man. This proved very satisfactory to the humans, but in their delight with each other they tended to ignore Raven, who felt the need for a mate of his own. He decided that the best method of obtaining such a one was to go to the Cloud Kingdom in disguise and steal the King's daughter, along with anything else that might be useful.

Raven arrived in Cloud Land through a hole in the wall and was unrecognized because he had assumed the form of a bear. He found that Cloud Land had greatly changed. It was ruled over by a King of Light who had created a peaceful place and brought light by the creation of fire and a huge ball of brightness in the sky. Raven, in his guise of a bear, was kept by the King of Light to entertain his children. The Raven used his time to decide what he wanted to take from Cloud Land.

On the day he decided to leave, Raven changed himself into a huge eagle. He grabbed the King's children and the fire-making stick under one

94

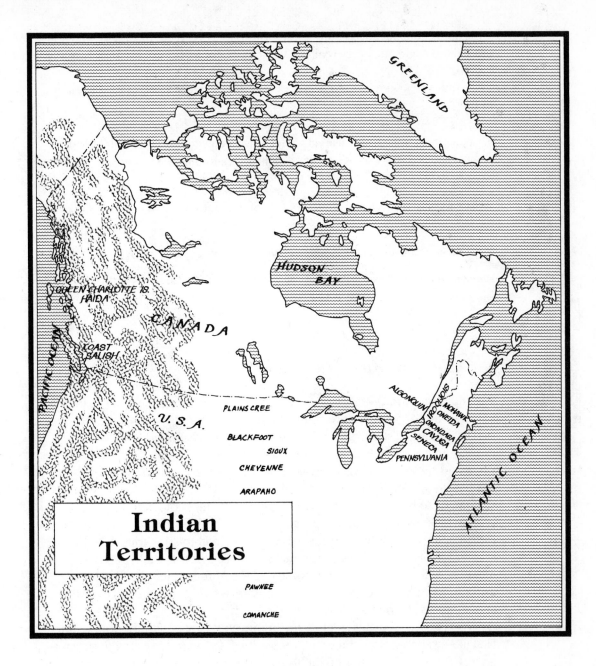

GREENLAND

HUDSON BAY

QUEEN CHARLOTTE IS. HAIDA

CANADA

PACIFIC OCEAN

COAST SALISH

U.S.A.

PLAINS CREE

BLACKFOOT

SIOUX

CHEYENNE

ARAPAHO

ALGONQUIN

IROQUOIS

MOHAWK

ONEIDA

ONONDAGA

CAYUGA

SENECA

PENNSYLVANIA

ATLANTIC OCEAN

Indian Territories

PAWNEE

COMANCHE

wing, and the ball called "sun" under the other. Everyone in Cloud Land chased the eagle once they realized what had happened, but he quickly made his escape.

Thus the Raven brought fire for his earthly kingdom and placed the sun in the sky.

What figure does the Raven remind you of in Greek mythology? It might interest you to know that the Raven's punishment in many accounts was never to be able to enter Cloud Land again.

What does this myth suggest about the relationship between people and animals in the Haida culture?

What do we learn are the basic human needs, according to this myth?

Why do you think it reasonable that Indians on the Pacific Coast of North America would call their sky world Cloud Land?

The Spirits

The Indians of the West Coast were hunters and fishermen. Although their villages were larger and more comfortable than those of the Eskimos, they too had to struggle to survive. Their myths were more developed than those of the Eskimos, for they had more time to tell stories and were together more often, but they still had very few gods as we know them. Interestingly, they too believed in an Old Woman of the Sea as did the Eskimos. It would seem that they also had a conception of a Supreme Being, about whom very little is known. However, many writers suggest that this idea became part of the Indian mythology only after the arrival of Christian missionaries. Like the Eskimos, the Haidas believed in animal spirits. This belief is easily seen in their creation myth. Animals could be appealed to in time of hunger. There were also stories about how the abuse of an animal would bring the wrath of the animal spirits. No one was to kill except out of necessity.

Everyone associates the Indians of the West Coast with the totem pole. First, it must be said that the tremendously high totem poles were constructed only after the white man brought his sophisticated tools. The original smaller totems were used as supports inside houses and as entrance supports. These were elaborately carved with the family crest (totem). Their connection to myth is indirect but worth mentioning. The tribes divided themselves into family groups and each group had its animal totem depicted by carving. Each village might have a bear family, for instance. Usually, it was said that some ancestor had had a mystical relationship with this particular animal spirit, but eventually the totem became a family identification sign only. But the fact that all totems were of animals such as bears, ravens, salmon, and so on, indicates the respect with which the people regarded the nature which surrounded them. In fact there are many stories of people being animals part of the time and animals being people part of the time. This indicates a harmony with nature that our culture lacks, but which is consistent among all Indian and Eskimo tribes.

Why do you think our culture lacks this quality of being in harmony with nature and being a brother of fellow animals?

Which outlook do you find most appealing?

How can you account for the similar belief of the Haidas and Eskimos in the Old Woman of the Sea?

Life

Nature and the Moral World

We have already seen that the world of nature was alive or animate to the Indian and the Eskimo, so this "science" myth of the Haidas should not come as any surprise.

After the world had been formed by the Raven, and men and women populated it, trouble began among the humans. They could not seem to get along although they had everything they could wish for. These humans were jealous of each other and one person wanted more than the other had. This

Witchdoctor and his vision of a wolf spirit, from an Indian carving.   97

resulted in quarrels and arguments. The creator told them that they must cease this strife, but although some tried, the situation seemed to get worse.

Finally, the creator tired of this and caused the islands of the Haida people (now the Queen Charlotte Islands) to be covered in darkness. When the darkness disappeared, all the evil people had been turned into trees. Their arguing became the sound of the wind through the leaves. The creator declared to the good people that they should see this as a warning for the future, and that they also should make use of this new tree in their daily lives. It was their reward for being good. The name of the tree was the cedar, and it is the most plentiful tree on the islands.

What is the obvious moral of the story? Can you compare this with any other similar stories? Why do you think this type of story is told so often?

Stories which tell of the origins of things as diverse as Niagara Falls and medicine bundles abound in all of North American Indian mythology. Many of the "explana-

Haida village at turn of the century.

tions" are ingenious and entertaining. We will be looking at one or two other science myths when we look at other tribes, but if you wish to read more, look at *Indian Legends of Canada* by E. E. Clarke. It tells many of these related stories. You could ask the same types of questions about those legends as we ask about the one we are studying here, and thereby learn a great deal more about Indian cultures.

THE SALMON'S REVENGE

It was mentioned earlier that the Indians were natural conservationists. It was considered a sin to kill more than one needed, or to offer an indignity to a dead or dying animal, for it too had a spirit. The following story, widely told in the coastal region, indicates the importance of not insulting a spirit.

Near the source of a salmon river there was a tribe whose members were able to catch so many fish that they were never hungry and could even trade with other tribes. The older people in the tribe were always careful to show respect to the salmon spirits and to give thanks to the other spirits of nature. But as time passed, the younger men of the tribe took this bounty for granted and refused to consider themselves lucky. They felt that the riches of the salmon were their due. Thus, in spawning season, they would catch fish just to mutilate them and watch their ingenious torture. The old people in the tribe warned them against such impiety, but they were ignored.

One day, a rumbling was heard in the distance, like the beating of a drum. This became progressively louder, and the Shaman said that it was the Supreme Spirit in his anger. Finally, a huge hill erupted in fire, and all the rivers seemed to turn to fire as well. This fire caused the trees to burn and almost all of the people in the village were killed.

What natural occurrence does the Supreme Spirit's revenge explain?

Compare this with the Eskimo story of the cave. Why do you think this type of story would be told by both cultures?

Do we have any similar "myths" today about this sort of evil? Should we?

THE FACE CHANGER

Another morality tale that concerns itself more with everyday life is told by the Coast Salish people, a tribe of the Northwest. This story, with many variations, can be found in a number of Indian tribes, perhaps because its message is universal.

Once there was a young girl who was beautiful, but because she was beautiful, she rejected all suitors. One young man was in love with her but she laughed at him. He begged her to tell him what he must do to win her love. She cruelly told him that if he would rub his body often with cedar twigs, she would love him. He did this, although the twigs were harsh and cut his skin. When he returned, she just laughed at his disfigurement and told him to rub his face with cedar branches. These harsh branches scarred his face even more. The maiden then laughed at his ugliness and would have nothing to do with him.

The youth was very sad, for his face was scarred. One day he heard of a spirit woman who lived somewhere in the forest. If he could find the way to her hut, she had the power to change faces.

After much traveling the youth found her hut and politely asked her to help him. She agreed to this and let him look at all of the faces she had hung on the wall. Finally, he chose one which made him look very handsome. Happily he returned, taking with him a good maiden who had saved his life from a bear during his journey home. There he and his new bride lived happily.

When the beautiful Indian maiden saw how the face changer had made him handsome, she was jealous. She wanted to be even more beautiful. So she set out to find the spirit.

Upon her arrival, she haughtily demanded a new face. The face changer took off her old face and replaced it with an ugly one which more truly reflected her character. Of course, the girl could not see her own face and it was not until she returned to her village and everyone laughed at her that she realized what had happened. No young man ever suffered again in pursuit of her love.

What is the obvious moral of the story? What other stories do you know that have this moral?

What does this story tell you about the Indian attitude toward love and beauty? Compare it with your own.

Left: Volcanic eruption.

The Indians of the Eastern Woodlands

Conception

Iroquois Creation Myth

Before the world was created, only water and water creatures such as the Great Turtle, otters, and muskrats existed. But one day, a beautiful princess fell out of the Sky World and surely would have drowned if two passing loons had not seen her falling and placed themselves so that she landed on their backs. (In some versions, swans break her fall.) Of course, they could not hold her forever, so they called upon the other water creatures. The Great Turtle took her for a time, while he told the others that they must find earth for her to live on.

The water creatures knew that there was earth at the bottom of the sea, but the sea was very deep. First the beaver tried, but he came to the surface and died from the effort, never having touched the bottom. The otter tried and met the same terrible end. Finally the toad dived down and, after what seemed a long time, came to the surface and also died—but not before he had given a small amount of dirt to the Great Turtle. The Great Turtle placed the dirt on his back; it grew and grew until it covered a good part of the ocean. This was the land where the princess and her descendants would live and it is still supported on the back of the Great Turtle.

The Great Turtle

Now it happened that the princess was pregnant with twins. Before they were even born, it was obvious that one was a good child and that one was bad. The bad child kicked and hurt his mother and finally killed her by bursting out of her side. His name varied from tribe to tribe, but we will call him Taweskare. The good twin was called Tsentsa. Their grandmother came down to earth to raise them.

Taweskare and Tsentsa

Always it was a contest between the two brothers to see who could make the earth pleasant for people and who could make it difficult. No sooner would Tsentsa create a beautiful meadow with rich soil than Taweskare would create a barren, rock-covered area where nothing would grow. On one occasion, it was said that the good brother made all rivers run downstream so that everyone could paddle with the current, but the other

102

brother made half of the streams go the other way. There are many stories about these two brothers in the Iroquois legends.

What does this creation myth suggest about the relationship of the Iroquois with the animals?

What are the similarities in outlook between this myth and the Haida creation myth?

Try to find other stories about the twin brothers Taweskare and Tsentsa. There are many. Where else have you seen this idea that there are two forces, one good and one bad, working on human beings?

The Spirits

Here, for the first time in our study of North American mythology, we are presented with what amounts to a pantheon of gods and a very organized religion where certain ceremonies were observed at certain times of the year and where there was a definite supreme power.

The Iroquois had a concept of a supreme being or Manitou who guided all of the world. He was prayed to, although he was not personified to any great extent. Offerings were made to him. The sun and moon were important deities and all of nature was invested with spirits. The spirits of plants such as the Corn Goddess were as important to the Iroquois as the animal spirits.

Because the agricultural life not only made these tribes less nomadic, but also more dependent on the consistent goodwill of nature, there were six major festivals a year to honor the gods of nature.

The first was the Spring Festival, which occurred at maple sugar time. All members of the tribe would meet with the Shaman or medicine man and confess their sins aloud while holding white wampum, a belt of white shells representing the purity each tribal member hoped to attain.

The next rite would be the Corn Planting Festival; then the Hope Festival as the first shoots of corn emerged. Offerings of tobacco would be made by the dancing Indians to encourage the spirits to allow the corn to grow.

Then came the Green Corn Festival when the corn was full-grown. This was a great festival of thanks, and there was much revelry and license permitted. Many of the Indians would dress in false face masks and dance. These false faces were supposed to represent a group of giant and malformed spirits who lived on the edge of the Iroquois world. The Seneca tribe in particular had many such masks. It was believed that by wearing the mask the dancer gained control over the spirits.

Then came the Harvest Festival, another time of thanks when the Indian tribes enjoyed the good part of life.

The last festival of the year was an interesting one. It was called the White Dog Festival and was held in the dead of winter. A white dog or grey fox was led through the village and everyone touched it, thus transferring their evil spirits to the animal. It was then killed and its mouth was bound so that the evil spirits could not escape from the carcass through this opening. Thus, the people were cleansed for a time, at least until the cycle should repeat itself with the Spring Festival.

What rite of thanks to our God have we borrowed from the Iroquois?

The use of wampum was widespread among the Indians, particularly the East Coast Indians and the Indians of the Eastern Woodlands. Many have the mistaken impression that wampum was money, but this was not so. Wampum was white and purple shells that were strung and woven into belts. These wampum belts were the political and religious history of the tribe. The designs were ceremonial and symbolic. Treaties were "signed" with the weaving of a wampum belt and its presentation to the other party. Noteworthy events were recorded in wampum belts. Unfortunately, it often happened that the medicine man was the only one who knew the meaning of the symbols, and those meanings are no longer known. There is an interesting story told of the wampum belt that was made for William Penn when the Indians sold him Pennsylvania. The belt depicted two men holding hands, one man considerably larger than the other. Although the white men just assumed that they were represented by the larger figure, the Indians made it clear that the larger figure was an Indian.

Why do you think most people would associate wampum with money?

The Indians of the West Coast and the Plains Indians had the equivalent of wampum in their use of *medicine bundles*. These were pieces of animal skin all bound in an intricate way and opened only by the medicine man, or initiates into the rites, on certain ceremonial occasions. No one who was uninitiated knew the meanings of the bundles except that they were a part of the religious life of the tribe. An excellent movie called *The Circle of the Sun* (National Film Board of Canada) tells the story of the Sun Dance of the Alberta Blood Indians and shows the ritual of the medicine bundle as it is enacted even today.

Medicine bundles recorded the political and religious history of the tribe by depicting ritual in ceremonial design. Often, however, rituals acquired independently of each other were common to many cultures. The idea of having an animal take on all of the ills of a society and then die in order to cleanse people of these ills was popular not only with the Iroquois but with other tribes and cultures. In Middle Eastern cultures the creature sacrificed was often a goat, and so the name for this creature in modern times has become the "scapegoat." Why do you think the idea of a scapegoat dying for the people would be so common? Does our culture have scapegoats? Why?

By examining the myths of the Eskimo, the Haida, and the Iroquois, we can see that there is a progression of sophistication and complexity from the first to the last. Can you make any general observations which might account for the fact that the Iroquois mythology would be the most complex of the three?

105

Life

Nature and the Moral World

We have seen that the formation of the constellations was important to the Eskimos. So it was with the Iroquois, not only because the movement of the constellations helped them determine planting cycles, but also because the placement of stars was an easy way of determining direction. According to the following Iroquois legend, this was not always the case.

On one occasion, a hunting party had gone so far away from the village that they were hopelessly lost. The chief warrior became ill from lack of food, and a council was called to determine what should be done. The pipes were lit and the drums began their throbbing, when out of the darkness a bright little creature, the size of a child, came up. This little person announced that she was their guide and instructed them to break camp and follow her. This they did and she led them to a magic food that made them strong and showed them where to find game.

Then the chief of the little people came. The Indians were courteous and thanked the chief, who promised that he would place a new star in the sky, a star that would stay in one place and not move as did the others, so that the Indians would always have it as a guide.

The Indian chief was grateful, and when he returned home he called all of the Iroquois tribes together to tell them of his adventure and to devise a name for the new star. They decided to call it "the star that never moves." And, of course, it never has.

Medicine bundles.

By what name do we call "the star that never moves"? What is our explanation for this?

To what other cultural groups do we attribute a belief in "little people"?

Look up some of the other Indian tales of little people and dwarfs.

THE CORN GODDESS

Corn became one of the most important crops to the Indians of the Eastern Woodlands. The following is one version of the story of a time when the Corn Goddess was among the Indians.

There was a great hunter named Gosadaya. He hunted all of the time, for this was the only way the Indians knew of obtaining food. One night, as he lay alone in the forest, he heard first a mighty crash, and then a mournful sound as all of the trees lamented the death of their great Chief, the mighty oak. Gosadaya joined the trees in their lament and offered a ritual sacrifice of tobacco which he burned on the trunk of the old tree.

After all proper observances had been made, he pointed to one of the nearby mighty oaks and suggested that this oak could be Chief. The grateful trees were pleased to have a new leader and thanked Gosadaya. He then returned to his hut, a temporary shelter he used while hunting in the area.

Soon after, a beautiful maiden appeared in his hut and told him that the Great Spirit was pleased with him because he had shown his reverence for the trees and helped them. She was to be his wife. The young man accepted this reward and they lived happily in the forest for a year before returning to his village.

Wampum belt.

The maiden then gave her husband some seeds that the Great Spirit had sent with her. She showed the village people how to plant them and how to harvest the corn that grew in the autumn. The people were very happy with this gift because the corn was nutritious and a far easier source of food than hunting.

But one day a relative of Gosadaya came to the village. He was still a hunter and had not heard of corn. When he asked for food, the wife gave him corn bread. He threw it to the floor in disgust. For this great impiety, the Supreme Ruler told the Corn Goddess, for so she was, to return to the Sky World. This she did sadly because she had been happy with Gosadaya. Just before she left, she whispered to her husband how he might follow her.

On the night that the Corn Goddess left, there was a great storm and all of the harvest was ruined. The corn actually disappeared from the stalks so that there was no seed for the following year. The men tried to hunt for game, but it was scarce and soon people were starving. Gosadaya determined to go to the land of the gods and seek his wife.

By following her directions, he found her and their reunion was a joyful one. He stayed with the Corn Goddess for a year, but when the time came for him to depart for his village, she tearfully told him the Supreme Spirit was still angry and would not allow her to return with him. But she gave him a few handfuls of corn so that he might plant them for his people.

When Gosadaya returned to the village, the people were glad to have the gift of corn again. They planted it and prayed diligently to the Corn Goddess and to the Supreme Spirit to make it grow. Because of their prayers, the corn grew and would continue to grow as long as the proper rites were offered to the deities.

In time Gosadaya became so lonesome for his wife that he left his tribe and went to live with her.

What would a bad harvest suggest to a people who believed in this myth?

What is the moral of the story?

THE THUNDERS There are many Iroquois myths about the Sky Beings or spirits of the sky. One such myth is the story of the Thunder Brothers. This myth was also told by many other North American Indian tribes.

108

Three young men were out hunting when one of them broke his leg. They were a long way from their village. For a time, the two friends carried their wounded friend, but soon they grew too tired and threw him over a cliff to die. They went back to their village and tearfully told his mother that he had died in a battle and that they had buried him according to the proper rites. This last statement reassured the mother, for if a person were not buried properly, his soul would never rest in peace.

But the youth did not die. An old man who lived in the valley saved him and made him his slave. The wound healed, but not well, and although the Indian boy was able to hunt game for the old man, he was not able to scramble out of the valley and escape. This new life was hateful to the boy, but he had no choice.

It happened that one day as he was out hunting, a wonderful event occurred. He had just killed a huge fat bear when four men, dressed in cloud-like robes, appeared to him. They explained that they wanted to kill the evil old man and asked the youth if he would help by leading the old man to the spot where the bear was. This he did. The old man, who was usually too sly to be caught, could not resist the idea of all of that bear meat and he knew that his crippled slave would not be able to carry it. As soon as he arrived in the place where the bear was, the Thunders stepped out of a cloud. The old man turned himself into a porcupine and tried to escape, but they killed him by throwing lightning bolts.

The four Thunders then gave the young Indian a cloud robe like theirs, healed his leg, and sent him home. He asked what he might do to aid them, and they said that they would call on him in the future. The young man returned to the village where he was met by his rejoicing mother. He never mentioned the treachery of his friends.

Often, after that time, the Thunders would ask the youth to fly with them. They always went on journeys to destroy evil people or to destroy the enemies of mortals. They told their friend that there was one enemy above all which they wished to destroy. This monster exuded an oily substance and caused people great harm. The youth found his hiding place at the bottom of a pond. The Thunders then made a huge thunderbolt and shot it at the monster. It was so powerful that it instantly killed the creature.

The Thunders then gave the Indian a message that would save his people much trouble and sorrow. They told the Indian that the spring lightning would kill the grubs in the garden if the people would turn the earth over each spring and expose the grubs. The young man delivered the message. From that time onward, the Indians revered the Thunders and always turned over the earth after the first thunder was heard in the spring.

What does this story tell you of the human conflicts between Indian tribes? You might be interested in looking up a similar story in the Old Testament, the story of Joseph and his brothers.

According to this legend, the monster was the father of all the cutworms that destroyed the plants the Indians needed for food. Why do you think this story would be so popular among the Eastern Woodland tribes?

THE SUN SHADOW

It should be obvious by now that the Indian myths were often intended to enforce certain activities and to encourage a high standard of moral behavior. The following is a Seneca myth.

The Seneca and Mohawk tribes had lived in peace and harmony for many years. This peace was broken by a band of young Seneca warriors who wanted a taste of war. They invaded a Mohawk village and stole several young girls and warriors to be their slaves.

The Mohawk chief sent a delegation of warriors to talk to the elders of the Seneca tribe. He reminded them of their long peace and told them that the hostages must be returned if war was to be avoided.

The Seneca stubbornly refused to give in and captured the delegation. War was declared.

As the Mohawk war party approached, the captives shouted them encouragement even though they knew they would be sacrificed before the battle started. But as the first Seneca knife rose in the air to kill a hostage, a miraculous event occurred. A shadow began to cover the sun until the sun completely vanished.

An Indian captive shouted that the Great Spirit was angry with the Senecas for breaking the peace. A wise old man of the Senecas told the warriors that the sun would no longer shine if the young men persisted in breaking the peace. Quickly the pipe of peace was passed among the warriors and, as this was done, the shadow slowly moved away from the sun. From that time forward, the peace was maintained between the Seneca and Mohawk people. In fact, it was not long after this that the union of the Six Nations occurred.

What natural phenomenon does this explain?

What cultural values emerge from this story?

After existing as separate entities for a time, many tribes of the Eastern Woodlands joined together in the federation which we know as the Six Nations. They had one of the most admirable alliances and one of the most democratic systems ever devised. There were elected representatives, women voted, and there was also a council under a constitution. Some of the ideas for federalism adopted in the American Constitution came from the studies of the Six Nations. Find out what you can about this aspect of the Six Nations culture and of the tribes which joined the alliance.

Death

Like the Eskimos, both the Indians of the Pacific Coast and of the Eastern Woodlands did not allow their thoughts to dwell on a complex concept of afterlife. They believed in ancestral spirits who could appear in dreams to their descendants. Like the Eskimos, the Algonquins had stories that the Northern Lights were the dancing souls of the dead.

The Haidas believed that the dead went into an underworld and that this underworld could be visited by the living under certain circumstances. However, if a living person ate anything in the underworld, he was never able to leave it. This sounds so remarkably like the story of Persephone in the Greek myth that one must either be amazed at the ways of the human mind or else suspect that the European recording the tale allowed his own knowledge of Greek mythology to influence him.

It is not surprising that the Iroquois should have the most sophisticated concept of an underworld, since they were the most sophisticated people in our study group. They believed that the dead lived in wonderful villages where they lacked nothing. These spirits would visit them in dreams. Some stories also talked of Warriors in the Sky, who were always there but who were only visible as Northern Lights.

In our study, only the Iroquois consistently saw life after death as a kind of reward. Why do you think that of the three native groups studied so far, it would be the Iroquois who came closest to our own culture's outlook.

The remarkable consistency in the myths of the North American natives shows their common environment. The Algonquin stories and the Eskimo explanations for the Northern Lights are good examples of this. What other similarities can you see?

Indian graves with family monuments.

The Indians of the Plains

Conception

A Crow Creation Myth

Long ago, before the world was destroyed, there lived a character named Old Coyote-Man. He built a boat, and when the boat was finished it began to rain. It rained so long that eventually all the mountains were covered with water except for one point on a high peak where Old Coyote-Man's boat eventually came to rest. Two ducks swam toward him, and he asked one of them to dive down and find some earth.

One dived three times unsuccessfully and was never seen again. Old Coyote-Man asked the other one to dive, and it was successful on the fourth try. Old Coyote-Man threw the dirt around him and it became the Earth. Then he traced out rivers and hills and all the landscape as we know it. From the mud he made the buffalo, horses, and all other animals. He fashioned a male and a female, and also a wife for himself. He made teepees for the people from leaves, and created bows and arrows and all the tools necessary for Indians to live.

When enough children were born, old Coyote-Man divided them into tribes and settled them in a great circle with one tribe in the center, the Crow tribe. All the other tribes became their enemies, and Old-Coyote-Man showed the Crows a dance that was to be performed over every enemy that was killed.

It is significant that every culture has a myth about a flood or a destruction of the universe. Compare this story with other flood stories. In what way is it different?

Many tribes had cultural heroes who taught the first peoples methods of survival, proper social customs, and ceremonial rituals. On the Pacific Coast, the founding father is a raven; farther south, he is a blue jay; in the plains, he is a coyote (prairie wolf); and in the east, he is a rabbit. Can you explain the choice of these particular animals? What does the use of such creatures as founding fathers tell us about the Indian's relationship with nature?

The Spirits

To the Plains Indian, everything was alive with gods and spirits. Ruling over all was an omnipresent Sky Father. Between him and the earth were powers, each governing their own realms, but sharing with the Sky Father the power to change into human shapes and come down to visit the earth people. These sky spirits (eagle, thunder, lightning, rainbow, sun, moon, planets) lived in the heavens in the same way as the Indians did on earth except that their homes were bigger and more beautiful.

Often the spirits interfered with humans by directing storms, causing rivers to dry up, or turning the buffalo herds. They even granted bravery to warriors. When evil befell a tribe, the only way the spirits could be appeased was through individual offerings from people who voluntarily suffered pain.

The Sun Dance ceremony, performed by a single warrior.

Thus, in the Sun-Dance, warriors would suspend themselves from poles by running wooden skewers through their chest muscles and looking straight into the sun. If a warrior could last all day, he became a medicine-man and brought prosperity to his tribe.

The Plains Indians had few sacred places, but where great events had happened they often celebrated their rituals in open buildings (such as the Sun-Dance Lodge) so that their physical sufferings would reach the spirits above. More often, though, the Indians worshipped their medicine-bundles (see page 106), which contained relics of their ancestors or objects given by the spirits to protect humans or to bring them good luck. Along with the medicine-bundles went the associated songs, dances, and costumes. Thus, myth and reality fused in a ritual drama where the past was brought to life and re-enacted in the present.

Explain why the spirits and the Sky Father are logical deities for the Plains Indians.

Life

Nature and the Moral World

THE NUPTADI
(YOUNG GRANDMOTHER)
ROBE OF THE
MANDAN TRIBE

Before the seventeenth century, the Plains Indians used dogs as beasts of burden. Horses were unknown to the Indians until the Spaniards brought them to America. After that, the Indians' life changed rapidly. Where before they had hunted on foot, they now became skilled riders in the buffalo hunt. Where before they had farmed the land, they now raided their enemies.

This is the story of a medicine-bundle (known as the Nuptadi), a very old and small apron-like garment worn by the tribes in ancient times. Because of the dog in the story, we know that it must have been told before the seventeenth century, which helps to explain this early custom. The story goes like this:

Coyote made a travois of wooden poles to help the first Indians transport their belongings while moving camp. One day, while a boy was sitting on a travois pulled by a dog, a coyote happened to appear. The dog chased it until both he and the boy were hopelessly lost. Looking around, the boy found a bow and some arrows. First he thanked the spirit who had left them for him; then he shot a buffalo, which died even though the arrow did not pierce its skin. With a sharp stone, the boy cut up the buffalo for food, and with its bones he attempted to make some tools. When he struck a big bone against a rock it broke, and where it fell he found a girl.

Since the boy had proved himself able to survive with the gifts of the spirit, Coyote appeared to him in human form and instructed him to gather some sage for a fire. When the fire was lit, Coyote passed the girl through the smoke four times. Each time the girl was passed through the smoke, both she and the boy grew older. Coyote knew that they both could now survive and look after each other, so he left them.

One day, after living well together in a teepee which they had made, the woman asked the man if it was not time for him to take a wife. She knew that two girls would arrive at their camp by the time they had built their winter lodge of earth and sod. When the girls arrived they agreed to be his wives.

Soon after, the wives warned the man that the woman needed an extra human scalp for a new rope she was making. Curious, the man looked in the bundle holding the robe and discovered that it was a shell robe with a man's scalp under each of the clam shells sewn to it. An empty space showed that it was awaiting another scalp. Recalling how the woman had cooked and eaten her meat secretly, he realized that she must be a spirit who ate human flesh.

When the woman came back, she passed her bundle and then accidentally touched the man's clothes. They instantly gave off a blue flame. He realized that he too must have supernatural powers and so, after running to the white teepee of his two wives for his weapons, he engaged her in combat. In the struggle he managed to shoot her with an arrow. Telling him that her time on earth had ended, she instructed him to take the magic shell robe and save it so that her powers might help the Mandan tribe. When she died, he took the robe and made the magic Nuptadi Robe bundle with it.

What ritual elements connected with the medicine-bundle can you discover?

This is both an etiological myth and a morality tale. Explain.

THE MAKING OF LAWS (Cheyenne)

In the beginning, there were no laws and people committed whatever injustices they wished. One man even killed his wife and abandoned his children. However, the children, a brother and sister, were able to find their way back to camp. The father rewarded them for their persistence by dragging them through the village, and in front of everyone, accused them of killing and eating their own mother.

Since there was so much crime, the people believed him and helped the father tie the children to stakes in the ground. Then the camp was moved and the two were left to starve. As soon as everyone was out of sight, a large black dog freed them by chewing through their ropes. When they got up, they saw a lodge with a bear and a lion in it, and although they were terribly frightened, they followed the dog's instructions to live in it.

When some buffalo appeared, the sister was instructed to look at them. Since her eyes now had a new power, the buffalo fell dead when she looked at them. The brother and sister quickly butchered the animals and sent a crow to their people with some of the meat. Since the tribe had had no luck in finding buffalo, they immediately returned for the food.

The father was the first to arrive. The bear and lion immediately killed and ate him. The girl, with her new powers, then called the whole tribe and told them that injustices had to stop. She said she would choose head chiefs and help set up laws. The first law they made was to banish for one to five years any person who killed a member of the tribe. She gave them a ceremony for choosing their chiefs, set up a special lodge for them, and constructed a peace pipe. She chose five head chiefs and made them take an oath to be honest and look after the tribe. Every ten years they were to choose new chiefs and have a renewal ceremony, but in order to maintain wisdom and stability, five of the old chiefs were to remain each time.

She concluded by giving them other sacred objects and taught them the special ceremonies needed to make the Cheyenne a great tribe.

What morality tale is told here? Do you know any similar myths? What is its Biblical counterpart?

Describe the relationship between the Indian and nature. What elements of ritual are present here that could be enacted as a live drama?

WHY THE BEAR WADDLES
(Comanche)

In the beginning, the sun was a problem. He would sometimes shine for a long time and then he would go away for a while. His irregularity caused problems for both the daytime and nighttime animals, so they decided to do something. Coyote suggested that one side choose whether to have the sun or not. Bear suggested that they play a hand game, with the winners having their choice. They got out the bones, some of which were marked and some of which were not. Coyote became the daytime scorer and Owl the night.

Sioux buffalo robe. The mythological significance of the sun is evident in the robe painting.

The day animals held the bones first and were so good at passing them behind their backs that it seemed as though they could not lose. Mole, however, was quick to guess who had the markers, and so the bones passed to the night animals. The game continued back and forth until even the sun got tired of it, and Bear, whose feet were cramped and aching, took off his moccasins to rest them.

Finally, the sun got so bored he decided to go and see who was winning. Crawling out from the under side of the world, he began to climb up his notched log ladder to find out the results. As he climbed, his light grew stronger and the night animals became frightened. In spite of the fact that the game was even, the night animals could take the sun no longer and ran away. Bear jumped up in such a hurry that he mistakenly put his moccasins on the wrong feet. All the other animals left Bear so far behind that he did not want to stop and change his moccasins. He waddled as best he could after them. Since he never did catch them, he has continued to walk this way ever since.

Since no one won the game, the daytime creatures took turns with the nighttime creatures, and that, too, has been the way it has been ever since.

What type of myth is this? What does it explain?

The hand game was a favorite of Indians all over North America and was played in some variation by all the tribes. Essentially, two people held counters, one marked and one unmarked, in either hand. The other side tried to find both marked counters in one guess. If successful, the counters were passed over and the other side tried to guess. If unsuccessful, the counters remained with the original side. Points were recorded. During the game, drummers and singers tried to confuse their opponents with distractions until finally a winner was chosen, and the losing side danced in honor of the other. What children's guessing game does this remind you of?

Death

Of all the Plains Indians, the Pawnee had the most sophisticated concept of death and the end of the world. Being astronomers, they saw the North Star as their creator god and feared its counterpart, the South Star, a god of the underworld. Morning Star was their protector because he led the sun up into the sky; conversely, Evening Star was their enemy because he pushed the sun down into darkness. Thus, a form of dualism was acknowledged by the Pawnees to help explain their world.

In Pawnee mythology the bodies of two dead star rulers were placed on burial frames in the sky. This reflects the Indian custom of placing the bodies of their dead on frames near the village.

MYTH OF THE MORNING STAR (Pawnee)

One of the more important medicine-bundles for the Pawnee was the "Morning Star" bundle. The story associated with it dealt with the dualism of good and evil. The story shows that the Morning Star was hindered by his daughter, since she robbed him of his creative powers (as evidenced in his spent energies at the end of the day). Since the story tells about the daughter of the Morning Star, the ritual connected with the myth always involves a captured young woman. This ritual occurred every four years and the story goes like this:

Young warriors had to creep into an enemy camp and capture a young woman alive. She was then brought back and treated kindly for a while so that she could carry good messages to the gods upon her death. On the appointed day, she was stripped of her clothes and painted half red (symbol of the Morning Star) and half black (symbol of the Evening Star). She was tied to a scaffold and the young warriors killed her with a shower of arrows. Her blood was allowed to seep into the ground to ensure a blessing for the tribe until the next ritual sacrifice.

This fertility myth has its counterpart in many mythologies. Read the discussion sections related to the Demeter and Persephone myth (pp. 23–26), the myth of Balder, the Theseus and Andromeda myth, and the Corn Goddess myth. What do all these stories have in common?

This is an excellent example of how the world of myth and reality fused in a deadly but ritual drama. What religious festivals do we celebrate that are similar?

THE FINAL DESTRUCTION (Pawnee)

Long ago, Tirawa Atius (the Power Above) was worshipped to the beat of the drums and the rattle of the gourds while the people chanted and sang before a medicine-bundle. The story of the end was seen this way.

In the beginning, Tirawa Atius placed giants on Earth, but because they grew too proud they had to be destroyed. A flood wiped them out, the last of the race dying on a hill in Kansas. Tirawa Atius then created humans. In the Northwest he set a great buffalo to hold a corner of the sky. Each year that the buffalo lost a hair, the world drew closer to the end. When the last hair fell out, all humans would be destroyed.

The Power Above placed four deities in the sky for each section of the heavens (the Evening Star, the Morning Star, the Sun, and the Moon). He promised to call a council with all of them if he had to destroy the human race. The Pawnee people believed that they would be warned when the end was near: the moon would change first to a dark color and then to black, the sun would lessen, and then instantly all would be blackness.

All this would be foreshadowed even in the heavens, themselves. When the Power Above was to call his council, the two star rulers would die. Their bodies would be placed on frames in the same way the Pawnee buried their dead—high above the ground so that their bones would be nearer the stars. The two burial frames were already in the sky (Ursa Major and Ursa Minor), moving around the North Star.

The North Star was important because it was aware of the Pawnee's fate and warned them that when the South Star moved through the heavens, it would one day swing high enough to capture Ursa Major and Ursa Minor (the People on the Frames). On that night the South Star would become the new ruler of the Earth. The final command to destroy Earth would then be sent out from the West and would be obeyed in the East. The North Star would give the orders and the South Star would carry out the commands on Earth. Meteor showers and stars would bombard Earth and all would be over. The Indians, however, would not die but would return to their original home by becoming stars, and would live in the territory ruled by the South Star.

The Pawnee believed that the giants' bones were left in the Kansas hills. Recent excavations have found these to be dinosaur bones. Does this seem like a reasonable explanation of the myth, or does the fact that the Norse, Greek, and other mythologies have stories about giants offer an alternative theory?

The Pawnees were astronomers. They believed that the sun, the moon, and the stars, in their regular patterns and movements across the prairies, revealed a relationship between the star-people and their own. The natural world and their own were interdependent, and so the worship of the Sky Father was a logical outgrowth of their world view. What "scientific" explanation could you give for some of the phenomena associated with the story of their end?

This myth has close parallels to the Norse vision of the end, to Ragnarok, and to a similar account of the Greek cataclysm, Zeus and Typhon. Compare these three

stories for similarities and differences. How do you account for three dissimilar cultures having a similar myth?

The Pawnee often saw the stars as warriors engaged in a dance, interrupted from time to time. In what way does this make the end of the myth seem more logical?

Postscript

There were many tribes who lived on the plains. In this short section we have tried to include a variety of their myths without being either superficial or all-inclusive. Those of you who are interested in these interesting people may wish to explore in some depth the complicated and unique myths of the Mandan tribe, particularly the stories dealing with Lone Man. Because the Plains Indians were both an agricultural as well as a hunting society, the stories of the Corn Mother are well worth investigating to see how important farming was to their culture. They should also be read in relation to the myths regarding the buffalo, the other chief preoccupation of the Plains Indians.

In the buffalo dance, led by the two esteemed warriors wearing whole buffalo heads, Mandans feign the milling movements of their prey.

Chinese Mythology

China has always been the center of culture for the East. As such, she has been influenced by her many neighbors, and in the process she has given as well as taken. Three great oriental religions have contributed to her rich cultural past and are the basis for Chinese mythology. They are Taoism, Confucianism, and Buddhism.

TAOISM The Tao is the universal energy behind all natural phenomena. It produced the *Yang* and the *Yin,* a dualistic concept for positive and negative, male and female—the alternating principles of nature (e.g., day and night). When the *Yang* and *Yin* came together, they produced heaven and earth, and, consequently, all human beings. This philosophical system is chiefly derived from the book *Tao-teh-king,* and is ascribed to Lao-tze, who lived between 604 and 517 B.C. After his death he was deified and became the inspiration for many miraculous stories about his life.

CONFUCIANISM Confucianism was founded by K'ung Fu-tse (551–479 B.C.) who, like Lao-tze, was deified after his death. Confucianism is a less emotional religion than Taoism or Buddhism, and more of a system of ethical teachings. It provided a basis for morality needed in its time. The sayings of Confucius and his disciples are contained in his book the *Analects*. His basic moral principal is the maintenance of *jen* (sympathy) between humans by keeping right relationships. The Confucian Golden Rule emphasizes the middle way and may be stated in this way: Treat those subordinate to you as you would be treated by those in positions superior to yours. *The Shu King,* another of the sacred books of Confucianism, contains most of their legends and stories about ancient China.

BUDDHISM Buddhism came to China from India. It provides an ethical philosophy based on self-denial and compassion. The "four noble truths" of Buddha are these: existence is suffering, suffering springs from desire, suffering ceases when desire ceases, the way to end desire is through the Buddhist way (the "noble eightfold path"). This way is made up of right belief, right resolve, right speech, right conduct, right vocation, right effort, right thoughts, and right ecstasy. The final goal is to reach *Nirvana* (blissful nonexistence). Each person is made up of energy that existed before birth and separates after death, and may be recombined in a similar fashion in other lives. Only through a religious life can people escape this chain and reach Nirvana. *The Three Baskets of Wisdom* are the sacred writings of Buddhism.

The Confucian longevity god.

A Taoist sage or deity.

Kuan-yin, Buddhist patron of mercy.

Taoism eventually merged with Buddhism, and a pantheon of gods was created which paralleled each other—that is, the names were different but the stories and functions were the same.

125

One story about Lao-tze states that he was immaculately conceived, and, after being carried in his mother's womb for seventy years, was born white-haired and wise. What does this tell us about the cultural values of the Chinese?

What is the Christian Golden Rule? How does it differ from that of Confucius?

Tou Mu, the Taoist goddess of life and death, parallels the goddess Kuan Yin in the Buddhist religion. What Greek gods and goddesses does she parallel?

A Confucian, a Buddhist, and a Taoist discuss the three ways.

126

The Creation of the World

Yang-Yin

In the beginning there was *Yang-Yin:* light-darkness, active-passive, heat-cold, dryness-moisture. The lighter part went skyward to form the heavens; the heavier went downward to form the earth. With this division, *Yang* and *Yin,* the male and female principle, came to be. *Yang* produced fire, hence the sun. *Yin* produced water, and hence the moon. Their active and passive forces mingled, producing the stars, the seasons, and all the products of earth (rivers, rain, dust, and all creatures).

A Ch'ing dynasty jade amulet shows
the Yang-Yin symbol surrounded
by the eight trigrams;
in each trigram Yang is represented
by an unbroken line
and Yin by a broken line.

P'an Ku

Some say that the world was created by a man, P'an Ku, who had horns projecting from his forehead and tusks projecting from his jaws. He lived for eighteen thousand years and every day that he lived he grew six feet. With his chisel and mallet he shaped mountains and chiselled out valleys or dug areas for rivers and seas. P'an Ku had help from four great beasts: the Dragon, the Unicorn, the Tortoise and the Phoenix. They were no help to him, however, when it came to putting the Sun and the Moon in their proper places. Consequently, the Sun and the Moon drifted into the sea and the world was left without light. P'an Ku had to go into the sea, and after placing his hands properly and reciting a powerful spell three times, the Sun and the Moon went into their places.

Phoenix.
Chinese ornamental inlay consisting
of a thin gold sheet, cut and incised.
T'ang Dynasty (618-906).

The universe was not complete until P'an Ku died. Then his breath became the wind and the clouds, his beard became streaming signs in the sky, his voice turned into the thunder, his flesh turned into the soil, his four limbs became the four quarters of the earth, his head became the mountains, his blood turned into the rivers, his hair became the herbs and trees, his teeth and bones became the metals and precious stones.

But this was not all. P'an Ku had built the world up into fifty-one levels: thirty-three were for the heavens; eighteen were for the hells beneath the earth. He left a great hole in the bottom of the world, which men and women often fell through. It was not until a woman, Nu-Ku, placed a stone over the emptiness that the world was completed and became well-ordered and harmonious.

128

The five-clawed feet of the dragon identify him as a symbol of the emperor, the Son of Heaven. Nonimperial dragons had four claws.

The Taoist influence in the myth is obvious. Some scholars, however, maintain that the story of P'an Ku came from outside China at a later date. What evidence can you suggest that would agree or disagree with this theory?

Compare the story of P'an Ku to that of Ymir (p. 49) in Norse mythology.

What etiological elements are contained in this creation myth?

The East views creatures differently from the West. In the Orient, the Dragon is the head of all creatures because it is filled the most with the _Yang_ principle. The Dragon has five colors in its body and possesses a pearl (the essence of the moon) and a charm against fire (the essence of the sun). It can make itself visible or invisible. In the spring it mounts the clouds; in the fall it lies dormant in the

waters. The Unicorn is strong and virtuous and therefore combines both principles of *Yang* and *Yin*. It eats no living vegetation and it never treads on green grass. The Tortoise possesses the secrets of life and death and with its breath can create clouds or palaces of enchantment. The Phoenix is the head of all birds. Its color is the blending of the five colors and its song is the harmony of the five notes. What values of the Chinese culture emerge from this description of the four creatures?

The Major Gods

TOU MU Tou Mu was the goddess of the North Star and was worshipped by both Buddhists and Taoists alike. She was the mother of nine sons and lived with her husband in the heavens, surrounded by stars which revolved around her palace. She is pictured sitting on a lotus throne and has three eyes and eighteen arms. In her hands she holds a bow, a sword, a spear, a flag, the head of a dragon, the disks of the sun and the moon, and five chariots. Since she rules over life and death, she is worshipped by those wishing long life.

One of the differences between the Greek and Chinese cultures is their attitude toward the deity of death. Tou Mu is pictured as kind and full of pity for human suffering. How is the Greek deity of death pictured? What, in each culture, would account for this difference?

MU KING Mu King (or Mu Kung, according to some) is the ruler of the gods and as such keeps a list of all the immortals. He holds the power of the *Yang,* the active male principle in nature. He lives in a heavenly palace colored in blue and violet, and is waited on by an immortal youth, Yu Nu, and the Jade Maiden.

An interesting creation myth surrounds this god. He was the first created from the primitive vapour and therefore is not only the purest creation but the highest product.

Since Mu King lives in the East and holds the power of the *Yang,* what type of god is he?

130

HSI WANG MU Representing *Yin*, the passive female principle in nature, Hsi Wang Mu was born of the Western air. She is the Golden Mother of the Tortoise and mother of twenty-four daughters and nine sons.

It is the union of *Yang* and *Yin* that produces heaven and earth. Compare this with the Greek creation story.

As a representative of the *Yin* principle, what kind of god was she? Why is this consistent, from what you know of mythology?

YEN-LO-WANG As god of the dead, the state of people's souls is a concern to Yen-Lo-Wang. He is king of the hells and is connected to nine other gods, forming a band called the Ten Kings.

Look up the story of Sun Hou-tzu (*Myths and Legends of all Nations*. Bantam), the monkey king, and how he became immortal and bested the god of the dead.

Life

The Natural World

SHEN I, THE DIVINE ARCHER One day, when the Emperor Yao ruled China, he came upon an archer wishing to serve him. The Emperor tested the archer's skills by commanding him to shoot an arrow at a pine tree growing on the top of a nearby mountain. The archer did so and hit his mark. But then a strange thing happened—the archer leaped upon the breeze, and flying upward, withdrew the arrow and returned it to the Emperor. Delighted, the Emperor enlisted the man and named him Shen I, the Divine Archer. Soon after, the Emperor made use of his servant.

One day, ten suns appeared in the heavens and burned up all the crops; fierce winds destroyed towns and the rivers flooded the country. Monsters appeared—a devouring serpent and huge boars—that played havoc with the country. The Emperor realized that it was the work of demons and commanded Shen I to take three hundred soldiers and destroy the monsters.

131

Shen I approached the problem methodically. First he stopped the destroying winds that were being sent forth by a mighty dragon's blast. He disabled the dragon by shooting it in the knee with one of his arrows, and then extracted an oath from it to live henceforth in friendship.

Next he tackled the problem of the nine suns. After leading his soldiers to the bank of a river, he saw three mountains close together in the distance. On the top of each mountain sat three huge birds sending out a scorching fire. He shot nine arrows at the birds, killing them and extinguishing the flames. When his troops reached the top of the mountains, they found nine red stones, each with an arrow through its center.

Shen I then tackled the floods. He shot an arrow into the waters, and they began to retreat. Out of the foam, however, emerged a man clothed in white and a woman, surrounded by twelve servants on milk-white horses. Shen I shot an arrow through the left eye of the man and another through the hair of the woman. Everyone retreated except the woman, who volunteered to be Shen I's wife, since he had spared her life. Shen I was not one to miss such an opportunity and he quickly married her. The ceremony of pomp and splendor was a gift from the Emperor for faithful service.

What scientific explanations can you give for this myth?

The story of the Ten Suns is very close to the Greek myth of Phaethon and the Sun Chariot. What explanation can you give for two different cultures having very similar myths?

For an interesting stellar myth, read the story of the "Celestial Weaver Maid and the Herdsman" (see *Myths of the World*. Grosset & Dunlap). It is about the stars Aquila and Vega.

THE METAL-BOUND CASKET

A wise and much-loved ruler, King Wu, fell ill and appeared likely to die. His three brothers were very concerned about the king, but only one, the Duke of Chow, did anything. In front of a series of altars he prayed to his ancestors to exchange his life for that of his brother. Upon finishing his prayer, he opened a metal-bound casket containing the holy writings of the kingdom and discovered that the signs within indicated that King Wu would recover. A recorder had written down the duke's prayer on a tablet, as a witness to the event. The tablet was placed in the casket and the chest was closed.

Chinese painting on silk,
attributed to Li Ch'eng (d. 967).
*Buddhist Temple Amid
Clearing Mountain Peaks.*

After five years, however, the king did die and was succeeded by his young son Ching. Because of the son's age, the Duke of Chow was appointed his advisor. The other two brothers became jealous of their brother's new power and started to spread rumors about the poor advice the Duke of Chow was giving. The Duke was so offended that he left the kingdom, knowing that the gods would prove him innocent.

That fall a great storm arose and ruined the crops and uprooted huge trees. The people became panic-stricken and went to the casket to consult the sacred writings. Upon finding the tablet with the duke's prayer on it, they realized the meaning of the storm and the Duke of Chow's innocence.

Ching quickly proclaimed that the Duke of Chow was faithful and that he had been wronged, and asked his loyal uncle to return. When the Duke of Chow was back in court, a favorable wind arose, the grain was restored and the trees replaced, and everyone benefited from a very productive year.

The Chinese were very fond of morality tales, and consequently a great many of these have been preserved. What moral does this myth reveal?

Death

The Chinese accepted death with a patience and understanding born of their long philosophical heritage. Here is a story of an old Taoist scholar, which helps us understand this attitude:

When the wife of an elderly sage died, his friends came to grieve with him. Instead of finding him in tears and wailing, they discovered the old man sitting on the floor, beating a drum and singing. When they inquired why he was so cheerful, he replied:

"At first I despaired at my wife's death, but then I realized that we are born to die and that this is a part of life we must face. I realized also that if I had died first, she would have had to remarry, perhaps to someone she did not love, and our children would have been ill-fed and ill-cared for. My wife is now at peace and my tears will not change life. If I were to make a great fuss, I would disturb her rest. It would show then that I know nothing of the ways of life and death."

Another example of this acceptance of Fate or Destiny is found in the myth of Shen I and the Gift of Immortality:

One of the daughters of Hsi Wang Mu wished to visit her mother. Mounted on a dragon, she flew towards the palace high on top of the Kiun Lun Mountains, leaving a brilliant streak of light behind to mark the way. The Emperor Yao saw this light and asked Shen I to find out what it was.

Mounted on the air, Shen I rode up to the light and was carried to the door of the palace. In front of the door was a hideous monster that ordered some huge birds to kill the intruder. Shen I routed the lot with one of his arrows. The door opened and Chin Mu, daughter of the goddess of the western air, invited the archer in. Shen I, seizing the opportunity, asked her if he could have one of the pills of immortality. She agreed, on condition that he build her a palace. This the archer did, choosing a site on White Jade Tortoise Mountain and accomplishing the undertaking in two weeks.

So pleased was the goddess that she gave him the pill of immortality, but reminded Shen I that a year's preparation was necessary before it should be taken.

Shen I returned home, told the Emperor all that had happened and hid the pill under a rafter in his house. He then began the diet and exercise program needed to help him achieve immortality.

Soon, however, he was sent on another adventure. While he was gone, his wife, Heng O, noticed a fine odor spreading itself around the house. Looking around, she saw a beam of white light coming from a timber under the roof, and unable to stem her curiosity, finally went to look. She discovered the pill of immortality (unbeknownst to her) and compelled by an irresistible force, swallowed it. Suddenly she found herself able to float freely. Before she could fly away, however, Shen I returned and discovered that the pill was missing.

Heng O realized what she had done. In terror she flew away from her husband and soon was out of sight. Shen I was prevented from following her by a mighty wind that spun him around and threw him on the ground. Meanwhile, Heng O came to rest on a huge crystal globe, cold and barren except for a few cinnamon trees. The icy air made her cough and the pill she had swallowed came up out of her throat. It changed into a pure white rabbit and quickly ran away, leaving her lonely and sad.

Shen I, however, had been caught in a whirlwind and carried up into the cloud palace of Mu King. There he told his story to the king of the immortals.

The king told him that soon he would become immortal and that he was not to blame his wife because fate had destined what she would do. He told Shen I that she was now an immortal living on the moon. As a reward for his faithful service on earth, Mu King promised him the Palace of the Sun.

Mu King gave him a sarsaparilla cake to eat, to protect him from the heat of the sun, and a lunar talisman to allow him to visit his wife. He reminded Shen I that he would be allowed only to visit her, and that she could never visit him. Mu King also gave Shen I the bird of the golden feathers to remind him of the laws of the sun's rising and setting. By the bird's notes, he would know morning, noon, and night.

Shen I lived happily alone on the sun, but after a time he decided to visit his wife. He forgave her and explained all that had happened. Shen I built a palace for her of diamonds, amethysts, rubies, and emeralds and called it the Palace of Great Cold. He returned to the sun and built a palace for himself,

calling it the Palace of the Lonely Park. After that, Shen I visited his wife regularly, on the fifteenth day of every month.

This is a science myth as well as a tale of immortality. What elements of geography and astronomy are explained? How logical are they?

What realities of existence and the human condition are contained in the myth?

Some of the Chinese deities, like the Norse, were capable of being killed. Read the story of "The Four Kings of Heaven" (*Myths and Legends of All Nations.* Bantam). What new outlook on existence does this story give?

Painted to illustrate a Taoist poem, a sixteenth-century scroll shows a Taoist scholar sleeping in his thatched cottage (center). The scholar dreams that he has attained immortality through magical practices; at left, he is shown blithely floating off over the mountains to the land of Immortals.

Part 3

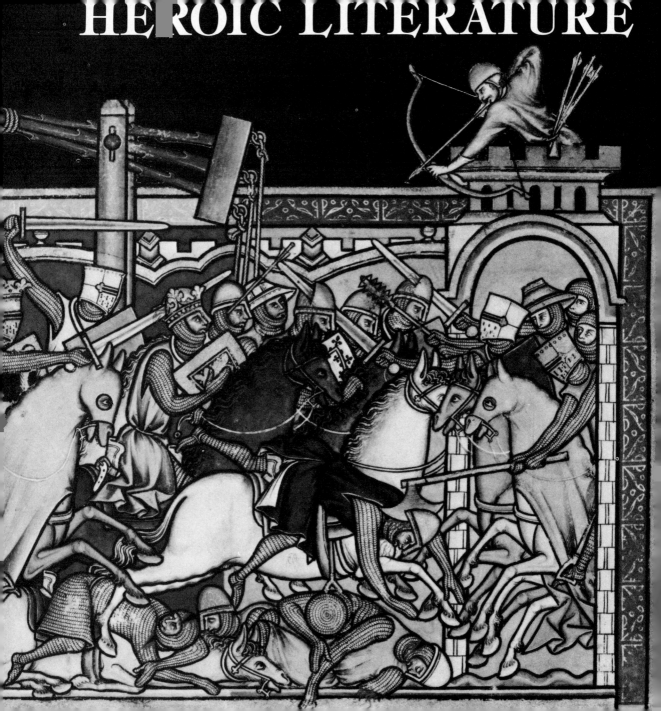

In Parts One and Two we worked on the principle that by studying the mythology of a culture, a great deal can be learned about that culture—particularly its interests, values, and ideals. In Part Three our purpose will be much the same, but our focus will be different. We will look at the heroic literature of the ancient Greek and the medieval Christian societies.

Although it would appear that the two societies about to be examined have little in common, being separated by time and religion, there is striking similarity in the needs of each society as reflected in much of its literature. Each society has a need to create heroes who embark upon adventures which reflect the aspirations of that society. Though the characteristics of the hero may vary, the need for a literature dealing with heroes remains constant.

Heroic literature is a specialized type of literature concerned with the adventures of a central figure who is somehow greater than ordinary mortals. This "hero" is set apart from, and above, the average person because of his almost superhuman courage, bravery, and cleverness. In fact, Hesiod, an ancient Greek writer, defined the word *hero* as a person whose status is between that of an ordinary mortal and that of the gods. Thus heroes are almost a link between human beings and the gods. They represent the ideal for their society. For this reason, a great body of literature is collected about their exploits. By recounting the adventures and triumphs of the hero, the society reaffirms its own values and allows the listeners or readers to identify with, and perhaps to emulate, the deeds of the hero. Heroic literature instills a sense of pride and imprints a value system on the audience.

It is far easier to study the heroic literature of the past because it is complete and because we have a perspective that is relatively objective. Studies of Greek heroes such as Perseus and Jason tell us much about the ancient Greek moral outlook and value system. By the same token, the Arthurian cycle reveals the values and aspirations of the medieval Christian society. Both of these bodies of heroic literature have a great deal in common because they offer us a view of two cultures that were secure in terms of qualities they valued.

Once we move into modern society, the whole question of heroic literature becomes problematical. For this reason, the section on modern heroes takes quite a different approach. This does not negate our findings, however, for it will soon become obvious that heroism is a pattern of behavior—a pattern that is easily isolated upon close investigation of the stories. Part Three, then, is also a study in literary theory and leads logically into Part Four.

140

Preceding page: Painting by a thirteenth-century artist of knights laying siege to neighboring lands.

The Classical Tradition

The later Bronze Age was the age of heroes in Greece. This was an age when the Greek city states were becoming a power to reckon with in the Mediterranean area. In many ways, the age of heroes was a celebration of the conquests of that time. The greatest heroes were Perseus, Bellerophon, Heracles, Jason, Odysseus, and Theseus. In each case, the hero was responsible for destroying the enemies of the Greeks and helping to unify the countryside; therefore, each was a kind of founding father.

The exploits of these heroes were recorded by many famous poets of antiquity. The most prominent sources are Homer's *The Iliad* and *The Odyssey*, probably composed in the eighth century B.C. But Homer is by no means alone. Euripides, the great tragedian of the fifth century B.C., is the only source for some of the exploits of Jason and Theseus. Hesiod's *Theogeny* (eighth century B.C.) and Pindar's *Odes* (sixth century B.C.) give us extra material for our study, while two very important authors, Apollonius of Rhodes (250 B.C.) and Apollodorus (first or second century A.D.), are the last of our important Greek sources. A great deal of material can also be found in the works of the Roman poet Ovid, who, although he was often skeptical of the Greek myths and legends, lovingly recorded them. He is a particularly valuable writer because many of his original sources no longer exist and therefore some legends remain only in his writings.

Two observations can be made from the above. One, there is no unified source for the stories of the Greek heroes. All of the literary sources were taken from an oral tradition as well as any writings available. Even at the time of writing, one must assume that each poet selected details which suited his temperament and purpose from the numerous accounts available to him. Therefore, although the stories agree in the main, there are innumerable variations in detail and emphasis.

Two, and most important, none of the writings are strictly historical. Rather, they are literary: they are works of the creative imagination. This does not mean that we can discern no historical validity in the accounts. Heinrich Schliemann, an archeologist, conclusively destroyed that theory when he followed the directions of Homer and discovered the buried city of Troy. As a matter of fact, a lot of our discussion will center on the historical. But this focus alone is far too limiting.

What makes these accounts so fascinating is that they are imaginative reconstructions of an earlier period as seen by a later age. The poets who wrote about the heroes were not interested in just recording facts but in creating the perfect hero for their own age. In heroic literature, the heroes became idealized as did the age in which they lived. They represented the height of attainment to the culture which delighted in telling of their exploits. The real character of a Heracles became less important than the more general heroic qualities that the poets ascribed to all heroes. We can then expect that the heroes will have many character traits in common with each other and will be involved in similar exploits.

It becomes obvious after reading much of the heroic literature of the ancient Greeks that a literary formula of heroism emerged which reflected not only what the Greeks demanded in their stories of heroes but what qualities of manhood they valued. The purpose of this section will be to see what pattern of heroism emerges and what the values of the classical age were.

There are many books which deal with these legends as history, though historians of this period are totally dependent on the literature for information. For example, historians suggest that the divine aid from Athene, mentioned in so many stories, was often, in reality, aid from Athens, one of the most powerful city states. An excellent book on the legends as history is Costa De Loverdo's *Gods with Bronze Swords*.

The Iliad and *The Odyssey* are both very long poems comprised of thousands of lines each. And yet, for two hundred years they were transmitted orally before being written down. The literature of our Western culture is rooted in this oral tradition. Consult the encyclopedia or any good dictionary of literary terms to find out how these poems were composed and how a bard could recite from memory hundreds of lines at a time.

For an account of *The Odyssey* as a real sea voyage, see Ernlie Bradford's *Ulysses Found*. Bradford confirmed the accuracy of Homer's sailing directions by taking the same odyssey himself. The voyage was made into the beautiful NBC film *The Search for Ulysses*.

It is significant that all heroic literature is an "imaginative reconstruction" of the

Schliemann's excavations of Troy.

past. It is imaginative in the sense that it views the past as an ordered glorious age, with clear-cut moral and social values, and easily recognizable heroes and villains. To what extent do you consider it important today that a culture have heroic literature?

The Greek Heroes

The Perseus Legend

Perseus was the earliest and one of the greatest heroes that Greece ever produced. He lived fifteen generations before the birth of Heracles, and in many ways was the prototype of all Greek heroes. Perseus was the son of **Acrisius** Danae and the immortal Zeus, and the grandson of King Acrisius of Argos. Acrisius was a descendant of the great house of Danaus, one of the earliest dynasties in the Peloponnesus. Typically, there was a struggle for control, a struggle in which only the strong survived. Acrisius had won the throne of Argos from his twin brother Proetus after a long battle. After much negotiating, Proetus, whose claim to the throne of Argos was almost as legitimate as that of Acrisius, was given the kingship of the nearby city of Tyrns. But Acrisius was worried. He knew that unless he had a son and heir, Proetus would just bide his time before taking over Argos.

The worried king decided to consult an oracle to find out if he would be blessed with a son who could ensure the continuity of his line. Much to his dismay, the oracle gave a terrible prophecy. Acrisius was told that not only would he never have a son, but that his daughter Danae would bear a child who would destroy him. In his fear, for Acrisius knew that an oracle was not to be taken lightly, he ordered that his daughter Danae be locked up in a room in the palace with her nurse and that no one should come into contact with her.

Danae   Danae was famous throughout the Peloponnesus for her beauty and grace. Unfortunately for Acrisius, the word of her beauty had spread even to Olympus and to Zeus. He looked down and saw the young girl in her prison and immediately desired her. No prison was strong enough to keep out the protean Zeus who could change his shape as he desired. For this occasion, he transformed himself into a shower of gold and entered one of the windows in order to possess Danae. Less romantic accounts suggest that the "shower of gold" went into the hands of the palace guards, and that Zeus entered by the door. The result of this union was Perseus.

Acrisius did not discover the ruse until after the child was born. He had not visited Danae in prison because of his feelings of guilt. It was not until he chanced to pass nearby one day and heard the infant's wailing that the horrible truth struck him. Immediately he had the nurse killed and called his daughter to appear before him. Upon questioning her, he learned that the child Perseus was the son of Zeus. He was too afraid to kill the child and Danae outright because of the power of Zeus, but he was also anxious to avoid his fate. The king tried to resolve the dilemma by having his daughter and grandson placed in a sealed trunk and letting them drift out into the Mediterranean. This way, he felt he would not be directly responsible for their deaths.

Polydectes   However, an oracle will not be denied. Danae and Perseus drifted to the island of Seriphos. There they were discovered by Polydectes, the king, who granted them asylum when he learned of their royal descent. As a sign

144

of his favor he adopted Perseus as his own son. Very little is recorded of the childhood of Perseus, although he was raised as a prince and learned the skills of the aristocracy of his day.

The ancient poets continue his story with Perseus as a full grown man at the court of Polydectes. Polydectes had fallen in love with Danae, possibly as a result of her beauty and possibly because of her dynastic connections with the house of Danaus after whom she had been named. Danae rejected his advances and Perseus swore to protect his mother's virtue. But Polydectes was so persistent that she had to seek asylum in the temple of Athene.

Temporarily thwarted, Polydectes plotted to get rid of Perseus, reasoning that once he was out of the way Danae would be his. Just as Acrisius had hesitated to kill a son of Zeus, so did Polydectes. He realized that the murder could not be direct, but that he must somehow force Perseus into a position where he would court death of his own accord.

Thus Polydectes pretended to fall in love with another princess. As was the custom, all of the kings and princes were obliged to offer him a wedding gift. Perseus was so relieved to see his mother safe that he committed a fateful error. He brashly boasted to Polydectes that in honor of his

Medusa wedding, he would be willing to slay even Medusa, the Gorgon. Of course, he had meant it only as an exaggerated boast, but Polydectes had been hoping for just such a slip from his exuberant and as yet uninitiated stepson. He quickly accepted Perseus' offer and, since it had been made in the presence of witnesses, Perseus was forced to undertake this quest. Moreover, Polydectes insisted that he would keep Danae hostage until the quest was fulfilled, secretly thinking that the task was impossible.

The king had every reason to feel confident that Perseus could never return. The Gorgons were three female monsters with horrible features and hair of writhing snakes. They were the children of Ceto and Phorcys, two children of Poseidon. From their islands, remote in the uncharted Atlantic, they plagued all sailors brave enough to venture out into that unknown sea. Medusa, the leader, was so terrible that anyone who looked at her directly was immediately turned to stone. Ironically she alone was mortal and, thus, could be destroyed.

To accomplish so great a task as killing this monster, Perseus would need not only all of the qualities of a hero but also the help of the gods. To aid his son in this quest, Zeus sent Hermes and Athene with divine advice.

Both were able not only to offer concrete aid but also to give Perseus more information about his monstrous enemy. They suggested to him that the best method of reaching and destroying Medusa was by seeking the aid of her other sisters, the Nymphs and the Graeae. The Nymphs could tell Perseus how to find Medusa, but the Nymphs could be found only if Perseus could persuade the Graeae to tell him where they lived.

Hermes was very vague concerning how Perseus was to find the Graeae. He would say only that Perseus must travel to the west as far as he could go and he would then encounter these strange "Gray Ones" who shared only one tooth and one eye among the three of them. Naturally, the Gray Ones would be reluctant to direct Perseus, a mortal, to their divine sisters, but Hermes told Perseus that if he should take their eye from them as they were sharing it, they would give him the information he desired for its return.

Hermes and Athene gave Perseus gifts to aid him in his quest. Hermes gave Perseus winged sandals to speed his journey to the Graeae. Athene presented him with a highly polished shield so that he could use it to mirror the face of the Gorgon when he reached her island and thus be protected from her direct glance.

With the aid of winged sandals, Perseus, after many days, found the Graeae, as Hermes had said, and by taking the single eye, learned from them the whereabouts of the Nymphs. He then went to their home, which many writers calculate to be near present-day Sicily, and tried to persuade them to help him in his cause. Perhaps because they saw the evidence of aid from the Olympians or perhaps because, as gentle spirits of the waters, they resented the terror imposed by their formidable sisters, the Nymphs agreed to help Perseus. They first gave him directions to the home of the Gorgons. Then they presented him with a pouch in which to place Medusa's head—for even in death it would kill any who gazed at it—and a helmet once owned by Hades which would make his approach invisible to the monsters.

Thus armed, Perseus was able to approach the Gorgons undetected. All three were sleeping, and Perseus managed to cut off the head of Medusa and escape before the other two awoke. Unaware that anyone had been approaching, since Perseus was invisible, Medusa had been unable to employ her ultimate weapon—her baleful stare. Perseus, careful to keep

146

The head of Medusa
from a painting by
Caravaggio.

the face hidden, placed it in the leather pouch given to him by the Nymphs. Thus the Greeks were saved from the terrible plague of the Gorgons, for without their leader, the other two lost much of their power.

On his way home to Seriphos, Perseus landed on the coast of Northern Africa. There he encountered another adventure. He was sailing somewhere near the coast of what is now Egypt. At that time the land was ruled by King Cepheus and his wife, Queen Cassiopeia. Cassiopeia was a beautiful woman, but she had foolishly boasted that she was more beautiful than the sea nymphs. Poseidon had taken this as a personal insult and had sent a huge sea monster to plague the coast. In his concern, Cepheus took the same step that many a king had taken before him in time of trouble and consulted an oracle to see how the monster from the sea might be appeased. He was informed that he must sacrifice his own daughter **Andromeda** Andromeda to the monster. Sadly, he consented to do this. Andromeda was chained to a rock facing the sea to await her death.

It was at this moment that Perseus landed on the coast. He saw the grieving parents on a nearby cliff waiting for the inevitable, but most of all he saw the beautiful Andromeda awaiting her fate in fear and anguish. Perseus decided at once that he must save this beautiful maiden, but he wanted to be assured that his labor would reward him, so he first approached the parents and made them promise that if he saved their daughter she would be his in marriage. Under the circumstances, they were only too willing to agree, and so Perseus arrived on Andromeda's rock just as the sea monster was emerging from the water to devour her. After a terrible battle, Perseus destroyed it and released the terrified girl.

At first Cepheus pretended delight and offered Perseus a great feast, but he wanted to refuse this Greek his daughter's hand in marriage. He realized that Perseus' claim to the throne of Argos was not certain and that, at any rate, such an alliance would not benefit the Egyptian throne as well as would an alliance with an African ally. In front of his assembled court, he told Perseus that Andromeda would never be his and ignored the threats of the angry hero. Unfortunately for Cepheus, he had underestimated the power of his young adversary. Perseus waited for the opportune moment and when all eyes were on him, he reached down and withdrew Medusa's head from its pouch. Everyone in the court gazed on it and was turned to stone. Perseus then sought Andromeda and sailed with her to the court of Polydectes where he demanded that his mother be freed.

Polydectes could not believe his eyes. In his opinion, the quest had been impossible. In the presence of his courtiers he foolishly accused Perseus of trickery. Perseus stated he would offer proof if all the courtiers but Polydectes would avert their eyes. They did so, and withdrawing the Gorgon's head, Perseus inflicted the same punishment on Polydectes as he had on Cepheus.

His quest fulfilled, Perseus left Seriphos with Andromeda and his mother to claim his rightful throne. He felt that the time was right since he was then at the height of his powers and his fame was spreading throughout the Peloponnesus. Acrisius, who realized his responsibility in denying the throne to his grandson, fled to Larissa in the north, and the crown of Argos was bestowed on Perseus without delay. He ruled in Argos as a just king and a good leader to his people. No longer needing the Gorgon's head, Perseus gave it to Athene, his patroness, and from that time forward she wore it and thus could turn her enemies to stone.

There is an interesting footnote to the Perseus legend. Perseus did not hold a grudge against his grandfather, realizing that his grandfather's actions were understandable and that perhaps they had indirectly allowed Perseus to gain fame. He therefore traveled to Larissa in order to offer Acrisius forgiveness. While there, Perseus entered the local games in honor of his arrival. Naturally, Acrisius came to watch. During the discus throw, Perseus, quite by accident, hurled a discus into the crowd and killed his grandfather, thus fulfilling the prophecy made before his birth.

The classical heroic literature offers an insight into the tribal structure of the royal houses which ruled the ancient city states. The rule was dynastic, the power being in the hands of a few influential royal families. This allowed for stability and continuity as well as permitting alliances formed by royal marriages. But the other constant fact of life was the dynastic struggle for power among the offspring of the rulers. What elements of this are evident in the Perseus legend?

Consider the function of the four Olympians involved in the fate of Perseus. Why is each a logical choice for his or her particular role?

Although the Olympians are supposed to be omniscient, Hermes has difficulty giving Perseus a geographical location for the Graeae. What reasons can be given to account for Hermes' haziness?

The women in this legend have very little control over their own fate. Look at the situations of Danae and Andromeda and draw some conclusions about the role of women in ancient Greek society.

From our point of view, many details in this story indicate great cruelty. However, since these legends were written to glorify the hero, the Greeks could not have had the same perspective. In the light of our values, what incidents or attitudes seem barbaric?

A number of words and concepts from the Perseus myth are still with us today. How are the following words or names used in a modern context: *aegis, nymph, protean, Andromeda, Medusa?*

The Jason Legend

Pelias

In Iolcus, a city in northeastern Greece, at the time when the wife of King Aeson was about to give birth to a child, a mutiny occurred in the royal household and Aeson was deposed by his brother Pelias. Unable to bring himself to kill his own brother, Pelias had Aeson and his wife imprisoned in a heavily guarded room. When Aeson's wife finally bore a child, they named it Jason and had it smuggled out of the palace in a closed casket, using the ploy that the baby had been stillborn. Pelias was then more at ease because he had no fear of anyone in the original royal line challenging his right to the throne.

Jason was taken to the mountains by loyal servants and given to the wise old centaur Cheiron to be raised and educated in the noble arts of his class. Thus Jason grew strong and became skilled in music and song, as well as in the art of warfare. When he reached maturity, Cheiron told him of the events surrounding his royal birth and sent him to reclaim his rightful throne.

On the way to his home, a fateful event occurred. When approaching a river, Jason met an old crone attempting to ford the swift current. Being strong and courteous, he instructed her to climb up on his shoulder so that he could carry her across. As they forded the river, she clung to him so tightly that he almost lost his balance. He saved himself and the crone but lost one of his sandals in the process. Upon reaching the shore, Jason set the

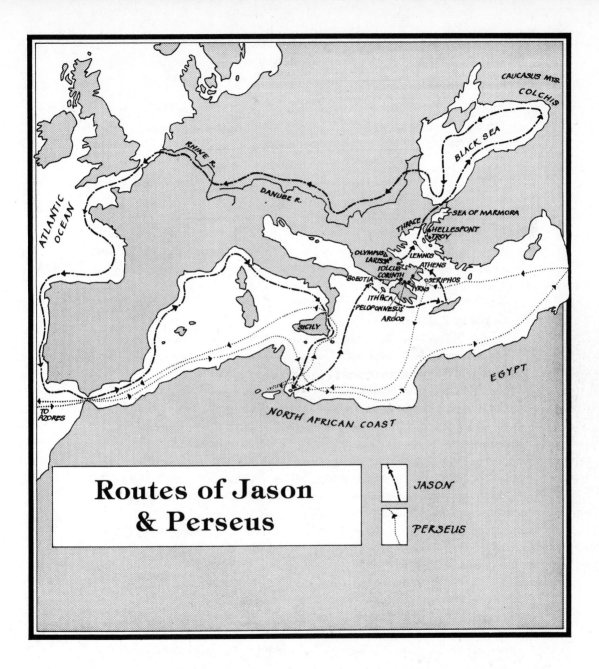

Routes of Jason & Perseus

JASON

PERSEUS

CAUCASUS MTS.
COLCHIS
BLACK SEA
RHINE R.
DANUBE R.
ATLANTIC OCEAN
SEA OF MARMORA
THRACE
HELLESPONT
TROY
OLYMPUS
LARISSA
LEMNOS
IOLCUS
ATHENS
BOEOTIA
CORINTH
SERIPHOS
ITHACA
TYRNS
PELOPONNESUS
ARGOS
SICILY
EGYPT
NORTH AFRICAN COAST
TO AZORES

woman down and continued on his way, unaware that he had aided both the divine Hera and an oracle which stated that Pelias would eventually be deposed by a man wearing only one sandal. Previously, Pelias had angered Hera by denying her proper sacrifice. The return of Jason to claim his rightful throne provided Hera with the opportune moment to begin to fulfill the oracle. (Some accounts have the disguised Hera reveal her identity to Jason in order to offer him advice on how he should confront his uncle.)

When Jason reached the market place in Iolcus, wearing the single sandal, Pelias was terrified. Realizing the danger he was in, Pelias contrived a plan to get rid of the stranger. He demanded an audience with Jason and asked him what he would do in his place if an oracle had stated that the king would be killed by one of his own citizens. Jason quickly replied, for Hera had put the words in his mouth, that he would send that person on a quest for the Golden Fleece. Pelias was pleased with this answer because he felt that such a quest could end only in death for anyone who undertook it. He told the youth about the oracle and demanded that he undertake the task as he himself had suggested it.

But before sending Jason on his way, Pelias asked him who he was. With no hesitation, Jason told him and his followers that he was the rightful heir to the throne of Iolcus, and after hearing the details of his birth, Pelias could not deny that it was so. However, he held Jason to his quest and promised him the throne only if he returned with the Golden Fleece.

The Golden Fleece was a legend even in the time of Jason. It was reputed to be the hide of a huge ram which had been sent by the gods to **Phrixus and Helle** save Phrixus and Helle, two children of the royal family of neighboring Boeotia, who were being sacrificed in order to end a famine then plaguing the land. It was not the fact of human sacrifice that so angered the gods, for this was not an unknown occurrence at that time, but it was an impious sacrifice, planned by the children's jealous stepmother merely in order to secure her own place in the dynasty. Hera was angered that such an odious crime should be committed in her name and sent the ram at the moment of sacrifice to carry the children off on its broad back to safety in the land of Colchis at the far end of the Black Sea.

On the journey, Helle lost her grip and fell into a sea which is now named after her. Phrixus, however, did reach Colchis and was welcomed by the royal family there. The ram was sacrificed in honor of Hera and the fleece placed in a sacred tree and guarded by a huge, ever-watchful serpent.

By bringing back the Golden Fleece to Greece, Jason would bring fame and fortune to himself. In preparation for his quest, Jason sent out runners to every city in Greece, asking for courageous men to join him in his adventure. At the same time he had a great ship built for the voyage, which he named the *Argo*. Soon he had assembled a great band of fifty men, including such famous heroes as Heracles, the two sons of Boreas (the North Wind), Orpheus, and many whose sons would later go against Troy. Never before in history had so many illustrious men gathered together in order to seek personal fame and glory. The quest would be difficult and dangerous, for although some contacts with the Black Sea area had been made by merchants, knowledge of the area was sparse, and the people living on the shores of the vast sea were known to be hostile.

Heracles

Upon completion of the ship, Jason and the "Argonauts" set sail toward the narrow entrance to the Black Sea by following the east coast of Greece. It was when they reached the island of Lemnos that they encountered the first of their many adventures. The women there, in a terrible grievance against their husbands, had killed every male on the island. Thinking that the Argonauts were enemies, they had donned their husbands' armor when they first sighted the *Argo* landing and rushed down to the shore to defend themselves. It did not take the Argonauts long to realize the true nature of their opponents, and this discovery almost ended the quest for the Golden Fleece. The Lemnian women were only too happy to invite the men into their city and their homes, realizing their potential as future husbands. Indeed, the Argonauts were so well treated by these women that they lost sight of their original purpose. That is, all except Heracles. Having grown impatient of the men's carousing, he knocked on every door in Lemnos throughout a single night, refusing to cease until every member of the expedition agreed to return to the ship. Sadly, they sailed away in the darkness leaving behind the beautiful and tempting women of Lemnos.

In order to raise the spirits of the men, a rowing contest was held. All night long the straining of the oars could be heard as Orpheus played his lyre in accompaniment to the beat of the blades. One by one, the men grew weary as the long hours passed until only Jason and Heracles were left. This was the first test of Jason's heroism against the greatest hero of the day. The name Heracles was known all over Greece and his deeds were sung by bards in all the royal houses. Compared to him, Jason was a mere unknown, and yet Jason was the leader of the expedition. It would have been disastrous for him to lose to Heracles in a battle of strength. As the contest went on, Jason felt his strength waning. Just as he was about to concede defeat, something so providential occurred that one suspects the interference of Hera; the huge oar being manned by Heracles broke and thus Jason was declared the winner. Perhaps this "defeat" sowed the seeds of discontent and in part accounted for Heracles' departure from the ranks of the Argonauts a few days later.

After the departure of Heracles, the ship continued eastward into the sea of Marmora, where it was necessary to land for supplies. There, the Argonauts were entertained by the kindly King Cyzicus and were able to depart the next day refreshed and well provisioned. They had just begun to continue on their way when they encountered a driving storm in which they lost their bearings and drifted helplessly. Forced to make a landing in the early dawn, they were immediately set upon by a band of fierce warriors. There was much bloodshed in the ensuing battle, but the Argonauts emerged victorious. As the sun rose over the battlefield, the Argonauts were horrified to see their host, King Cyzicus, lying mortally wounded on the blood-soaked ground. He and his men had mistaken Jason's crew for a band of pirates attempting to invade their coast under cover of darkness. Overwhelmed by this tragic mischance which had pitted friend against friend, Jason ordered proper funeral observances to be held, including the traditional holding of games in honor of the dead. After all of the time-honored rituals were completed, they sailed off towards Colchis with heavy hearts.

Phineas

The Harpies

Before entering the narrow channel that separated the Sea of Marmora from the Black Sea, the Argonauts stopped in the land of Thrace to seek the advice of the blind King Phineas. They sought Phineas not only because he was a famous seer and could possibly foretell any further obstacles, but because they also needed directions in the uncharted waters of the Black Sea. He promised to help them if they would rid his kingdom of the Harpies. These were gruesome females with wings and eagle-like talons who descended at mealtime and carried off the best of his food. Because of the terrible odor that lingered from their attacks, the remainder of the food was unbearable.

Jason accepted the challenge and commanded a large banquet to be prepared in order to entice the Harpies. Just as Phineas and his court were seated, the Harpies appeared and began to snatch up the best morsels. But Jason was ready for them. The two sons of Boreas, Calais and Zetes, had

154

agreed to blow up a fierce wind between them. At Jason's signal, they attacked the Harpies with such ferocity that they were immediately lost to view and never returned to plague the table of Phineas again.

In gratitude, Phineas told Jason how to avoid the great clashing rocks, the Symplegades, guarding the narrow entrance to the Black Sea, and how to navigate to Colchis. He also gave him one more piece of advice that Jason did not understand at the time: to put his faith in Aphrodite once he arrived at his destination.

Sailing eastward with renewed confidence, the Argonauts soon came to the Symplegades, which were enshrouded in mist and high waves. Even for the Greeks, renowned sailors that they were, this passage had proved to be an impossibility in the past. No one had ever navigated these waters without the destruction of his ships, for before the navigation was completed the rocks had always come together, only to spring back after their destructive action to wait for the next expedition.

As Phineas had suggested, Jason released a white dove at the entrance of the narrows and closely followed its course. By doing this, he could not only choose the same course as the bird but also gain some idea of the amount of time he would have before the rocks could clash together again. As the bird flew, the rocks began their terrible movement but only managed to clip its tail feather. Immediately as the rocks separated Jason's crew followed, pulling with all their might. Just as the rocks were about to crash again, a great wave pushed the ship safely into the Black Sea. The Symplegades sprang back and have remained immobile to this day because a prophecy had decreed that once a ship had escaped their grasp, their tyrannical rule would end forever.

The Black Sea, with Colchis at its far extremity, was literally the end of the earth as far as the early Greeks knew. As Jason set across its waters, he would surely have lost his way had it not been for Phineas. After many days of steady sailing in the vast, unknown waters, they finally sighted the Caucasus Mountains, home of King Aeetes, the protector of the Golden Fleece. Jason had made tentative plans for the confrontation with his host. He proposed to be direct and honest with the king, hoping to persuade him that his quest for the Golden Fleece was a just one. However, if this failed, he then proposed to get it by guile or even warfare if necessary.

Upon sighting the huge *Argo*, King Aeetes and his court assembled to greet the strangers and make them welcome, providing that they came in

Aeetes

peace. Jason and his crew were happy to accept the hospitality of their host, hospitality which according to custom had to be extended before it was considered proper to ask strangers the purpose of their mission. When the proper time came, Jason explained the nature of his quest. Aeetes was first enraged and then amused at the presumption of Jason, but because he could not offer violence to a guest, he proposed a contest and promised that if Jason were successful, the Golden Fleece would be his. Jason was, in one day, to yoke together two fire-breathing bulls which had been made by Hephaestus, and then to plow a huge field sacred to Ares, the god of war.

Once the furrows were open, an even more challenging and seemingly impossible task was to be his. The king presented Jason with the teeth of a dragon which, when sown, would immediately produce a race of huge fighting men, one for each tooth sown. Jason was to engage them in combat and either destroy them or be killed himself. Aeetes made the challenge even more compelling by boasting that he had accomplished the same task himself. This was true, but what Aeetes had neglected to mention was the fact that he was a magician of great power, as were all members of his royal family, and that no mere mortal could hope to equal this feat. Although Jason accepted the challenge, courageous as he was, he knew inwardly that he would fall without divine aid. He therefore prepared to place his trust in Aphrodite as Phineas had suggested.

This trust was not misplaced, for Hera had been making plans on behalf of her favorite and had enlisted the aid of Aphrodite. They realized that to help Jason they must counter the magical power of Aeetes with an even more powerful force: Eros. The two goddesses instructed Eros to go to the court of Aeetes and loose his magic arrows on the unsuspecting

Medea   Medea, the king's daughter. Medea was a powerful sorceress herself and quite able to challenge her father's power if she so desired. Thus, while her father was offering the challenge to Jason, Medea was struck by the arrow of Eros. Even as Jason accepted the terms of the contest, she was instantly and helplessly in love with him and determined to pit her power against that of her father.

That night Medea met Jason secretly and told him of the magical powers she had acquired as a priestess of the witch Hecate. She revealed her passion for the Argonaut and promised to help him face the impossible challenge of her father, providing that he would take her with him when

156

he succeeded in his quest. It would be obvious to all at Aeetes' court that she had helped him and her life would then be in danger. Jason, fascinated by her charm and power, agreed to this condition. Medea gave him a magic ointment which, when applied, would make him invincible for one day. This would enable Jason to yoke the terrible bulls and to plow the field. To defeat the armed warriors, Medea suggested the old rule of divide and conquer. By throwing a stone into their midst, they would become confused as to who their enemy was and would begin fighting among themselves.

The next day, Jason, anointed with the potion, faced the bulls and easily subdued them. After yoking them to a plough, he proceeded to sow the dragon's teeth as Aeetes looked on in uneasy silence. When the giants arose, Jason did as Medea had instructed and the giants began fighting each other. In the resulting confusion, Jason entered the fray and was able to destroy the warriors who were left.

Aeetes was furious, for he knew that Jason had help from some immortal source. But, because of the bargain, he promised that he would give Jason the Fleece the next day. Realizing that this was a ruse to gain time, Jason determined to act immediately and again enlisted the aid of Medea. Under cover of darkness, she led Jason and Orpheus to the sacred garden which contained the Fleece.

Orpheus

As the legend had described, the Fleece was hanging in a tree guarded by a huge serpent which never slept. It was in order to nullify the power of this serpent that Medea had insisted Orpheus come with Jason. She ordered Orpheus to begin singing his softest and most soothing songs as he had once done for Hades. She used her magic to make herself and Jason immune to his enchanting lyrics. Just as all men and animals responded to the songs of Orpheus, so too the serpent was captivated by the music and fell into a deep sleep. By climbing up the coils of the slumbering serpent, Jason was able to reach the Golden Fleece, glittering in the pale moonlight. With the prize in hand, they quickly left the sacred garden and boarded the Argo which had been made ready for the flight. Medea joined Jason and, in order to further insure their safety, she arranged for her brother Apsyrtus, a child much loved by his father, to be kidnapped and held as a hostage during their escape.

When Aeetes discovered the duplicity of Jason and Medea, he immediately set sail in pursuit, sending his entire navy in every direction to find them. Spurred on by the anger of their leader, Aeetes' crew soon came within sight of the fleeing *Argo*. Medea had anticipated this and evolved a terrible plan to prevent capture. With Jason's approval and in plain sight of her father, she slaughtered her helpless brother Apsyrtus and cut his body into pieces which she then threw into the sea. She knew that Aeetes would have to pause to gather up the pieces of his beloved son in order to give him a proper burial, according to the custom. By the time Aeetes had completed this gruesome task, the *Argo* was out of sight, lost in the vast expanse of the Black Sea.

Although Jason and Medea had escaped for the time, there were many trials yet confronting them. Jason realized that the ships of Aeetes would be waiting for him at the narrow entrance between the Black Sea and the Sea of Marmora. He therefore devised a daring plan. From ancient accounts, he knew that a huge river was said to empty into the Black Sea and that this river, if followed, led to another sea. Jason mistakenly reasoned that this was another route into the Mediterranean for he knew of the existence of no other large body of water. He found the mouth of this river (now known as the Danube) and followed it to its source. There the crew made a long portage to another river and found themselves in a cold, hostile land. Sailing northward, they did reach a sea, but it was vastly different from the Mediterranean. Although he knew little of the geography of this area, Jason reasoned that by sailing with the land on his left, he and his crew would again reach the Mediterranean. No doubt he was encouraged in this theory when the climate continued to become warmer as they sailed due south. They reached the famed pillars of Heracles, the entrance to the Mediterranean, and reentered the familiar sea, far from the waiting ships of Aeetes. After much buffeting from island to island, and many adventures, they reached Iolcus where Jason received a hero's welcome from the populace who had heard of his exploits but had given him up for lost.

Jason's happiness was soon turned to rage when he discovered that Pelias had caused the death of his parents. He enlisted the aid of Medea to seek his revenge. This proved to be an error in judgment on Jason's part, for Medea, as a true daughter of Hecate, exacted a revenge so horrible that the Greeks of Iolcus were sickened by the deed and later banished the two, reasoning that Medea's crime was greater than Jason's right to rule. She had tricked Pelias' two daughters into believing that by killing their father and boiling the pieces of his body in a huge cauldron, she could, by

Medea killing her children,
from a painting by Delacroix.

incantation, bring him back to life as a young man. Previously, as the daughters looked on, she had convinced them of her powers to rejuvenate by performing the same feat on an old ram. Now, to their horror, once they had performed the grisly deed, Medea was nowhere to be found. The citizens of Iolcus were not so much horrified by the death of Pelias, which they knew was just, as by the terrible demonic quality of the eastern priestess whom Jason had brought home as his queen. Banished from his own court, Jason went to Corinth with Medea in the *Argo*. There he was greeted royally. The *Argo* was placed by the temple of Poseidon and dedicated to that god.

For a short time Jason endured his exile and Medea bore him two sons. But it became increasingly apparent to Jason that he would never regain his rightful throne as long as he was married to Medea. The Greeks feared her dark, magical powers. A solution to this situation was offered to Jason by the king of Corinth. He realized the advantages of having a hero of Jason's reputation and stature as a member of his royal household and suggested to Jason that he divorce Medea and marry his daughter Glauce. Jason realized the advantages of such a match, and long proximity with his wife caused him to forget that her awesome powers could also be used against himself. He repudiated Medea and announced his intention to marry Glauce. Medea realized that without Jason she would no longer be safe in Corinth and felt with some justification that Jason was treating her unfairly. She killed Glauce by devious means and punished her husband by killing her two children as well. Some accounts have stated that Medea boiled her children and served them to Jason for dinner. Medea then left Corinth, aided by a chariot and flying dragons sent by Hecate, leaving Jason to brood over the ruins of his plans.

Jason, whose kingship had been so shortlived, was doomed to spend his waning years wandering, a lonely man without a country or a home. Finally, he found his way back to Corinth and his old ship, the *Argo*. Possibly musing about his heroic quest and its unfortunate aftermath, he sat in the shadow of the old and rotting timbers. Falling into the sleep of the very old, he was struck dead by the great oaken prow of his ship which had rotted through and fell at that fateful moment. Thus ended the life of one of the great heroes of the ancient world.

Phases of the Heroic Pattern

This ending is only the beginning of the Jason story. What follows is a number of observations about the hero, the heroic pattern, and the relevance of all this discussion to literature, to the Greeks, and to us.

THE BIRTH   As we have seen in the case of Perseus, the birth of someone destined to do great things was enshrouded in the mystery and intrigue of a royal court. The child was of divine and/or royal parentage. His birth was the cause of a dynastic struggle for power and consequently his young life was in jeopardy. Often a ruse was required to suppress the identity of the child and thus save his life.

Compare the births of Jason and Heracles with the above formula. Naturally, not every hero will fit this pattern detail for detail, but it is a surprisingly consistent one.

What do these facts tell us about the Greek royalty and their relationship to the gods on Olympus? Why do you think the Greek authors insisted on these conditions surrounding an heroic birth?

What heroes' births in other cultures and religions follow all or part of this formula?

It is a consistent fact that the childhood of the hero is rarely mentioned in heroic literature. It is merely suggested that the child, who had been either spirited away or brought up in seclusion, was raised in a manner consistent with his future role of greatness. What are some possible reasons for this absence of detailed information?

DESTINY   Destiny played a very great role in the lives of the Greek heroes. As the poets saw them, these men were fated to be great, and to be great meant that their lives were inextricably entwined with the interests of the Olympians. In the case of Perseus, his birth was the result of a divine oracle. In the case of Jason, not only was there an oracle, but the goddess actually advised him directly and took his part.

Document the oracles which affected the lives of heroes. What does the fact that these oracles were always fulfilled tell about the Greek concept of the divine law? Why do prophecies and oracles figure so strongly in the narratives of the great heroes of the past?

Document the direct intervention of gods in the life of Jason and any other hero. In each case, try to decide why that particular god is involved and why the Greeks would naturally assume that this deity would be intervening.

Obviously the Greeks did not feel that divine intervention took away from the greatness of the hero. Rather, it was a mark that the gods recognized the potential of the hero. Would this be true for a modern concept of heroism?

161

THE QUEST   According to the classical tradition, in order to prove his status as hero and thus claim his throne, the young man had to undertake a dangerous quest on behalf of his people. Sometimes the aim was to save the people from a terrible plague or tyrant; sometimes it was for material gain. Usually the successful completion of the quest fulfilled both objectives. Quite often the task was set by the usurper who considered the quest an impossibility. This added a strong element of adventure to the narrative, as well as reinforcing the difficulties entailed in success.

A quest is literally a search for something. We tend to associate it today solely with a religious or a moral purpose. But this concept was not paramount in ancient Greek values. For them, a quest meant a challenge to be sought out and a goal to be achieved. The hero's quest became of vital importance to the culture and to the people. Through the story the audience was able to identify with his character and to reaffirm its own cultural values.

In the case of each hero studied, identify the quest and account for the reason why it was an important objective to the society. This is not as simple a task as it may first appear. For instance, taken on a literal level, Jason was in search of a ram's hide. But the Golden Fleece could be taken symbolically. There is the implication that the fleece, because of its religious associations, is part of a religious quest for the people of the Greek mainland. Its return could represent an atonement for the deaths of Phrixus and Helle.

It is possible that the Golden Fleece was a euphemism for the wealth of Colchis and that Jason was really on a raiding expedition to try to gain a portion of the rich eastern trade. The acquisition of such a rich trading area would make Jason a very popular leader. There is also a theory that the thick wool of the ram was merely one of many such fleeces used by the eastern people to pan for gold in the mountain streams feeding the Black Sea. Thus, it is also possible to see the fleece as the proverbial pot of gold found at the end of many a journey of exploration. Quite possibly the search for the fleece was really the story of the first Greek exploration of the mysterious and then uncharted eastern sea. One could even argue that the search for the fleece was a combination of all of these.

There are possibilities for similar conjecture concerning the symbolic meanings behind all the heroes' quests. The reader must look at the facts of the quest very carefully and then attempt some conclusions.

In classical heroic literature, the hero always encountered several difficulties and overcame them before reaching his primary objective. Each difficulty revealed his physical prowess and his mental capabilities as well as making the story more exciting and suspenseful for the listener. Thus by the time the hero actually reached the object of his quest, his heroic stature had already been firmly established. Look at the difficulties encountered by the heroes and try to decide what qualities the Greeks would have considered heroic.

The appearance of a monstrous creature which must be overcome is a remarkably consistent fact in these classical legends. In fact, the heroes in this study are all forced to overcome a monster or monsters in some form. We have seen that Medusa was part serpent and that the fleece was guarded by a huge unsleeping serpent which had to be overcome by magic. Document the appearance of other monstrous figures in the heroes' quests. How could their recurrence and especially the fact that so many are snakes and so many are female be accounted for? In what other types of literature does the hero kill a monster to save the people and get the girl?

THE JOURNEY HOME

After the object of the quest had been attained, many of the heroes found themselves confronted with an arduous journey back to their homeland. In many cases, they met new adventures and hardships. For instance, Jason found the journey home even longer than the journey to Colchis. Obviously, this was an opportunity for the early poets to expand upon the tale of the hero as well as to explain the almost legendary travels of early explorers.

But there is another reason why this tale of the hero's return was often stressed. To the Greeks, the homeland was a very important part of their life. A person was identified by his lineage in a particular area and by his ties to one city state. Greece was still very much a tribal society, and one of the worst punishments a person could undergo was to be exiled from his home. Thus the tale of the hero's difficulties in returning would be very compelling and significant to the Greek.

The Odyssey of Homer is fascinating in that it deals exclusively with the return of the hero, the hero in this case being Odysseus (Ulysses). One might argue that the defeat of Troy was the object of his quest since he engineered that victory, but because he had offended Poseidon, he was forced to wander for ten years before arriving home in Ithaca.

Find out all that can be found about Odysseus' difficulties with the following in his efforts to return home: The Lotus Eaters, Polyphemus, Aeolus, Circe, Tartarus, the Sirens, Scylla and Charybdis, Hyperion, and Calypso. In many ways Odysseus met all of the trials of a Jason or Perseus, but all on the way home. After having considered the difficulties of the return home, compare the qualities of character displayed by Odysseus with the qualities of the other heroes. In what ways is he typical?

THE REWARD   In each case, the hero gained the rewards of his labors. This usually meant that the hero became the king, although in the case of Heracles, he merely gained fame and a very high place of honor. However, it was a feature of these legends that this height of power was very short-lived. Perhaps the poets who had created heroes felt compelled to destroy them as well. Jason was faced with exile; Perseus killed his grandfather in error; Theseus inadvertently caused the death of his father.

The old age of the hero is also something that is treated in a similar way in all of the legends. It was either obscure or inglorious. For instance, Jason wandered the earth a dispossessed old man. It was almost as if the old age of the hero was an embarrassment.

Compare the endings of these heroic tales. What factors could be found in ancient Greek society as well as in basic human nature that would account for this phenomenon?

ROMANTIC ELEMENTS   No adventure story would be complete without the element of love. Anyone with any knowledge of mythology will be aware that this is particularly true in the case of the ancient Greeks. Perseus had his Andromeda, and Jason his Medea. All of the heroes had encounters with many women, and it is clear that they were considered lovers of rather heroic proportions. Certain interesting attitudes towards females and their traditional place in ancient society emerge if one examines the role of women in the classical tradition. It is significant that there are no women heroes. We will leave the reader to draw his own sociological conclusions about this fact. When we examine the stories closely, certain attitudes become evident.

Document the plight of the following women: Andromeda, Penelope, Danae, Ariadne, and Phaedra. Discuss to what extent they had any control over their own destiny.

Another sort of woman figures very prominently in these stories: the witch or priestess. Medea, Circe, Calypso, and the Sirens fall into this category. The hero was clearly attracted to these women, but their power was regarded as evil or demonic by the hero as well as by the ancient poets. These women were the prototype for the *femme fatale* so popular in all literature. What does the fascination with the "enchantress" reveal about the ancient Greek attitudes towards women? To what extent has this idea about women persisted? Why?

In this study of the classical heroic tradition, we have looked at the heroes under such categories as their birth, their quest and its problems, and their rewards. Although we have tried not to force conclusions, we have attempted to point out certain consistent patterns—patterns that will recur in the medieval heroic tradition. The discovery of the "pattern" and its cultural implications has been our focus, but we hope that this introduction to classical literature will encourage further reading of original and critical sources and will point the way to parallels in the literature of every age.

The Medieval Tradition

Everyone has some familiarity with medieval heroic literature. It is associated in our minds with the enchanting tales of childhood, of knights in shining armor and damsels in distress. Many of our fairy tales originate from this heroic tradition. Of all the stories told, the legends of King Arthur and the Knights of the Round Table are best known. The success of the musical *Camelot* has shown the interest still generated by this age of chivalry and romance.

Currently several attempts are being made to "find" Camelot in much the same way that Schliemann sought to discover Troy. But the fact remains that historically Arthur's existence is as problematical as that of the Greek

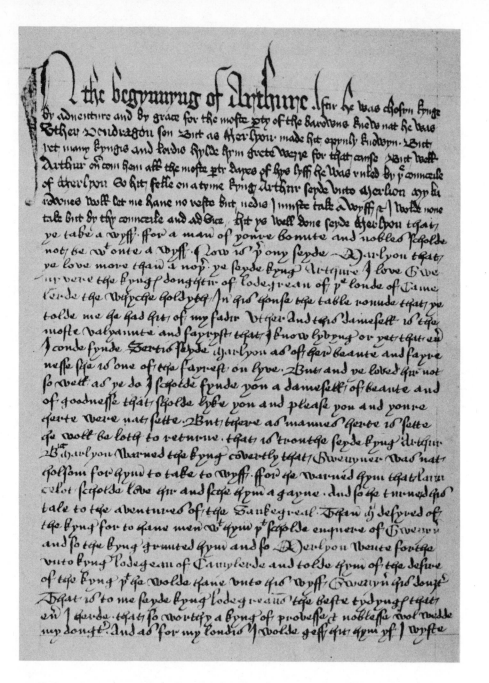

Manuscript page from Malory's *Le Morte D'Arthur*, approximately 15th century A.D.

heroes. In Nennius' *Historia Brittonum,* written in 800 A.D., there was mention made of a King Arthur who defeated the Saxons in England in the late fifth century A.D. But the other historical commentaries that so many of the poets claim as sources no longer exist, leading many scholars to suspect that this listing of sources was a literary convention. And there is no doubt at all that even if Arthur did exist, he certainly did not accomplish all of the feats attributed to him.

The Arthur we know is a product of the poetic imagination, a literary manifestation of medieval society's desire to create a heroic figure who could "carry" the values of the culture and whose stories would delight and instruct. The historical Arthur was the catalyst for an entire literary cycle which developed over a number of centuries. This growth of the Arthurian cycle is well documented since in this case, unlike the classical poems, we are dealing with a written, not an oral, tradition.

Arthur and his knights first gained literary prominence in the *Historia Regum Britanniae* of Geoffrey of Monmouth in 1135. It was this writer who began the elevation of Arthur to heroic stature. Instead of having Arthur defeat only the Saxons, Geoffrey had him defeat the Scots, French, Norwegians, and even a Roman Legion. Monmouth also added details about Arthur's supernatural birth and death and his defeat by his own kindred. Although Geoffrey of Monmouth related the history of Arthur in a very direct way to the classical heroes, it was even more significant that he sought to relate Arthur to Christ. This change in emphasis placed Arthur very definitely in the Christian tradition. His values as a hero and his exploits became a reflection of a Christian culture.

In many ways, Arthur was more sophisticated than the Greek heroes because the culture that created him was more sophisticated. This was the era of the chivalric code and courtly love. Form was all-important. Loyalty to one's love or to one's king was not only a social obligation but a profoundly religious one as well. Monmouth created Arthur in the image of the perfect medieval knight. It was only a matter of time before the great poets in France began to add to his story.

Chrétien de Troyes, a twelfth century French poet, was responsible for adding more romantic elements to the story of Arthur and reinforcing Arthur's role as a Christian hero. He introduced the love affair between Launcelot and Guinevere, as well as the stories of the quest for the Holy

Grail. In the following years, many writers were to add to the stories of Arthur and Launcelot as well as the other knights of the Round Table.

All of these writings culminated in the great prose work of Sir Thomas Malory published by Caxton in 1485 under the title *Le Morte D'Arthur*. Like authors before him, Malory interpreted the stories in a way which reflected his own interest. But his work was also encyclopedic in that it included most of the cycle from Monmouth and French sources. It is his work which has made the greatest contribution to our knowledge of the Arthurian legends.

Since Malory's work alone involves twenty-one books, we are making no attempt to be all-inclusive. The wonderful, romantic story of Tristram and Isolde is left out entirely, as are many of the stories about the knights of the Round Table. The following stories are meant to introduce only the main strands of the Arthurian legend and to act as an introduction to further reading.

There has been a tremendous resurgence of interest in Arthur during this century. Two works which describe the search of archeologists and historians for evidence of the historical Arthur are *The Search for King Arthur* by Christopher Hibbert and *King Arthur in Fact and Fiction* by Geoffrey Ashe. These books are particularly interesting because of their beautiful illustrations and their clearly stated text.

The ideal of courtly love and the chivalric code permeated the medieval aristocracy in both France and England. Both of these ideals represent very complicated forms of behavior and much has been written about them. Since an appreciation of these is important to an understanding of the Arthurian cycle, the reader should look up the basic tenets of courtly love and the chivalric code in one of the larger encyclopedias.

Just as the Greek heroes embodied the cultural values of their time, so did Arthur for the Middle Ages. The poets purposely created in Arthur a Christlike figure because Christ represented the epitome of goodness and order. What qualities of character and behavior would you therefore expect Arthur to have that would not be found in the Greek heroes?

The Arthurian legend is no different from any other heroic tradition in that its writers sought as their hero not a contemporary leader but one who existed in the past. Why is it necessary for an historical figure to be safely dead before such literature can create a legendary hero? What evidence is there for this same tendency in modern society?

Arthur's Rise to Kingship

Uther Pendragon

The Arthurian cycle begins with the lust of Uther Pendragon, high king of South Wales in the fifth century A.D. Uther had acquired the generic name of Pendragon because he was the leader of all the British kings during the wars against the Angles and Saxons. With the collapse of the Roman Empire in the fifth century, Britain discovered she was very much alone and was forced to protect herself from the heathen barbarians of the European mainland. The remaining British kings, who were Christian and comparatively civilized, were forced to rally in order to fight the invaders.

Merlin

At the same time, there were tremendous power struggles among the kings of each area in Britain to gain control. Uther was supreme for a time, but Britain was in need of a warrior who could unify the country more permanently. No one was more aware of this need than Merlin, the most famous magician of his day. It was he who realized that Uther could produce the hero Britain required.

Ygerne

It began thus. Uther had called all of the allied nobles to his castle for a feast. There he spied Ygerne, the beautiful wife of Gorlois, the Duke of Cornwall, and was overcome with desire for her. She rejected his advances and told her husband, who immediately insisted that they leave Uther's court. In his anger, the Duke of Cornwall did not observe the proper leave-taking formalities. This omission provided Uther with the necessary excuse to declare war on the Duke. But Uther realized that merely defeating Gorlois would not gain him the virtuous Ygerne. At this point Merlin offered his assistance. He agreed to help Uther, but only under certain conditions. Merlin predicted that a child would be born from Uther's union with Ygerne and specified that this child must be given over to him at birth. So great was his desire for Ygerne that Uther agreed to this condition.

Merlin was able to capitalize on a miscalculation made by Gorlois. The duke had placed his wife in one of his isolated castles while he and his troops occupied another castle. He hoped to trick Uther into believing that

Ygerne was with him. This ruse might have succeeded were it not for Merlin's alliance with Gorlois' rival. Merlin cast a spell on Uther so that the high king would appear at Ygerne's castle in the guise of her own husband. The unsuspecting wife slept with Uther and only discovered the truth of his identity when news of her own husband's death reached her the following morning. During the night, Uther's forces had attacked and killed Gorlois as he ventured forth from his castle. Thus, this propitious death prepared the way for Uther to marry Ygerne.

As Merlin had predicted, a son was born of this union. Keeping his promise, Uther had the unchristened child delivered in secrecy to Merlin who entrusted him to Sir Ector, an old and faithful knight. Sir Ector was to raise Arthur, for so Merlin had christened the baby. Thus, Arthur was educated in the best chivalric tradition but was saved from the danger and intrigue that would normally surround a royal heir.

When Arthur was fifteen, Uther Pendragon died, and for a time the land was torn by warring factions, all attempting to gain control. This civil war threatened the entire social and religious structure of Britain since the Saxons were quick to take advantage of the situation and renew their efforts. At Merlin's suggestion, the Archbishop of Canterbury commanded all of the warring leaders to come to London at Christmastime, on pain of damnation. He held a service on Christmas eve and at that time prayed for a miracle. The Archbishop beseeched God to proclaim a Savior for Britain on the same day that He had brought forth a Savior for the world. And during this Christmas service, the miracle did occur.

A great stone appeared in the churchyard. Embedded in it was an anvil with a mighty sword protruding from it. Underneath the anvil was written: WHOSO PULLITH OUT THIS SWORD OF THIS STONE AND ANVIL IS RIGHTWISE KING BORN OF ALL ENGLAND. All of the mighty contenders to the throne tried to pull the sword from the stone and failed. Thus a leader was not chosen at that time and the Archbishop declared that a further contest would be held at Easter and at Pentecost so that more knights could attempt the seemingly impossible feat.

In the natural course of events, it is unlikely that the young Arthur would ever have been offered the opportunity to test his strength. He was too young and his royal parentage was known only to Merlin. But destiny (or Merlin) would not be denied. Tournaments were held near the churchyard, and Arthur attended the games as valet to his older step-brother, Sir

Uther consults Merlin with Ygerne watching, from a thirteenth-century manuscript.

Sir Kay   Kay. During the games, Sir Kay sent Arthur to obtain a sword. As he passed the church, he chanced to see the sacred stone. Foreseeing no harm in borrowing this sword, he easily pulled it from its resting place and presented it to his kinsman. Kay perceived which sword he had and immediately claimed to all the lords that he should become king.

None of the lords was prepared to believe Kay's claim without proof. They insisted that he reinsert the sword in the anvil and draw it out again. Of course he would not do this and was forced to admit that it was Arthur who had accomplished the feat. Arthur was put to the test and succeeded a second time. With great joy, the archbishop declared him high king. Merlin chose this time to tell the true story of Arthur's birth. Thus Arthur's right to rule was established, not only by his royal lineage but also by Divine consent.

King Arthur   The lords, jealous of their power, refused to be ruled by one so young and obscure as Arthur. Arthur therefore had to establish his right to rule by his prowess in an ensuing civil war. His main allies were Sir Kay, Sir Ector, the Archbishop, and Sir Bors and Sir Ban from France. His main enemy was his uncle Lot. In all accounts of this war, Arthur was depicted as saving the land from destruction, a land laid waste by warring factions. Tennyson, in his account of Arthur's rise, accurately described the country before Arthur emerged victorious:

> For many a petty king ere Arthur came
> Ruled in this isle, and ever waging war
> Each upon the other, wasted all the land;
> And still from time to time the heathen host
> Swarmed overseas, and harried what was left.
> And so there grew great tracts of wilderness,
> Wherein the beast was ever more and more,
> But man was less and less, till Arthur came.

Arthur's prowess in this war was stressed by Malory: "King Arthur did so marvellously in arms that all men had wonder." Because of his prowess and Merlin's advice, Arthur prevailed and gradually the countryside became peaceful.

In the legends, Arthur never totally unified his kingdom. He and his followers constantly had to fight wayward lords, evil monsters, and barbarian hordes. But Arthur did manage to create for a time, through his

172

extreme goodness and heroism, an almost ideal society amid the surrounding chaos. He married the beautiful Guinevere, established the court at Camelot, and instituted the order of the Knights of the Round Table. It was a time of happiness, where chivalric acts and brave deeds predominated and where high adventure and love became the highest ideal.

Arthur's birth occurred in the course of a struggle for power and as a result of supernatural forces. Compare Arthur's birth with that of his counterparts in Greek heroic literature. Why do you think the pattern repeats itself in a different cultural context?

Arthur's rise to kingship follows the classical pattern of the trial, in this case pulling the sword from the stone and fighting to unify the country. But, as was mentioned in the introduction, the identification of the medieval hero with the Christian ideal was also an important factor. Where in the account thus far do you see the writers attempting to relate Arthur to Christ?

In the cycle there are curious remnants of pagan rites and preoccupations which persisted in the Middle Ages and coexisted very amicably with Christianity. A good case in point is Merlin, the magician and Arthur's mentor. In our story of Arthur's birth, which follows Malory's account, it is obvious that the writer attempted to make Merlin a sort of agent for God. He not only planned Arthur's birth, but he also had him christened and even became advisor to the Archbishop of Canterbury —an odd role for someone who was so obviously initiated in the arts of white and black magic.

Merlin was probably of Druidic origin since one of the most consistent claims about him was that he had magically built the magnificent Druid temple at Stonehenge. He was said to be the son of an incubus, a spirit of the air. It was also said that his mother, a mortal, had him baptized and sent him to a monastery to be raised, thus accounting for his Christian attributes.

Merlin was such an interesting figure that writers began to add more and more stories about him. The best known is his fatal love affair with Vivian, one of the Ladies of the Lake, a group of mystical beings who appear in medieval stories from time to time. For a quick review, the reader will find Bullfinch's *Mythology: The Age of Chivalry* an excellent summary of Merlin's career.

Each century has tended to identify with different Arthurian characters. For instance, in the eighteenth and nineteenth century, stories of Launcelot and Guinevere were the most popular. Merlin is the Arthurian figure who seems to command as much or more interest in our modern society. Why do you think this is so? Mary Stewart's *The Crystal Cave*, and its companion *The Hollow Hills*, are good examples of the new fiction centering on Merlin.

The World of Camelot

Arthur reigned over a great deal of territory during his kingship and thus held court at several different places. But the most famous site of Arthur's court was Camelot. Even now the name Camelot evokes a feeling of romance and enchantment. In the Middle Ages it represented the embodiment of the chivalric ideal and the height of medieval sophistication. Beautiful ladies in rich and colorful apparel spent their days delighting in the spectacle of tournaments and jousts and in listening to stories of the hunt or of knights' adventures. Feasts were held and religious festivals observed, all under the benevolent eye of King Arthur and his beautiful Queen Guinevere. But the main attraction in Camelot was Arthur's Order of the Knights of the Round Table. This Order drew young men from far and wide to Arthur's court.

The Round Table   The Round Table had been made by Merlin's magic and had traditionally belonged to the high king. Arthur obtained it from Guinevere's father as part of her dowry. The number of knights who actually sat at the Round Table varied from story to story, but the qualifications for obtaining a place remained constant. To become a member, a knight had to prove his valor, and once membership had been bestowed by Arthur, a knight would remain so honored until someone else showed himself superior in battle. The number of knights who sat at the Round Table at any given time was limited, and membership was a prize greatly sought after.

Each Knight of the Round Table was charged to observe the highest code of chivalry. He was to be loyal and virtuous, to avoid cruelty, to offer mercy, and to always grant the wishes of any lady in distress. Although it was perfectly acceptable for a knight to leave Camelot in order to seek

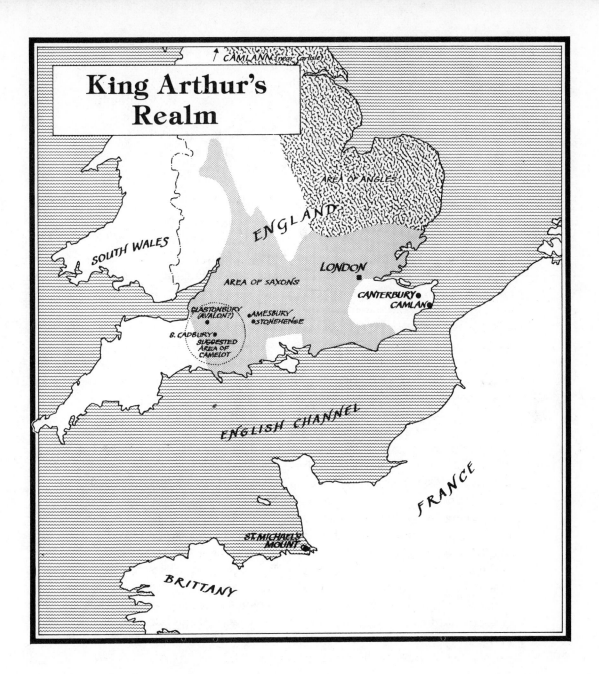

King Arthur's Realm

CAMLANN (near Carlisle)

AREA OF ANGLES

ENGLAND

SOUTH WALES

AREA OF SAXONS

LONDON

CANTERBURY
CAMLAN

GLASTONBURY
(AVALON?)
●AMESBURY
●STONEHENGE

S. CADBURY●
SUGGESTED
AREA OF
CAMELOT

ENGLISH CHANNEL

FRANCE

ST. MICHAEL'S
MOUNT

BRITTANY

adventure for its own sake, he was charged never to take part in a battle for personal gain or for any unlawful reason.

As the epitome of knighthood, Arthur presided over the Knights of the Round Table. In the early legends, such as the accounts of Monmouth, Arthur's own adventures were at the center of the narration, but as the cycle grew, more and more stories dwelt on famous knights such as Sir Launcelot, Sir Tristram, and Sir Galahad. The following two stories will focus on Arthur's adventures as a Knight of the Round Table.

EXCALIBUR Throughout his leadership, Arthur had the advice and magic powers of Merlin to aid him. It was through Merlin that he acquired Excalibur, the famous sword which made his chivalric efforts so notable. One day when Arthur was touring the countryside in search of adventure, he chanced to come upon three serfs chasing Merlin with cudgels. As soon as they saw Arthur, mounted and in full armor, they quickly abandoned their attack. The King, who was pleased to have been able to help the magician, jokingly reminded him that it was his prowess and not magic that had saved him. Merlin reminded Arthur that he could have saved himself if he had wanted to but that, in effect, he had used this situation to draw Arthur to a place where the king's own prowess was to be challenged.

The king suddenly noticed a knight, fully armed, guarding a pass. Upon cautious inquiry Arthur learned that no one could pass without first jousting with this knight. Arthur responded to the challenge. Three times the lances of the king and knight crashed upon each other, shattering against the heavy shields. Whereupon, they both began to fight with their swords, matching stroke for stroke until Arthur's blade broke. The knight offered to spare the king if he would admit to being defeated and cowardly. Arthur was willing to assent to the first, but his pride would not allow him to admit to the second. He made one last attempt to overcome the knight with his strength, but the knight managed to make Arthur, whose armor was heavy, fall backwards to the ground.

Just as he was about to raise the king's helmet to cut his throat, Merlin cast a spell causing the knight to go into a deep sleep. Arthur became very distraught, for he thought Merlin had killed this knight who had officially been able to best him. Merlin assured Arthur that he was just asleep and

176

would awaken in three hours. The knight's name was Sir Pellinore, and Merlin prophesied that thereafter Sir Pellinore and his sons would do Arthur great service as members of the Round Table.

The two then went on their way, with Arthur lamenting the fact that he was unarmed and without a sword. Merlin promised to help, and they rode until they came to a lake. In the middle of the lake Arthur saw a wonderful sight: an arm clothed in white samite rose out of the water, and in the hand was a sword. Merlin said that he must ask the permission of the Lady of the Lake to obtain it. Upon receiving her permission, Arthur rowed out and took the rich sword in its jeweled scabbard from the hand, which then sank beneath the waves. "As long as you have this scabbard," Merlin said, "you cannot receive any harmful wound from any knight." Thus

Arthur came into the possession of Excalibur, which was the name of the weapon, and kept it until his final battle.

Arthur then returned to the Round Table and told of his adventures. This greatly pleased the company, for not only were they amazed that he, a king, would jeopardize his person by entering into single combat, but they were delighted that his own chivalry was the same as he had demanded from them.

While on a campaign in Brittany, Arthur was accosted by a peasant who requested aid from the renowned champion. A giant lived in a nearby cave on the mountain known as Saint Michael's Mount. The people in the surrounding countryside lived in constant fear of this creature, for the giant would kidnap their children and devour them. This time he had carried off the Duchess of Brittany and no one had been able to stop him. Arthur was horrified that such a terrible thing should happen to a gentlewoman and immediately sought directions to the giant's lair. These were readily given, along with the warning that the giant would most likely be found feasting near the two huge fires that guarded the hoard of treasure in his cave.

Arthur charged Sir Kay and Sir Bedivere to arm themselves and accompany him. However, when they arrived at the foot of the mountain, he would not let them ascend with him but requested that they remain below. Arthur climbed until he came near the great fires, and there he found an old woman bewailing the untimely death of the Duchess. Determined in his faith, he boldly went forth and found the giant surrounded by his booty and three newly found victims, three damsels bound in preparation to be roasted on the fire and eaten. At such a sight, Arthur was sorely troubled by the evil of the man and quickly challenged him.

The giant rose up with a great club and struck Arthur so hard that he knocked his helmet off, but Arthur had managed to strike him a blow with his sword before being knocked over. A great wound opened in the giant's stomach, causing him to throw away his club and in a wild rage to wrestle with the fallen king. He jumped on Arthur, crushing three of his ribs. The three maidens began to pray for Divine aid and, as they encouraged their champion, Arthur managed to draw his dagger and stab the giant. Together they rolled down the hill until they arrived at the spot where Sir Kay and Sir Bedivere were waiting. The two knights freed Arthur, and at the king's command Sir Kay smote off the giant's head, placing it on his spear for all to see.

The people came from all around to marvel, whereupon they thanked both God and the king. Arthur caused the giant's treasure to be divided among the people and decreed that a church be built on the mountain. When this was done, the church was dedicated in the name of Saint Michael.

The Marriage of Arthur

At the same time that Arthur was becoming established in his realm, it came into his mind that he should seek a wife. The loyal barons were in favor of this resolution and encouraged Arthur so that the kingdom might have a queen and future heir. Accordingly, Arthur sought the advice of Merlin, telling him that of all the beautiful maidens in the land, he preferred **Guinevere** Guinevere, the daughter of Leodegrance, king of Cameliard.

Merlin warned Arthur that although Guinevere was beautiful, there were many other ladies in the land and that Guinevere was not the best choice. Merlin knew that Launcelot, one of Arthur's greatest knights, would fall in love with Guinevere and that she would eventually return that love. Because of his faith in goodness and his great love for Guinevere, Arthur resolved to ignore the advice of Merlin and took Guinevere to be his wife.

Arthur's wedding was a day of great pomp and ceremony. All of the lords and ladies attended, and every knight of the Round Table swore to fight to the death for his new Queen. Arthur and his lady lived in supreme happiness until that time when the dreadful prophecy of Merlin began to be realized.

LAUNCELOT Because of his valor, Launcelot was the greatest knight of Arthur's Round Table. Malory describes Launcelot as follows:

> *Sir Launcelot Du Lac . . . in all tournaments and jousts and deeds of arms, both for life and death . . . passed all other knights, and at no time was he never overcome but if it were by treason or enchantment, so Sir Launcelot increased so marvelously in worship and in honor, therefore is he the first knight that the French book maketh mention of after King Arthur came from Rome. Wherefore Queen Guinevere had him in great favor above all other knights, and in certain he loved the queen again above all other ladies and damosels of his life, and for her he did many deeds of arms, and saved her from the fire through his noble chivalry.*

Launcelot and Guinevere did not consummate their love immediately, but finally their desire for each other overcame their sense of propriety. It was not long before their affair became a scandal of the court, although for a time Arthur was in ignorance of their love. Launcelot was torn between his two loyalties and often left Arthur's court to seek adventure. Guinevere accused Sir Launcelot of loving her less because he absented himself from her presence so often, but he was quick to reply that he did this only so that the shame of their alliance should be less obvious. Guinevere was unimpressed with this explanation and in a jealous rage ordered him to leave the court forever, an order she was to regret very soon after.

On the occasion of a great feast, Sir Pinel, jealous of Sir Gawaine, plotted to poison him. He reasoned that Sir Gawaine, because of his eminence and because Sir Launcelot was absent from court, would be seated beside the queen at the dinner. So he poisoned a choice-looking apple and placed it in a dish beside the queen, knowing that it was her custom to bestow the best fruit to the person beside her during the dinner. Much to Pinel's dismay, when the guests were seated, the place of honor beside Guinevere had been given over to Sir Patrise, a visiting knight from Ireland. Sir Pinel kept his silence as the innocent queen offered the poisoned apple to the visitor, who fell dead immediately upon eating it. Since no one in Arthur's court had any quarrel with Sir Patrise, suspicion immediately fell on the queen, for everyone had seen her choose the apple and offer it to him.

Sir Patrise's kinsman came to Arthur's court and demanded vengeance on the queen unless some knight was so convinced of her innocence that he would do battle for her. The challenger's name was Sir Mador, a knight famous for his ability in close combat. All of the Knights of the Round Table were reluctant to champion the queen, whose reputation had been stained by the stories of her amorous adventures. In the absence of Launcelot, only an older knight, Sir Bohort, felt any pity for her and offered her his aid. Sir Bohort knew he was no match for his opponent, as did Guinevere. Thus she had cause to regret her treatment of her lover.

On the day of the contest, Sir Bohort went with his loyal retinue to a hermitage in the woods, there to be shriven before his death. Luckily he encountered Launcelot and quickly told him of his lady's peril. Launcelot sent Sir Bohort back to Camelot and promised that he would follow in time to take his place in the battle with Sir Mador.

Launcelot and Guinevere, from a line engraving based on a French eleventh-century miniature.

As all the nobles gathered, a tearful Guinevere was led in and placed near the stake on which she was to be burned if Sir Mador was victorious. As the trumpets signaled the beginning of the combat, a knight in strange black armor rode in on a white horse and offered to fight for the queen. In the ensuing battle, both men fought valiantly, receiving many wounds and cuts, but finally the black knight defeated Sir Mador, who was forced to sue for pity. This request was quickly granted, providing that the queen be acquitted of treason and no mention be made on any monument to Sir Patrise that Queen Guinevere had had any part in his death. To this Sir Mador agreed and the queen's champion revealed himself as Launcelot. Thus Queen Guinevere was saved from the fire, and Launcelot was back in favor once again.

Not long after this, the crime of Sir Pinel was discovered and he was punished for his evil deed.

The Death of Arthur

Although Launcelot and Guinevere's love for each other was sincere, the medieval writers saw their adultery as the source of the moral decay which led to the decline of Camelot and the death of Arthur. For, as long as Arthur and the goodness he represented had predominated, his enemies, led by Lot and Arthur's nephew, Modred, were held at bay. But Guinevere's crime caused divided loyalties and encouraged others to follow suit. Many writers claim that Arthur's spirit was broken when he himself discovered the pair together. At this discovery, the trust and loyalty which had held the Round Table together was shattered. Launcelot was forced to flee to France and Arthur followed with an army.

This provided the opportunity that Lot and Modred had been waiting for. Because it had been Modred who had led Arthur to discover the lovers together, Arthur had made him Regent in his place before leaving to attack Launcelot. This was exactly what Modred had calculated would happen, and he was quick to use the situation to his own advantage.

As soon as Arthur was in France, Modred announced that the king had been killed in battle and claimed Arthur's throne as well as Guinevere's hand. Guinevere fled to London with her supporters to try to defend herself and Arthur, for she still loved him. Word was sent to Arthur that his kingdom was in danger.

When Arthur received news of the revolt, he returned to Britain, landing with all of his forces at Dover. It was at Camlan, near Dover, that the final battle was fought.

The fight raged for several days, with Modred's forces gaining much ground. One by one Arthur's loyal friends were slain. Sir Gawaine was victim to Modred's sword and thereafter appeared to Arthur in a dream warning him that to fight the next day would mean certain death. He told Arthur that Launcelot had been informed of his plight and in his remorse was coming to his aid.

Armed with this knowledge, Arthur called a truce, hoping to gain time until Launcelot's forces could arrive. Modred agreed. As they met, their armies on each side of them, one of Modred's men unthinkingly drew his sword to kill an adder which had bitten him. This act was misinterpreted by Arthur's army, who drew their arms and entered the fray.

After long, single combat, Arthur killed Modred but not before Modred had given him a mortal wound. Thus it happened that Sir Arthur lay in his death throes, amidst a field of dead men, accompanied only by his loyal friend Sir Bedivere.

Arthur charged Bedivere to take him to a chapel at the nearby lake and to throw his sword Excalibur into the water. Bedivere left his king to do the deed, but just as he was about to throw the sword into the waves, he hesitated. It seemed foolish to throw away such a beautiful work of art at the whim of a dying king. So he returned to Arthur and told him that he had done as Arthur had commanded. Arthur berated his old friend for this lie and sent him to the lake once more. Again Bedivere returned and falsely claimed that the deed was done. Arthur sadly chastised him for refusing the wish of his lord. Convinced at last, Bedivere returned to the lake and did as he had been bidden.

As Excalibur arched through the air, an arm clothed in samite rose out of the water, grasped it, and disappeared beneath the waves. With that, a funeral barge appeared out of the mist, bearing weeping ladies dressed in mourning. They landed in stately procession and placed the dying Arthur on his bier. And so Arthur was taken on the ship, which slowly disappeared into the mist to the lake isle of Avalon, there to remain until the world should be ready for a man of his goodness to return again. On his memorial were written the words, "*Hic jacet Arthurus, Rex quondam, Rexque futurus:* Here lies Arthur, the once and future king."

After the death of Arthur, the world of Camelot was no more.

Queen Guinevere spent the rest of her life in deep penance at the convent at Amesbury. Upon her death, she was taken and buried at Glastonbury, some say beside Arthur. Many accounts suggest that his mortal remains had been placed there in the care of the monks. Launcelot became a hermit until the death of his lady and then returned to France, where he died shortly thereafter.

The Quest for the Holy Grail

By the time of Malory, many stories and adventures had been added to the earlier accounts of Arthur. Such a case was the addition of the Launcelot and Guinevere love story. Added in like manner was the tradition of the quest for the Holy Grail.

The Holy Grail, known as Sangreal, was the cup from which Christ drank during the Last Supper. According to the sources, a pious Jew named Joseph of Arimathea secreted the cup away after Christ's crucifixion and brought it with him to Glastonbury in England where he preached the gospel of Christ. Upon his death, the care of the sacred relic was given over to his descendants. All truly pious people who had seen the Grail at that time were full of wonder, for it seemed to radiate a kind of inner light and created a sense of well-being in all who gazed on it. But as the Dark Ages descended and people forgot the teachings of Christ, the holy vessel disappeared from view. The legend was that it would return only if a man were born in England worthy to seek it out and thus restore its blessings to the land.

There were many legends about European knights searching for the Grail, but it was not until the writings of Chrétien de Troyes that the quest for the Holy Grail became part of the Arthurian Cycle. When Malory wrote his *Le Morte D'Arthur*, he included the Grail Quest, thus giving the great romance a Christian framework and interpretation even more strongly than had previously been done. The quest for the Grail became a test of a knight's true character and worth. If he was a true Christian, he would gain a glimpse of the Grail; if not, the revelation was denied him. It was this last great quest which finally foreshadowed the failure of Camelot. Arthur knew that

few of his knights had the purity of heart to be deserving of this vision and that the many who wished to quest for it would never return.

During Arthur's time, a man was born worthy to attempt the quest. Pelles, a descendant of Joseph of Arimathea, had a son by Sir Launcelot whom she named Galahad. When he became a knight in Arthur's court, he brought to the Round Table a natural piety and goodness, as well as valor.

Sir Galahad

One miraculous proof of his goodness was given to all of the knights. Merlin had constructed a special seat for the Round Table called the *Siege Perilous* and warned that any unworthy and impious knight who sat there would instantly be killed. A haughty and faithless warrior had once laughed at this warning and sat in the seat—only to disappear into the ground. But one Pentecost, when Galahad sat in the *Siege Perilous,* these words appeared, emblazoned on the back of the seat: "This is the Siege of Galahad, the haut prince."

Shortly thereafter, as all of the knights were seated at the Round Table, there was a great clap of thunder. Suddenly, in the midst of an unearthly light, the faint outline of the Grail appeared suspended above the table. It was enshrouded by costly white samite so that no one could see it clearly. Then it was gone. This appearance of the Grail in veiled form prompted first Sir Gawaine and then others to vow to quest for it until they should see the Grail in its full glory. In spite of his fears for their safety, Arthur sadly consented to their desire for the quest by granting them leave to go. And so each knight went his separate way.

On his journey, Sir Galahad came to an abbey and learned that it possessed a wondrous white shield emblazoned with a red cross which no man should bear unless he were pure in heart. A certain King Bagdemagus believed he was qualified and had taken the white shield, after which he was attacked by another knight whose lance had pierced the white shield as if it were not there. King Bagdemagus was sorely wounded and took the white shield back to the abbey, admitting that it was not for him. Sir Galahad took this same shield, and as he rode forth he met the same knight. But this time the knight, who recognized Galahad, greeted him in a friendly manner and explained that the shield, which had belonged to Joseph of Arimathea, had been placed in the abbey after his death and that Joseph

Sir Galahad in the *Siege Perilous,* from a fourteenth-century French manuscript.

had prophesied that Galahad would be the man worthy to make it his own. The knight then disappeared, leaving Galahad to pursue the Grail once more.

Sometime later, Sir Gawaine came to the same abbey and heard the story of Sir Galahad's good fortune. Believing that Galahad must be on the right track, he determined to catch up with him and thus share in his glory. Before he left, an old monk at the abbey warned Gawaine that unless he was willing to do just penance for his sins, the goal of his quest would forever elude him. Sir Gawaine was too proud and vainglorious to listen to this simple holy man and impatiently went on to seek Galahad. Before long he came to a castle where a tournament was being held. Gawaine could not resist the challenge and entered the contest. He defeated all of the knights except the last. This knight was protected by a white shield bearing a red cross, and its owner was able to overthrow him completely. Gawaine did not realize that his opponent had been Galahad any more than Galahad had recognized his visored friend. But this defeat wounded Gawaine's pride; he determined that the old monk was right and returned to Camelot, renouncing his quest.

Launcelot, too, had joined the quest for the Holy Grail. But after many an adventure he realized that his sins, especially his love for Guinevere, would prevent him from ever reaching his goal. Seeking a holy hermit in the forest, he did great penance for his past. As a reward for his great remorse, and because he was a great champion, he was offered another glimpse of the samite-shrouded Grail at the enchanted castle of Carbonek, beside a great sea, but this was the most that he could ever hope for. Like Gawaine, Launcelot returned to Camelot.

In the end, only Sir Galahad, Sir Bors, and Sir Percivale managed to attain a vision of the sacred vessel. They, too, arrived at the Castle of Carbonek. There, as they gazed at the shrouded vessel, a vision of Christ appeared to them and told them that England was still too full of sin to be worthy of the Grail. He then directed them to a ship and led them to the Spiritual Palace in the city of Sarras. There Sir Galahad was crowned king and all three were permitted to see the Grail one more time. But only Galahad was allowed to see into the Grail in all its purity, for of the three, only he was completely worthy. Galahad died before he could say what he had seen, and the others watched as angels escorted his soul to Heaven. At the same time, the Grail was also taken into Heaven, never again to be seen on earth.

Sir Percivale elected to stay and eventually died near the holy city. Sir Bors returned to Camelot where he recounted all of the events that had taken place. Everyone rejoiced at the news of Galahad's success, but Arthur knew that this quest had sadly depleted his band of warriors and clearly shown to them their unworthiness. Ironically, the quest for the Grail signaled the decline of the world of Camelot.

We have already seen that Camelot has been the subject of extensive archeological investigation. This search has been expanded to include Camlan, the lake isle of Avalon, and even Arthur's possible resting place. These explorations have produced remarkable results, leading many to suspect that more of the Arthurian cycle has an historical basis than had hitherto been thought.

The *Search for King Arthur* by Christopher and Thomas Hibbert, and *King Arthur in Fact and Fiction* by Geoffrey Ashe, are the best nonfiction sources for the Arthurian Cycle. Eleanore Jewett's *The Hidden Treasure of Glaston* is an excellent fictional account of the search for Arthur's grave at Glastonbury. This last book might be considered juvenile, but the story is fascinating to Arthur buffs. Even today, visitors at Glastonbury Abbey are shown the places which are believed to belong to Arthur's reign. Three other well-known fictional accounts of the Arthurian Cycle are *The Sword at Sunset* by Rosemary Sutcliff, *The Sword in the Stone* by Terence White, and *The Hollow Hills* by Mary Stewart.

The medieval romances abound with magical weapons. Excalibur is the most famous. As long as he had the scabbard, Arthur was invulnerable. Our account does not include how the scabbard was stolen by his evil kinswoman, Morgan le Fay (see *Book Four* of *Le Morte D'Arthur*), but this loss explains his death. At first glance it would seem that a magic sword gives a hero an unfair advantage, but if you compare Excalibur with various magical resources of the Greek heroes, it becomes obvious that this supernatural aid was a consistent factor. Why do you think this was so?

Using all of the stories recorded here and any you may have read on your own, list the qualities of the medieval hero that emerge. The stories of Tristram's heroism, omitted in our account, could also be consulted. Compare these qualities with those of the classical hero. To what extent is one type of hero more or less attractive to you than the other?

The world of Camelot reveals a great deal to us about the world of the medieval aristocracy. What sort of world emerges when you read between the lines? You might consider especially the code of behavior, the attitude towards women, and the place of Christianity.

There are many cycles in the medieval heroic tradition which have not been mentioned here. Because the Arthurian legends deal not only with Arthur, but with Launcelot, Tristram, Galahad, and a myriad of others, it is a much more diffuse and complex series of stories than the Greek tales of Perseus or Jason. The accounts of the Greek heroes focused more on the main character and changed less as time passed. The medieval heroic tradition was expanded in an infinite variety of ways during the entire medieval period.

Some of the other medieval cycles describe the world of Charlemagne and El Cid, two historical figures who were made into literary heroes after their deaths. The Arthurian legend is a good introduction to the medieval outlook, since the qualities of heroism and the lifestyle reflected here are the same as those established in the other cycles. You may wish to read the story of Charlemagne in *The Song of Roland*, translated by R. Harrison, or the story of El Cid in *Poema del Cid*. Norma Goodrich's *Medieval Myths* is an excellent account of all the major heroes of the period from Beowulf to El Cid.

Heroic Literature in Modern Society

At the beginning of Part Three we commented that societies need to create literary heroes who reflect the societies' own cultural values. In the two societies studied thus far, the cultural values described were relatively simple and straightforward. These were people who felt sure of their values and whose literature reflected the tastes of an aristocracy that had common bonds of religion and politics. Although our society today does not operate under any such certainties, this type of traditional hero—today a hero for the dominant middle class—can still be found.

Superman is a perfect example. Not only does he follow the traditional pattern of the special birth, but he updates the tradition by coming from outer space. Like the knights of the heroic tales, he undergoes trials and saves maidens in distress. In Superman comics, values, to put it mildly, are not complex. Superman is on the side of goodness; his enemies are always evil and their motives clearly malignant. As a modern type, Superman is representative of all of the other comic book heroes from Batman to Tarzan.

Not only comic books but much of our other reading matter preserves elements of this very black-and-white value system. In mass paperbacks, figures like James Bond and Mike Hammer represent modern heroes fighting against evil for the good of their society. They may not be born of gods, but they are the next best thing—supermen who are always stronger, more cunning, and better lovers than anyone else.

Television and films carry this superman hero as well. The western, for example, offers all of the elements that heroism thrives on: enemies to be conquered, rewards to be won, and women to be saved. In fact, the western has become a heroic genre all by itself. The interest in this pattern can best be seen in the long runs that programs such as *Gunsmoke* and *Bonanza* have had.

Modern technology has fostered this desire for new heroes, but the pattern they follow is also in the old tradition, changed only by slight modern touches. One of the new heroes in the mass media is the doctor: Doctor Kildare, Doctor Gannon, Doctor Welby. His tools may be space age, but he goes through the trials of a Jason and rushes off to rescue people in a sports car (or ambulance) instead of on a horse. He is good and he is conservative, upholding the values of Western society.

Whether or not one accepts comic books, detective stories, films, or television serials as "literature," one must accept the fact that these media heroes are culture carriers for the twentieth century and that their exploits *do* reflect the aspirations of many people. However, one cannot help feeling a little disturbed at the idea of a society idolizing Superman, James Bond, and Doctor Kildare. While such a simple value system is emotionally appealing because it offers solutions, it is intellectually unacceptable.

We live in a complex world of shifting values, where easy solutions no longer apply. Religion is not the cohesive force it once was; the old stable aristocracies have collapsed, and different social systems have arisen, systems often in conflict. Mass education has created a large group of people who question everything, including the role of human beings in society. For these reflective people, the old concept of the hero may be enjoyed on one level as a comfortable and appealing fantasy, but ultimately it is rejected as simplistic and naive.

The old heroes are out and a new hero is in. This new hero is reflected in the *serious* literature, drama, and media of the twentieth century. One has only to look at the course of study in the average high school English program. There are no traditional heroes to be found in novels such as *1984, Catcher in the Rye,* and *The Pearl,* or in drama such as *Death of a Salesman, Look Back in Anger,* and *Zoo Story.* On the contrary, much modern literature presents a type of protagonist who would be better classed as an "anti-hero."

In this tradition we are given central figures who are trapped by forces greater than themselves and who have almost no real hope of being saved, let alone saving others. They have not been born of gods, for no gods exist in the anti-heroes' world. They are on their own, nor do they easily fit into the existing social structure. They are outcasts, like Holden Caulfield in *Catcher in*

190

the Rye and Willy Loman in *Death of a Salesman*. There are dragons, but the dragons have taken over in society and choked out individuality. Or worse, the dragon is inside the anti-heroes' mind; they are unable to come to terms with their own problems. Above all, anti-heroes lack self-confidence and direction.

Anti-heroes exist in a world where there is no real meaning, no clear distinction between right and wrong. All of these attitudes are characteristic of a modern philosophy of life that is almost as pervasive today as the values exemplified in Greek or medieval societies. This is the philosophy of existentialism, made famous by writers such as Sartre and Camus. The existentialist philosophy sees people as simply existing in a universe out of which they themselves must make their own meaning. There is no heroic pattern to follow: humans must constantly make their own decisions and their own choices each time they encounter a problem. For some time now, this literary tradition has dominated because it expresses so much of the modern uncertainty as to our purpose on earth.

There are some signs that the literary tradition of existentialism is also unsatisfactory. It is a depressing view of life: few of these "heroes" succeed and we require heroes to succeed for us where we cannot. Hero worship is, after all, a positive, vicarious experience.

If one rejects the negative quality of this anti-heroic literature, there are several ways to regard the heroic tradition in our modern society. We could simply say that the heroic tradition is dead, that there are no true heroes any more; that the anti-hero, as his name suggests, is merely proof of this fact.

However, we can see trends now in literature for intensely personal solutions to life's problems, usually solutions involving individual relation-

ships. Perhaps the new hero is the "everyman" who finds life's meaning through individual love. D. H. Lawrence is a writer who best exemplifies this trend. His heroes find the meaning of the universe in the love of another. In the movement away from the sterility and alienation of the anti-hero, love may become the new god in this tradition.

Then again, the new heroic tradition may lie in a return to old values such as religion or a return to a simpler past. Novels such as *The chosen* by Potok, and *Jonathan Livingston Seagull* by Bach, reflect this, as do plays like *Jesus Christ Superstar* and *Godspell*. The urge to seek a simpler life, often by retreating into past values, is seen in the popularity of Thoreau's *Walden Pond,* Whitman's poetry, and the renewed interest in the literature of native Indian and Eskimo populations. Whether or not this retreat is possible is not the issue; the fact that it is seen as desirable is what makes it so interesting.

The renewed interest in the study of mythology is in itself an expression of this urge to define our values. Myth has always been society's attempt to formulate or come to grips with its own cultural outlook. Twentieth century mythology and its heroes will only be seen in its entirety at a future date.

"Cowboys and Indians are old-fashioned. You be the president of GM and I'll be Ralph Nader."

"Here comes your knight in shining armor."

Cartoon by Doug Sneyd. Reprinted courtesy of *Toronto Star.*

Cartoon by Stan Hunt. Reprinted courtesy of *Toronto Star.*

However, the roots of our mythology are starting to grow and some of its offshoots are worth considering, even if the main trunk is not yet visible. Perhaps a Jason or an Arthur will emerge as the hero who will represent our age for future generations, and we just cannot see him (or her) at this point in time.

We have suggested some of the modern heroes in comic books and paperbacks. Take any one which appeals to you and discuss how each conforms to the elements of the old heroic tradition. Sometimes the similarities are quite literal. For instance, in *Doctor No*, the first of the James Bond series, Bond attacks a fire-throwing tank, painted as a dragon, to save the beautiful girl. Of course, he uses a bazooka instead of a sword, but that's progress.

Our study is of literary heroes, but in the past these heroes were historical figures. We can see this same mythological process at work today, especially in the mass media. What modern people have been "mythologized" in this way? To what extent have they been made to fit the traditional heroic pattern?

Existentialism as it has been incorporated into the literature and films of our time has had a tremendous impact on our cultural outlook whether we agree with it or not. While existentialists disagree on parts of this very complex philosophy, the attempt should be made to find out what various writers say about it. A reasonable place to begin your own study of this philosophy would be with a good encyclopedia or a comprehensive dictionary of literary terms.

If you had the power to shape a cultural hero for our time, what would he or she be like? Consider personality, the goals this person might consider worthwhile, and the problems he or she might need to overcome.

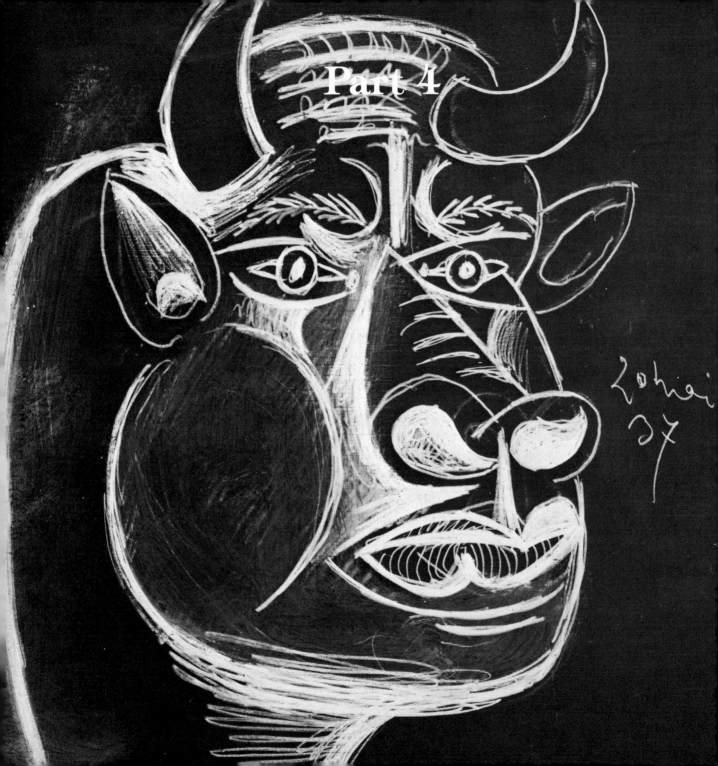

Part 4

APPLICATIONS
OF MYTH

Part Three concluded with an examination of the concerns of serious literature. Part Four carries on that examination. But Part Four takes quite a different
approach from the preceding three. It assumes that the reader now has a
reasonable background in mythology and is somewhat versed in the mechan-
ics of literature. Thus, this chapter is the logical outgrowth of the first three in
the search for the meaning behind the past and its relationship to the present.

Part Four begins with a look at the impact that myth has had on some of
our great writings. For simple examination, we have chosen poetic literature,
though novels, plays, and short stories have also utilized myth and, if space
had permitted, could have been used equally well. A brief survey of the
Classical Allusion section will indicate that it covers poems from many ages
as well as poets from many lands. Mythology has had this universal appeal.

A natural extension of these poems is, of course, the use of archetypes
in literature. We have included an examination of some archetypes as well as
illustrated them at work in poetry. The reader will be surprised at how much
mythology actually underlies most of our literary tradition. We would be
remiss, therefore, if we did not include a sample of archetypal criticism,
simplified as it is, and explain its part in our mythological heritage.

Closely allied to this is the use of mythology in the study of psychology.
No student of myth can avoid the tremendous influence of Freud and Jung,
not only on literature, but on our whole attitude to our cultural and
mythological past.

Finally, Part Four concludes with a brief study of some of our modern
mythographers. The last few years have seen inroads into the interpretation
and understanding of mythology that have caught the fancy of the reading
public. Several writers stand out in this regard, not because they are popular
in the narrow sense of a fad, but because they write with conviction and
dedication. It is not our purpose to take sides with the authors concerned;
we wish only to record what they have said. It is the reader's job to be critical,
in the most comprehensive sense of the word.

In its complete form, Part Four is vital to a mature understanding of myth
and provides, to a great extent, the reason for this book.

Preceding page: Pablo Picasso. *Study for Bull's Head* (1937) for *Guernica* Studies and "Postscripts."

Myth in Literature

Classical Allusions

ON FIRST LOOKING INTO CHAPMAN'S HOMER

Much have I travelled in the realms of gold,
*   And many goodly states and kingdoms seen;*
*   Round many western islands have I been*
Which bards in fealty to Apollo hold.
Oft of one wide expanse had I been told
*   That deep-browed Homer ruled as his demesne;*
*   Yet did I never breathe its pure serene*
Till I heard Chapman speak out loud and bold:
Then felt I like some watcher of the skies
*   When a new planet swims into his ken;*
Or like stout Cortez when with eagle eyes
He stared at the Pacific—and all his men
Looked at each other with a wild surmise—
*   Silent, upon a peak in Darien.*

John Keats

Keats' poem is a very good starting point for this unit. Here we have a nineteenth century poet, praising the creative ability of a seventeenth century poet to bring to life, in translation, the great writings of the eighth century B.C. poet, Homer. This is an attitude that any writer would understand: literature is a product of the imagination and knows no boundaries of border or time. Great literature is concerned with the illumination and understanding of the human spirit. The writer must regard the use of previous insights or experience as legitimate sources for his own creative powers.

It is not surprising, therefore, to find a tremendous number of references to classical mythology and literature in writings of all periods. No one can tell of the fall of Troy better than Homer, and no one can write the myths quite like Hesiod, but any writer can use the characters and events of their stories in his own writing.

This use of classical writings in subsequent literature is referred to as the use of classical allusions. The new writer does not copy the myth; he uses the reference to enhance his own work. When he does so, the myth undergoes a metamorphosis, a developmental change, retaining its familiarity but gaining greater dimensions.

Thus there are two reasons for the study of classical allusions. One is for the pure pleasure of being able to identify such a source. The second is more important: to see why the reference is being used and to discover how the poet has filtered the "old story" through his own creativity and made it a new and richer experience.

The following selection of poems illustrates the tremendous variety of ways in which poets have made use of classical allusions.

PAN'S SONG

Pan's Syrinx was a girle indeed,
Though now shee's turn'd into a reed,
From that deare Reed Pan's pipe does come,
A Pipe that strikes Apollo dumbe;
Nor Flute, nor Lute, nor Gitterne can
So chant it, as the pipe of Pan;
Cross-garter'd swains, and Dairie girls,
With faces smug and round as Pearles,
When Pan's shrill pipe begins to play,
With dancing weare out night and day;
The bag-pipe drone his Hum lays by,
When Pan sounds up his minstrelsie.
His minstrelsie; O Base! This quill
Which at my mouth with winde I fill,
Puts me in minde, though Her I misse,
That still my Syrinx lips I Kisse.

John Lyly

How has Lyly developed the Pan-Syrinx myth in order to make a statement about his own love life?

Why would Lyly want to identify himself with the figures of Apollo and Pan?

What elements of his own contemporary setting has Lyly introduced in the poem?

ESCAPE

(August 6, 1916. Officer Previously Reported Died of Wounds, Now Reported Wounded: Graves, Capt. R., Royal Welsh Fusiliers)

. . . But I was dead, an hour or more:
I woke when I'd already passed the door
That Cerberus guards and half-way down the road
To Lethe, as an old Greek sign-post showed.
Above me, on my stretcher swinging by,
I saw new stars in the sub-terrene sky,
A Cross, a Rose in Bloom, a Cage with Bars,
And a barbed Arrow feathered with fine stars.
I felt the vapors of forgetfulness
Float in my nostrils: Oh may Heaven bless
Dear Lady Proserpine, who saw me wake
And, stooping over me, for Henna's sake
Cleared my poor buzzing head and sent me back
Breathless, with leaping heart along the track.
After me roared and clattered angry hosts
Of demons, heroes, and policemen-ghosts.
"Life, life! I can't be dead, I won't be dead:
Damned if I'll die for anyone," I said . . .
Cerberus stands and grins above me now,
Wearing three heads, lion and lynx and sow.
"Quick, a revolver! but my Webley's gone,
Stolen . . . no bombs . . . no knife . . . (the crowd swarms on,
Bellows, hurls stones) . . . not even a honeyed sop . . .
Nothing . . . Good Cerberus . . . Good dog . . . But stop!
Stay! . . . A great luminous thought . . . I do believe
There's still some morphia that I bought on leave."
Then swiftly Cerberus' wide mouths I cram
With Army biscuit smeared with Tickler's jam;
And Sleep lurks in the luscious plum and apple.

He crunches, swallows, stiffens, seems to grapple
With the all-powerful poppy . . . then a snore,
A crash; the beast blocks up the corridor
With monstrous hairy carcass, red and dun—
Too late: for I've sped through.
                              O Life! O sun!

Robert Graves

Cerberus, from a
William Blake drawing for
Dante's *Divine Comedy*.

Graves makes use of a wide range of mythical allusions in this humorous account of his imagined death. The entire poem is an extended metaphor; that is, he has taken the classical idea of the hero's journey into the Underworld (see Heracles, Theseus, and Orpheus) and applied it throughout the poem.

What are the advantages of the use of the following classical allusions? Lethe, Proserpine (Persephone), Cerberus, Morpheus (a Roman god).

No poet feels constrained to stick with only classical allusions once he has started this process. So it is not surprising that Graves uses other allusions. How do the following contribute to the poem: a cross, a rose, a cage, a barbed arrow, the lion and lynx and sow?

Just as Vergil in *The Aeneid* used the journey into the underworld as a conscious imitation of the Greek heroic pattern, so does Graves. For what other reasons does Graves use the journey into the underworld?

200

THE GOLDEN SHIP

There was a fine Ship, carved from solid gold,
With azure-reaching masts, on seas unknown.
Spreadeagled Venus, naked, hair back-thrown,
Stood at the prow. The sun blazed uncontrolled.

But on the treacherous Ocean in the gloom
She struck the great reef where the Sirens chant.
Appalling shipwreck plunged her keel aslant
To the Gulf's depths, that unrelenting tomb.

She was a Golden Ship: but there showed through
Translucent sides treasures the blasphemous crew,
Hatred, Disgust and Madness, fought to share.

How much survives after the storm's brief race?
Where is my heart, that empty ship, oh where?
Alas, in Dream's abyss sunk without trace.

Emile Nelligan
Translated by P. F. Widdows

Ulysses and the Sirens,
from a Greek vase
of the fifth century.

Nelligan, a French-Canadian poet, is famous for his poems about the inner soul. This poem is interesting because it uses the sonnet form for structure and meaning, while at the same time using classical allusion to illustrate a very private concept.

What do the references to Venus (Aphrodite) and the Sirens contribute to the total meaning of the poem?

The use of "golden" and "ship" images here is not only classical, but universal. How does each image add to a deeper understanding of the poet's theme?

THE MINOTAUR

The labyrinthine forest's spoor
leads to the patient Minotaur.
Deep in the dark and structured core
the bull-man waits inside the maze
and he who dares explore will raze
the beast of fear behind the door.

No Ariadne and no crone
will point the way. Each man alone
must thread his path, unreel his own
life spool and fumble to the lair.
Each man must journey naked there
nor arm himself with wing nor stone.

For he who goes his armor shed
and walks with all that once he fled
that man will face the horned head
the unimaginable eyes
and find there where the monster dies
the ichor that the terror bled.

Isabella Gardner

One of the most common ways people have seen their own lives is in terms of a journey or a quest. (The quest motif is discussed in detail in Part Three.) In this modern poem, Gardner uses the journey motif to express a psychological process. She literally remakes the myth.

Review the classical myth to familiarize yourself with the following: Daedalus, the maze, Theseus, Ariadne, the thread, and the Minotaur.

Although Gardner follows the actual story line, she consistently forces the reader to see the narrative in a different perspective. What new meaning emerges because of the following phrases: the patient Minotaur, the beast of fear, his own life spool, and find there where the monster dies/the ichor that the terror bled? (Ichor is one name for the blood of the immortals.)

What has the Minotaur become? Why is Theseus never mentioned by name?

Minotaur, from a William Blake drawing for Dante's *Divine Comedy*.

Archetypes

Archetypes are special symbols. As their name suggests (arche = original or first; type = stamp or model), they derive their origin from associations in our distant past and, hence, mythology. For example, if a young man with a twinkle in his eye were to offer his girlfriend a luscious red apple instead of a flower, he would either get a smack in the face or a coy thank you.

Why would an apple elicit such a response? Well, for a beginning, the apple is often depicted as the fruit Eve ate and then offered Adam in Paradise. The apple is associated with temptation as well as the fall from favor. This association takes us to another old story, that of Helen and Paris. If you remember that Aphrodite, goddess of love, won the golden apple in the first beauty contest by promising the most beautiful mortal woman to the young prince, it is not surprising that, for the Western world, the apple has had sexual associations.

Consider, too, how it draws more meanings. As a luscious red fruit it attracts to itself the symbolic ideas of that color: passion, mystery, blood, and ecstasy. These symbolic values have been with us for as long as recorded memory. The ripe, juicy fruit is itself a product of the fall of the year, plucked in the prime of life when it has come to full fruition. Thus, the fruit is associated with the seasons and is part of that great analogy connected to birth (spring), youth (summer), maturity (fall) and death (winter). The apple is a Western archetype because of its collective focus of meanings.

Naturally, not all of these images run through the girl's mind as the young man offers her an apple, but with experience and the ability to think in abstract or symbolic terms, she has learned of the collective associations connected with the apple and reacts accordingly.

Other archetypes spring easily to mind. The garden, for example, existed in classical literature. The Blessed Isles were obviously gardens, as was the Land of the Lotus Eaters, so attractive to Ulysses and his crew. We find constant reference to gardens in the media as well as in modern literature. Films like "Woodstock" (and the line from the song "We've got to get back to the garden") and "The Garden of the Finzi-Continis" are a few examples. Advertisers make use of the various garden associations to sell their products. Collectively then, the garden means unspoiled innocence, freshness and purity, spring and summer's growth. It could just as easily take on demonic

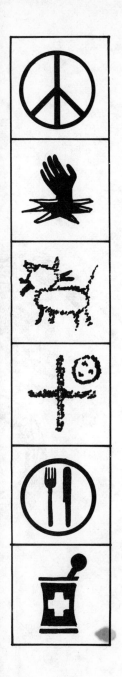

associations, however, if the context were to change. In that case the garden would become a desert full of cactus and scorpions, a wasteland unfit for the human condition.

All archetypes exist in two forms, the context determining their meaning. Water is a good example. Archetypally, it can be a life-giving force teeming with activity or it can be a flood, a tidal wave ready to destroy. In context, the reader can easily discern which symbolic function or archetypal association it will have.

Because our literary heritage in the Western world traces its origins from the Graeco-Roman and Judeo-Christian cultures, our archetypes are rooted in the *Bible* and the Classics. To understand how archetypes work, it is necessary to have an extensive knowledge of mythology and the Old and New Testaments and then to connect this knowledge to our present literature.

The following are literary examples of two archetypes: the snake/serpent and the rose. The reader must keep in mind that they are just a taste of the many that do exist. They establish, first, that archetypes exist in a multitude of ways and, second, that their mythological heritage is so far in the past that we now accept the association without fully realizing the initial connection. Thus, the myth, itself, is often overlooked.

For the Western world, the snake as something evil or sinister needs no introduction. In classical and religious writings, serpents (and, by extension, dragons) are constant villains. There is the serpent in the Garden of Eden. Medusa has hair of writhing snakes; Perseus slays the dragon; a serpent guards the Golden Fleece. Saint George saves his people from a dragon. The Arthurian cycle abounds in tales of dragon slayers.

We have included in this section two modern poems which indicate that this archetype is still as compelling as ever.

THE SNAKE / SERPENT

Visual symbols (top to bottom): Peace; thin ice; hobos' symbol for "kind lady lives here"; hobos' symbol for "doctor here won't charge"; restaurant; pharmacy.

THE SNAKE

A narrow fellow in the grass
Occasionally rides;
You may have met him,—did you not?
His notice sudden is.

The grass divides as with a comb,
A spotted shaft is seen;
And then it closes at your feet
And opens further on.

He likes a boggy acre,
A floor too cool for corn.
Yet when a child, and barefoot,
I more than once, at morn,

Have passed, I thought, a whip-lash
Unbraiding in the sun,—
When, stooping to secure it,
It wrinkled, and was gone.

Several of nature's people
I know, and they know me;
I feel for them a transport
Of cordiality;

But never met this fellow,
Attended or alone,
Without a tighter breathing,
And zero at the bone.

Emily Dickinson

FILLING STATION

With snakes of rubber and glass thorax,
like dragons rampant,
statistical, red with ambush,
they ambuscade the highway.

Only in the hinterland, and for neighbors,
the extant blacksmith drives
archaic nails into the three-legged horse.

But on route 7
the monsters coil and spit from iron mouths
potent saliva.

(Beyond the hills, of course;
the oxen, lyric with horns, still draw
the cart, and the limping wheels.)

A. M. Klein

In "The Snake," Emily Dickinson points out that although she feels kinship for other creatures, she does not for the snake. Why do you think the snake has always had negative associations?

How has Klein updated the archetype and still retained its traditional associations?

How is the role of the snake/serpent in these two poems similar to its role in the Garden of Eden?

207

Although most snake/serpents in literature are evil, one well-known poem, "Snake" by D. H. Lawrence, takes the archetypal associations and reverses them. Lawrence chooses to reject the traditional meaning and to see the snake as good. He blames the prejudice against snakes on "the voice of his education," that is, on the archetypal associations.

This raises an interesting point about archetypes. If taken literally, they can be harmful. In order to express evil, snakes are useful; but to kill a snake for this reason is absurd. A snake exists outside of our moral categories. We instinctively read ourselves into nature, but we must remember that not all lambs are white, nor all owls wise.

"Polly" by Mal. Reprinted courtesy of the Chicago Tribune—New York News Syndicate, Inc.

"B.C." by Johnny Hart. Reprinted courtesy of John Hart and Field Enterprises.

"Of course, they're made of plastic . . . They're symbolic of my love, which does not wither away, but endures forever."

THE ROSE "A rose is a rose is a rose," said Gertrude Stein. But roses have archetypal associations as well. If lions are king of the beasts, then roses rule the flower hierarchy.

Imagine Burns saying "My love is like a yellow, yellow chrysanthemum" or a lover receiving celery stalks as a gift of endearment. Of course these gifts are not impossibilities but they might give the receiver pause whereas roses would not.

Likewise, the following poems depend on our acceptance of the archetype.

ONE PERFECT ROSE

A single flow'r he sent me, since we met.
    All tenderly his messenger he chose;
Deep-hearted, pure, with scented dew still wet—
    One perfect rose.

I knew the language of the floweret;
    "My fragile leaves," it said, "his heart enclose."
Love long has taken for his amulet
    One perfect rose.

Why is it no one ever sent me yet
    One perfect limousine, do you suppose?
Ah no, it's always just my luck to get
    One perfect rose.

Dorothy Parker

roseroseros   erose
roseroseroseroserose
roseroseroseroserose
roseroseroseroserose
roseroseroseroserose
roseroseroseroserose
roseroseroseroserose
roseroseroseroserose
roseroseroseroserose
roseroseroseroserose
roseroseroseroserose
        eros

Timm Uhlrichs

210

A RED, RED ROSE

O my Luve's like a red, red rose
*   That's newly sprung in June.*
O my Luve's like the melodie
*   That's sweetly play'd in tune.*

As fair art thou, my bonnie lass,
*   So deep in luve am I,*
And I will luve thee still, my dear,
*   Till a' the seas gang dry.*

Till a' the seas gang dry, my dear,
*   And the rocks melt wi' the sun!*
And I will luve thee still, my dear,
*   While the sands o' life shall run*

And fare thee weel, my only Luve!
*   And fare thee weel a while!*
And I will come again, my Luve,
*   Tho' it were ten thousand mile.*

Robert Burns

What qualities does the rose have, that it occupies such a high place in our symbolic language?

Why does Burns choose a *red* rose to describe his love?

The first two poems demand our acceptance of the meaning of the archetype and then provide a "twist." How does Dorothy Parker regard the rose? What association does Uhlrichs cleverly weave into the fabric of his rose poem?

What other flowers, besides the rose, have the status of an archetype?

The rose has religious connotations as well. According to the *Bible*, God made the promise that "the desert shall bloom as the rose." In the medieval world, Christ was often associated with the rose. This motif is also seen in Dante's great religious poems.

We chose the few examples above because of their prominence, but no doubt other archetypes in literature will spring to mind from your own experience. The main thing to realize is the importance of the archetypal symbol in communicating, and to understand how we express our own nature through the medium of the world outside ourselves. The following poem expresses the significance of archetypes to the human experience. Follow closely how the archetypes and symbols work in almost every stanza, and examine the wealth of associations they bring to the poem.

ADVICE TO A PROPHET

When you come, as you soon must, to the streets of our city,
Mad-eyed from stating the obvious,
Not proclaiming our fall but begging us
In God's name to have self-pity,

Spare us all word of the weapons, their force and range,
The long numbers that rocket the mind;
Our slow, unreckoning hearts will be left behind,
Unable to fear what is too strange.

Nor shall you scare us with talk of the death of the race.
How should we dream of this place without us?—
The sun mere fire, the leaves untroubled about us,
A stone look on the stone's face?

Speak of the world's own change. Though we cannot conceive
Of an undreamt thing, we know to our cost
How the dreamt cloud crumbles, the vines are blackened by frost,
How the view alters. We could believe,

If you told us so, that the white-tailed deer will slip
Into perfect shade, grown perfectly shy,

The lark avoid the reaches of our eye,
The jack-pine lose its knuckled grip

On the cold ledge, and every torrent burn
As Xanthus once, its gliding trout
Stunned in a twinkling. What should we be without
The dolphin's arc, the dove's return,

These things in which we have seen ourselves and spoken?
Ask us, prophet, how we shall call
Our natures forth when that live tongue is all
Dispelled, that glass obscured or broken

In which we have said the rose of our love and the clean
Horse of our courage, in which beheld
The singing locust of the soul unshelled,
And all we mean or wish to mean.

Ask us, ask us whether with the worldless rose
Our hearts shall fail us; come demanding
Whether they shall be lofty or long standing
When the bronze annals of the oak tree close.

Richard Wilbur

Archetypal Criticism

NORTHROP FRYE   One of Canada's best known literary critics is Northrop Frye, renowned for his monumental work on myth and archetypes, *The Anatomy of Criticism*. In his book, Frye places the critical study of literature on a scientific footing by defining, through the images of myth, the various literary origins in ritual and folk tale. He then tries to fit these origins into a classification system to help identify the various forms of literature that exist and thus to help understand some of their meaning.

The critic, says Frye, must stand back from the work, examine through the imagery the basic plots, and comprehend the entire range of patterns that emerge. By knowing the original or archetypal plots of mythology, the critic can be aware not only of the relationship of a present work to its beginnings, but also the more subtle meanings related to it in the present.

For example, if we are reading a poem, story, or play that has images of sunset, fall, or retirement, we can be fairly certain that the work is a tragedy. It will, therefore, be related to the myths of the fall: the dying god, sacrifice and violent death, the isolation of the hero and his/her subsequent overthrow. We can expect to find minor characters equated with the traitor and the siren, people who lead the "lamb to the slaughter." The animal images will be of beasts or birds of prey: the wolf, vulture, serpent, or dragon. The setting will take place in a sinister forest or its equivalent: the heath, wilderness, or tree of death. In the city, the setting will be in terms of modern deserts, garbage heaps, ruins, or sinister geometrical images like boxes or transfigured crosses. It cannot be otherwise, for these are the archetypes of tragedy.

The archetypal critic comprehends all this because he is able to get to the informing substructure of the work and because he knows there is a continuing relationship in all the great works of literature. His task is to point out this structure to the reader and, in so doing, enrich the reader's understanding and appreciation of the writer and his work.

Substituting spring and winter as organizing categories, compile two charts similar to the chart below.

Season: summer.

Time equivalents: Afternoon (day), youth (ages), zenith or growth, marriage or its equivalent.

Setting/rural images: the garden or grove, flowers, a world of green and gold, the tree of life or life-giving rivers.

Setting/urban images: a glowing, alive city with precious stones, parks; wood or ancient materials replace concrete.

Animal associations; a community, hence peaceful; flocks and domesticated animals, pigeons and doves, deer and faithful animals.

Type of hero myth: wish-fulfillment myths, especially of order and love, hence

divine or superhuman communities; the birth of the hero or re-birth with the defeat of the powers of darkness and winter.

Subordinate characters: the father and mother or their surrogates.

Literary forms: all romance and most rhapsodic poetry.

(This is based on a chart from Northrop Frye's *Fables of Identity*.)

Modern Mythographers

Before the twentieth century, scholars regarded myths as stories that had to be studied in the course of one's education. They saw in mythology little more than fanciful tales, useful for literary allusions. Then along came Schliemann's discoveries (1871), Sir James Frazer's *The Golden Bough* (1890), and Freudian psychology (1911–1913). The study of mythology has never since been the same.

These three pioneers saw in mythology underlying truths that allowed them to use myth in a historical, sociological, or scientific way. Hence, we have seen fit to include several twentieth century writers who have contributed to a new understanding of our world by their re-examination of mythology: two psychologists and a social anthropologist/literary scholar.

All of these writers have taken different approaches in their use of myth and, in most cases, have written quite voluminously about their theories. What we have tried to do here is to review those theories by paying specific attention to one of their more popular or more readable books and, where appropriate, we have referred to some of their other works.

Each author is treated briefly for several reasons. There is no intent on our part to substitute for the original work, with its many proofs and examples; instead, it is our intention to state the writer's theories and to encourage the reader to use his/her knowledge of myth and tradition to understand how an author has arrived at such views.

Myth and Psychology

Our study of mythology has revealed to us only some of the various interpretations and explanations at work behind the actual narrative accounts. It should not be surprising, therefore, that there is a relationship between the unconscious and subconscious states of our personality and the actual stories from our mythological past. Psychologists were the first to see this relationship and from their work evolved a gradual understanding of the language and symbol systems common to both. To see how these forces of man's inner fears, drives, and motives have been interpreted, it is necessary to look at the work of two great psychologists: Sigmund Freud and Carl Jung.

SIGMUND FREUD   Freud, an Austrian psychiatrist, was initially influenced by a fellow physician, Joseph Breuer, who was treating his patients by using hypnosis. Freud used Breuer's treatment on people suffering from various anxieties, particularly hysteria. From this work he discovered that the symptoms of hysteria could be traced to an earlier age when the patient had suffered severe psychological strain or trauma. This discovery was the beginning of Psychoanalysis. Eventually, Freud abandoned hypnosis in favor of a method called "Free Association," which allowed his patients to recall their past while talking to him. Through this free association process, Freud became more and more convinced that most of his patients' problems were sexual in origin. This led to his most famous (and somewhat controversial) theory of the Oedipus Complex, a theory at the heart of Freudian psychology and, perhaps more important for our study, a theory which has had a tremendous impact on writers and critics since the turn of the century.

Essentially, the theory has its origin in the Greek myth of Oedipus. Laius and Jocasta were the king and queen of Thebes. Laius was warned through an oracle that if he had a son, he would be killed by him. When Oedipus was born, Laius, fearing the prophecy, secretly ordered his son's feet bound and the baby left to die on a mountain. However, Oedipus was found and taken to Corinth where he was raised as the son of the kind Polybus. When Oedipus grew up he, too, consulted an oracle about his future and was told that he would kill his father and marry his mother. To avoid the prophecy, Oedipus ran away from the only home he had known. While wandering towards Thebes, he was forced off the road by a chariot. In the

Surrealist paintings capture mythical and symbolic elements similar
to those in the dream or the unconscious.

argument that followed, he killed the driver who, unknown to Oedipus, later was identified as none other than Laius. At Thebes he became king by solving the riddle of the Sphinx and later married the widowed Jocasta, his mother. Two sons and two daughters, Polyneices, Eteocles, Antigone and Ismene) were born to them. Eventually, however, the king and queen discovered the truth of their marriage. Jocasta killed herself and Oedipus blinded himself to avoid seeing his children, the truth of his past. He left Thebes in exile (according to some authorities) with his daughter, Antigone.

Freud translates the original myth of Oedipus in the following fashion: In the development of personality, the child is dominated by incestuous wishes for the parent of the opposite sex and feels jealous of the parent of the same sex; this behavior is characterized by disassociation or extreme dislike. However, the fear of punishment makes the child suppress these wishes. Eventually, by identifying with the commands and prohibitions of the father, the male child overcomes his dislike for him and replaces it with the wish to be like his father. The strength and success of this identification influences the nature of his attachments, hostilities, and degree of masculinity in later life. Thus, the development of a social conscience is the result of this complex.

The Oedipus Complex applies in a reverse way to females, and is sometimes called the Electra Complex. Students interested in psychology might like to look up the differences, as seen by Freud. Students of mythology might wish to investigate the mythical elements surrounding Electra and her mother, Clytemnestra.

Because of his Oedipal theory, Freud sees the majority of symbols as sexual in nature, expressing only certain primitive desires or wishes. Since Freud assumes that dreams are always the expression of the irrational part of personality and that they are repressed during conscious hours, he tries to interpret their meaning. A knowledge of myth and an appreciation of its symbolic language becomes necessary for a basic understanding both of Freud's psychology and of many writers influenced by psychoanalytical theory.

CARL JUNG   Carl Gustav Jung broke with Freud, his teacher, in 1913, after a close association with him for six years, and formulated a different approach to psychology. Initially Jung believed, as did Freud, that complexes had their origin in painful psychological experiences in early childhood. This was essentially an environmental phenomenon because it was subject to external experiences (stimuli) that were subtly working on the infant psyche. Jung felt that there must be something else working on the unconscious psyche that went deeper than these early childhood experiences. He began to think that the mind, in its evolution, had been shaped by powerful physical and organic forces that were so awesome that our mind still bears the imprint or vestiges of them today.

This placing of the psyche within the evolutionary cycle was Carl Jung's central achievement. It meant that individuals were linked with their past: not only with the past of childhood, but with the past of biological evolution. The very forces that shaped the brain and allowed early "humans" to survive were the forces that shaped each brain itself; the potential (or the predisposition) for experiencing and responding to the world today was the same as that for early primitive beings.

He felt that we constantly carry with us the memories of our race, not just as inherited genetic particles but as the shaping forces that forged our very psyche. Jung called this force our "collective unconscious." It differed from the personal unconscious in that it was a deeper stratum that went back to the beginning of creation—it was, in effect, a type of biological conditioning. It was an *internal* complex, because one was born with it; Freud dealt with complexes that were *external* in that they developed because of the early environment.

Jung called this form of conditioning by the past *archetypal*. (See also page 204, the archetype section, for another application of this theory.) According to Jung, archetypes were the inborn forms of intuition, perception, and apprehension in the unconscious. Archetypes may be experienced, therefore, as emotions. Most commonly, however, they are identified as images, particularly in our dreams, and often in association with the transitional stages of life, such as those involving birth or death. Other archetypes include rebirth, power, magic, the hero, the child, the trickster, God, the demon, the wise old man, the earth mother, the giant; and many natural objects such as trees, the sun, the moon, wind, rivers, fire, and many created objects, such as rings and weapons.

It is important to realize that Jung's archetypes are not fully developed pictures in the mind, like memory images of our past; rather, they are like a negative that is developed by experience. It is only when our conscious is awakened to the archetypal image or experience that we are in a position to

219

evaluate its importance. This is where myths and Jung's theory interact.

Although myths may be primitive attempts to explain natural phenomena, they can also be much more than that. They may be expressions of how early people experienced these things, and consequently their emotional or psychological quality is significant. Since many myths are similar around the world, Jung sees this as a direct expression of the collective unconscious in action.

An example of this collective unconscious can be seen in Jung's examination of the universal or earth-mother symbol—the tree of life. He suggests that the tree of life is like a fruit-bearing geneological tree and hence a kind of tribal or mythic mother. This symbol is evident in many myths, since a number of them have the first mortals being born from a tree. Many also tell how a hero was enclosed in a maternal tree trunk, like the dead Osiris in the cedar tree or Adonis in the myrtle. Also, numerous goddesses were worshipped in tree form and this gave rise to the cult of sacred groves and trees. Stories of wooden caskets, chests, or barrels are seen by Jung as female symbols for the womb, in which the hero emerges in a type of rebirth (for example, the myth of Perseus). Jung sees common factors basic to human experience behind many of these stories—so basic that they had to be recorded. Thus, we have myths.

In modern society, archetypes are best expressed psychologically when they appear in dreams or through the fantasies of people in a maladjusted state of mind. Images such as the square, circle, or wheel; and others, such as those that appear as human or semi-human form (gods, giants, dwarfs, and real or fantastic creatures), are important symbols that recur endlessly in mythology as well as in psychoanalysis. The shaping forces that form these unconscious recollections in dreams are the same that created the world's great myths. Jung says that an understanding of their basic truth leads to an understanding of ourselves, and that this is what makes the study of myth so important.

Myth and Archeology

James W. Mavor, Jr., of the Woods Hole Oceanographic Institution, is an oceanographic engineer and one of the designers of the famous submarine *Alvin* that found the missing H-bomb off the coast of Spain. In 1965, his interest in the sea led him to begin investigating the riddle of Atlantis. Since then, he has led two international archeological expeditions to the Aegean Sea, where he believes that he, together with Dr. Galanopoulos, has discovered Atlantis on the volcanic island of Thera. But before examining Mavor's findings, it is worthwhile to consider the myth itself.

Although many writers have been captivated by the myth of Atlantis, few details are actually known about it. Indeed, most of our facts come from the Greek philosopher, Plato, the first to describe the Lost Continent in his two books, *Critias* and *Timaeus*. Plato's account is told through Critias, a character in the two books. It goes like this:

Long ago the gods divided the earth among themselves. Poseidon received the island of Atlantis, among other areas. In the middle of Atlantis was a great plain and in the center of the plain was a mountain. A young woman, Cleito, lived there, whom Poseidon eventually fell in love with and married.

Afterwards, Poseidon divided the island Metropolis into alternating circles or zones of land and water, three of each, in order that no one could get to Cleito's home in the mountain. He then created two springs out of the earth, one of warm water and one of cold, and made every variety of food and plant spring up from the earth.

Poseidon and Cleito had ten children. When they were of age, Poseidon divided his kingdom into ten portions and gave one to each child. To his eldest son, Atlas, he gave the center of Atlantis and made him king over all the rest. To the second, Gadir, he gave the eastern part of the island as the way to Gades on the coast of Spain (now called Cadiz). To the rest he gave smaller portions and some islands in the open sea.

Atlantis lay outside the Straits of Heracles (thought to be Gibraltar) and was approximately 2,650,000 square miles in size (about the size of Australia) and, some think, stretched from the Azores to the Canary Islands. The kings of Atlantis were extremely wealthy and possessed many of the world's valuable metals, which were abundant on the island. These metals included not only gold, silver, copper, zinc, and iron, but a rare metal, orichalcum—

thought to be a shiny copper or a type of brass. In addition, the island was abundant in animals (especially horses, which were sacred to Poseidon), grains, fruit, and timber.

Atlantis was an extremely happy place and as long as the gods intermarried and retained their divine spirit, it stayed that way. But through marriage with mortals, their divine portion was gradually diluted until at last the people became cruel and greedy for power. Zeus, aware of how they had become, decided to punish the people of Atlantis. He sent a huge flood and an earthquake that destroyed them and caused Atlantis to sink into the sea.

With Plato's story in mind, it is now possible to consider Dr. Mavor's findings as related in his book *Voyage to Atlantis:*

While in Greece in 1965, Dr. Mavor was introduced to a Greek seismologist, Dr. Galanopoulos, who told him of his theory about Atlantis. Dr. Galanopoulos identified the culture of Atlantis with the ancient people of Crete, the Minoans, the richest and most advanced nation of the ancient world. They had colonies all over the Aegean Sea, including those on the island of Thera (see map on page 3), or Santorini, as it is now called. Thera was a volcanic island with a long history of eruptions. Galanopoulos interprets Plato's story as descriptive of two islands, the "royal state" (Crete) and a "smaller metropolis" (Thera). Central to his theory is the enormous catastrophe that destroyed Atlantis so quickly. He suggests that the island of Thera erupted in the fifteenth century B.C. and that the high, densely populated central portion of the island collapsed into a sea-filled trough, or caldera, some 1300 feet deep and ten to eleven miles across.

The second part of his theory deals with the island of Crete, which, he proposed, fitted the description of the plains and is the shape of Atlantis. To deal with this, however, Dr. Galanopoulos had to use another theory: that Plato's figures were inaccurate. The error can be explained in terms of the confusion between the English billion (a million million) and the American billion (a thousand million). The ancients, in translation, rendered measurements of 100 as 1000, which is entirely plausible if one remembers that in ancient times numbers were imprecise and easily mistaken. When the figures were revised, measurements and dates coincided consistently with all the known facts of Plato's story and with the history and geography of the ancient world.

Dr. Galanopoulos refutes the location of Atlantis as being in the Atlantic on the following grounds: One, most of Heracles' feats were performed in Greece and had no connection with Gibraltar. Two, he believes that the Pillars of Heracles actually refer to Cape Malea and Cape Matapan on the Peloponnesus, and not to Gibraltar. Three, the disappearance of large land masses is geologically possible only over a long period of time, whereas smaller land masses have been known to disappear suddenly. Four, the oceanographic data for the area around the Azores shows no evidence of sunken islands in the last 72,000 years. Five, the earth's crust in the Atlantic Atlantis region is too thin to support such a huge continent. Six, Thera was more the center of the ancient world and therefore would give rise to more stories like that of Atlantis than would an area out in the Atlantic. Finally, Atlantis may be one of a series of related stories having their origin in the eruption and collapse of Thera: Deucalion and the Flood, the Epic of Gilgamesh, and perhaps even the Exodus and the Red Sea crossing.

With Dr. Galanopoulos' theory of Atlantis, Dr. Mavor set out to raise funds and find scientists to help him. He wanted to start an underwater archaeological expedition to discover if there were Minoan remains on the sea bed of Thera. He also hoped to discover the original shape of Thera and to excavate five underwater locations where ruins might be found.

In August, 1966, the first expedition set out for Thera using five basic instrument systems:

1) a sonar system—to measure depth
2) the seismic profiler ⎫
3) the magnetometer ⎬ to measure the nature of the earth's crust
4) the gravimeter ⎭
5) a gravity coring system—to analyze samples taken from the bottom of the sea

The results of that first expedition confirmed the following:

1) that the Thera cataclysm was a collapse of the central core of the island rather than a huge central explosion;

2) that rambling waterways surrounding the ancient volcanic cones of Thera coincide with Plato's geometry of the "metropolis";

3) that the original size of the island corresponds to Plato's description;

4) that there was enough evidence (pottery, wall remnants, and other findings) to show that Thera had been heavily populated in Minoan times.

The expedition also brought world renown to the two doctors, in that *The New York Times* (September 4 and 10) reported their finds as Atlantis "discovered."

The following year Dr. Mavor was back again, this time to do a detailed land survey and archaeological excavation. His scientific team uncovered a Minoan palace and a large town buried beneath the volcanic ash near the town of Akroteri, proving that royalty had lived on Thera and enjoyed a standard of living equal to that of Minoan Crete. Dr. Mavor concluded that Thera must have been a strategic maritime center and, as Plato said, probably a religious center as well. These factors would have accounted for the ancient conflicts that the Atlanteans engaged in as they faced increasing pressure from Eastern and Western population movements and which finally ended in warfare and plans for conquest just before the island exploded.

Since 1968, recent excavations on Thera have tended to support Dr. Mavor's theory. Unfortunately, the work has been "inadequately engineered, funded, and staffed" and the expedition has run into problems. Dr. Mavor is confident, however, that the additional proof needed by archaeology will be forthcoming and his research substantiated.

For a full, day-by-day account of Dr. Mavor's exciting story, read his book *Voyage to Atlantis* (G. P. Putnam's Sons). It is straightforward, clear, and complete with many pictures, charts, and diagrams necessary to support his findings. It also includes an excellent bibliography of books and articles written about Atlantis.

The best collection of Atlantean accounts and theories, told in clear, simple style, is James Wyckoff's *The Lost Continent of Atlantis* (G. P. Putnam's Sons). He also includes Dr. Mavor's theory, but as only one of many.

For students interested in scientific detective work, Henry Chapin's *The Search for Atlantis* (Macmillan, Inc.) is an excellent account. Starting out with a detailed study of the past, he shows how anthropologists, archaeologists, geologists, meteorologists, and oceanographers investigate clues from the earth, the atmosphere, and under the sea, as well as from oral tradition and written reports. One day these studies may solve the mystery of the myth of Atlantis.

Students of psychic phenomena may be interested in the "life readings" of Edgar Cayce, as his son tries to prove the existence of Atlantis in *Edgar Cayce on Atlantis*

(Paperback Library). The son suggests that Atlantis was the first place on earth where man changed from spiritual to human form, and thus a study of Atlantis may save us from our future holocaust since we are the reincarnated forms of previous Atlanteans. He also suggests that Atlantis must have had a fantastic technology of TV, laser rays, death rays, and atomic energy before being destroyed.

Myth and the Human Condition

JOSEPH CAMPBELL One of the leading authorities on myth is Joseph Campbell, Professor of Literature at Sarah Lawrence College in New York. He has written and edited over twenty books on mythology including his four-volume study of world mythologies, *The Masks of God* (1959), and his most famous, *Hero with a Thousand Faces* (1972), which is an examination of ancient hero myths and the eternal human struggle for identity. One of his latest books is *Myths To Live By*, a collection of essays in which Campbell examines the myth-making process. Each essay is quite distinctly his, yet shows the influence of Freud and Jung on his theories.

Campbell's thesis is that myths and religions have always followed the same archetypes and can no longer be the exclusive right of a particular race, region, or religion in a modern scientific world. He forces us to see these common denominators we all share because of the myth-making process, and concludes that people must see themselves as part of a world family and allow this knowledge to be of use in fulfilling our human potential. He suggests that since we have a basic need to create myths, these myths should be used constructively as a creative force.

According to Campbell, a myth should fulfill at least four human needs:

(1) Instill a sense of awe or rapture in the human relationship to the mysteries of the universe.

(2) Provide an understanding of the world in accordance with the scientific knowledge of the time.

(3) Support the social order through rites and rituals.

(4) Guide the individual through the psychological traumas of living.

For Campbell, the study of mythology is an extremely important field to examine. It is the cornerstone for building a better society in this modern world still beset with ancient problems. A study of myth is the key to the door of insight. Every person must unlock the door and walk in.

For an interesting review of Campbell's theories, read the *Time* article "The Need for New Myths" (January 17, 1972) or one of his essays in any of his books. To what extent do you agree or disagree with his theories?

Take any myth and find several counterparts to it from other cultures. Try a Campbell analysis of this phenomenon by examining its psychological motivations, its aspect for good or evil, its counterpart in modern society. How does the myth fulfill Campbell's four criteria?

PROJECTS

Part 1.   Greek Mythology

1. Like the early Greeks, we, too, invest lifeless objects with a spirit or human quality. The scarecrow and the pumpkin on Halloween are good examples of this. Make a list of several other objects to which modern man attributes lifelike qualities.

    How is animism used in literature? Write a short description in which you give life to an inanimate object.

2. A science myth, such as the myth of Charybdis and Scylla, is a story that tries to explain the occurrence of a natural phenomenon. Write your own science myth. Here are some suggested topics:

    The Origin of the Stars
    The Creation of Maple Syrup
    How the Salmon Became an Ocean Fish

    Be sure to use a Greek god in your story.

3. Science students would enjoy reading Isaac Asimov's *Words from the Myths* (New American Library). The first four chapters discuss words our language still uses from early myths. Divide the class into small groups and give an illustrated report, using charts, maps and slides, on word origins and scientific explanations.

4. Discuss with your science teacher the origin of the names of the following chemicals:

mercury	promethium
niobium	tantalum
plutonium	titanium
uranium	

5. Make a chart of all the symbols connected with the gods that were used by the early alchemists (e.g. ♂ = Mars). Relate some of these to astrology by

forecasting the characteristics of your classmates born under these planets or signs.

6. Give a report on the significance of the Olympic Games in Greek mythology.

7. Debate the cause of evil in the world and whether man or woman is most responsible for it.

8. Improvise a skit between Prometheus and Epimetheus arguing about the qualities of woman. Be sure to portray the personalities of Prometheus and Epimetheus by using speech characteristics, costumes, and props.

9. Read the story of *Pygmalion* by George Bernard Shaw or listen to a recording of *My Fair Lady*. Compare these versions with the Greek myth of the creation of Galatea.

10. Dionysus is a god who still holds a strong appeal, especially in the theatre. Draw a diagram or show slides of the ancient Greek theatre and explain its connection to Dionysus. How has it evolved from its primitive beginnings?

11. Artists have always used myths for their subject matter. Look up Goya's painting of Cronus eating his children ("Saturn Devouring a Son"). Discuss whether myths were meant to be taken as literally as this. Is there a political metaphor involved in the painting? in the original myth? Draw a picture on a mythological theme or give a talk on the use of myth in art.

12. Give a visual presentation of the Greek Hades and its characters. Use the facilities of your nearest art museum, make slides from your library's art books, or use an opaque projector. How have modern artists depicted death?

13. Draw a magazine cover for *Mad Magazine* or *National Lampoon* which parodies one of the gods. See *National Lampoon* (May, 1972) for its version of the birth of Aphrodite.

14. Using stage makeup and costumes, show how you would portray the character Death for a scene on a battlefield. A picture of Death from Ingmar Bergman's film, *The Seventh Seal* (Janus Films, N.Y.), may be of some help. How does this compare with the Greeks' conceptualization of death?

15. A collage is an artist's attempt to use various materials glued together in an artistic fashion to present a picture or theme. By cutting from magazines,

228

newspapers, and travel folders, make a collage of mythical themes or names of pictures (or all three) to make a point about the modern use of myth in our culture and language.

16. Cut out pictures from advertisements of women generally considered to be beautiful and categorize them according to the characteristics of Hera, Aphrodite, and Athene. Why do people, especially in the Women's Liberation Movement, object to these types of classifications?

    To what extent are attractive woman used as part of the selling feature of a product? How do you feel about this type of advertising?

17. Design a product and invent a name for it, based on one of the Greek gods, his symbol, or a story connected with him. The product may be one of the following: a soap, a car, a newspaper, bubble gum, or one of your own choosing. Then design a print ad campaign using mythology copy and visuals to sell the product.

18. Midas and Epimetheus are similar characters in that they both represent the unthinking buffoon or clown. Make a list of all the movie or television personalities you know who would fit this type and discuss it with the class. Could a similar list be made for the hero or wise man?

19. Film fans will find a wealth of material based on the stories of ancient Greece. *Black Orpheus, Ulysses,* and *Hercules* are some that spring to mind. Using a guide to TV films, look up as many as you can find that utilize myths as a storyline or theme.

20. Plan a film script based on an encounter with one of the gods (for example, a scuba diver discovers Poseidon's palace). Make a short film from this script if you have the equipment available. See the illustrated article on the film *The Birth of Aphrodite* in *The American Cinematographer* (September, 1971).

21. Opera lovers may wish to listen to Gluck's "Orfeo et Eurydice," Monteverdi's "Orfeo," or Offenbach's "Orpheus in the Underworld." Students interested in this music should share their knowledge of the story and the music with the class.

    What other types of music utilize mythology in some manner?

22. Read the poem "The Story of Echo" by John Godfrey Saxe. Write your own poem or ballad about Echo and Narcissus or any other mythological couple.

229

23. Recite the "Ballade of John Barleycorn" or tell the class the story of "The Pied Piper of Hamelin" by Robert Browning. Discuss to what extent they reflect elements similar to Dionysus and his background.

24. Limericks are short five-line poems with a specific meter and rhyme scheme. Compose some myth limericks based on your reading of the myths.

25. Graffiti are short, witty sayings often found on walls, old buildings, or other public places. Using your knowledge of the myths, write a page of myth graffiti. Here are some examples:

> Achilles is a heel
> Clotho spins a mean yarn
> Pan blew it
> Cronus was fed up with his kids
> Prometheus was a pyromaniac
> Narcissus shouldn't make waves

26. Stamp and coin collectors will find much material depicting figures from mythology. Invite a local dealer to illustrate this for you. Perhaps someone you know has such a collection and can explain the myths connected with the images. (See page 10.)

27. Make a mythology scrapbook. Use the following suggestions as a guide for your collection:

   a. art and sculpture of the gods
   b. illustrations and cartoons similar to those in this book
   c. selections from Shakespeare and poetry that name the gods
   d. scenes of Greece and photographs of Greek temples
   e. advertisements
   f. stamps and coins
   g. scientific names from the Greek

Part 2.   Comparative Mythology

Norse Mythology

1. The Viking gods were the gods of Scandinavia. Make a list of the archeological findings in America that are thought to be Viking settlements. See *Reader's Digest* (March, 1973) article "Who Really Discovered America?"

2. Using any of the Thor myths, write or improvise a comedy scene in which all of his impetuous nature, his frustration, and his impatience are brought out. Do not hesitate to exaggerate his good-natured, buffoon-like characteristics or pit him against clumsy, voracious giants. This should be pure slapstick.

3. Make a comparison of the mythical elements in the Anglo-Saxon poem "Beowulf" and those in the myths of the Norse. What Christian elements exist in both? Make a dramatic tape recording of some of the more interesting episodes from "Beowulf."

4. Investigate the religion of the Druids and their center at Stonehenge. Compare your findings with those in an article in *The Catholic Digest* (February, 1971) about "America's Stonehenge."

5. Dualism is a philosophy which states that life is made up of opposite elements: good and bad, love and hate, life and death, etc. Debate this philosophy in light of the two types of gods found in Norse mythology, the Aesir and the Vanir. Be sure to explore where they live and what they stand for.

6. Moral sayings from the Norse are comparable to the Greek fables (Aesop) or the wisdom literature of the *Bible*. Make a comparison of wisdom literature and relate it to the type of culture and environment that must have produced such an attitude toward life. (See page 72.)

7. Design and write a class newspaper based on the news events surrounding Ragnarok. Write from a Norse point of view, the day after the disaster has taken place. Include ads, comics, and sports.

8. Make pendants or *papier mâché* jewelry of the runic letters. Find out what

charms and stories are associated with each letter. Share your findings with the class.

9. Richard Wagner's operatic Ring Cycle, "The Ring of the Niebelungen" is his masterpiece of mythological interweaving of Norse myth and his own interpretations. Musically oriented students might present selections of the opera, synopses of the plots, or production pictures for the class to see and hear.

   The Time-Life four-volume record set is an excellent aid, as it includes notes, pictures, and fine music. The Time-Life three-volume companion set of books on Wagner and his famous opera is also an excellent reference.

Eskimo Mythology

1. There are many articles on the Eskimo, his environment and culture, in past issues of various magazines. Locate these articles in the library using the *Reader's Guide to Periodical Literature*. Through library research make a pictorial essay for a classroom display to help explain Eskimo mythology. *National Geographic* will also be helpful.

2. Eskimo art is admired for its simplicity and its primitive power to capture the spirit of the North. Make a slide presentation of various art museum collections (slides are often available for rental from the museum or they may be made from original art), and tell your own version of an Eskimo myth. Be sure to use sound effects. Pictures on an opaque projector may be substituted for slides.

3. The relationship between Eskimo art and myth may be studied through the following films available from the National Film Board of Canada, New York, N.Y.

   How To Build an Igloo
   Kenojuak: Eskimo Artist
   The Living Stone

4. *Nanook of the North* (Budget Films, Los Angeles) is the original predecessor of the film documentary. In spite of the fact that the filmmaker Robert Flaherty staged much of the footage, this early film (1922) paved the way for many of our attitudes toward the Eskimo today and should be discussed from that point of view.

North American Indian Mythology

1. Compare the myths of other North American Indian tribes with the accounts given in this book.

2. Make an Indian diary or journal in which you record a ten-day trek, under the watchful eye of your gods, to a favorite hunting ground and back. Be sure to record events that show your kinship with nature and the animism that you believe in.

3. Draw or make from papier mâché or plaster surgical dressings some replicas of West Coast Indian masks. Explain the myths connected with them.

4. Astronomy students might report on the various star myths of the West Coast Indians.

5. Write a skit or ballad based on one of the harvest festivals so that you bring out either the ritualistic or the functional aspect of the myth.

6. Make a tape recording of as many Indian songs, records, and taped sound tracks from films as you can locate. Give a presentation explaining their meaning to the class. Scholastic *Scope* (January 31, 1972) has an excellent issue on the Indian, his music and poetry.

Comparative Mythology

1. Define myth in a large enough context to explain the conclusions you have reached from reading comparative mythology.

2. Write an original science myth for any culture you wish. Explain how your myth is consistent with the culture and environment you are writing about.

3. The following books have myths from many countries. Read one of the books and lead a discussion of some aspect or theme that runs through all myths, by using many examples from the stories to prove your point.

> David Creighton, *Deeds of Gods and Heroes* (St. Martin)
> Padraic Colum, *Myths of the World* (Grosset & Dunlap)
> Eth Clifford, *The Magnificent Myths* of Man (Globe)

4. Trace the development of the alphabet by drawing (or copying) the various letters, from Egyptian picture writing to late Roman, on overhead projectuals. For ease in presentation, choose only a few letters and trace their complete development.

5. Go through art books in your local or school library and look for all the symbols that stand for evil or malevolence (e.g. snake, serpent, apples, etc.). Show the pictures and try to explain why these figures stand for the negation of the good life in Western society. What myths do you know that also use these symbols?

6. History students might investigate the historical authenticity of myths of any culture they are interested in. Make an attempt to be a Schliemann by suggesting where some historical finds might be discovered.

7. Geography students might draw topographic maps of the region for a mythological culture they are interested in. Explain what type of myths you would expect to find in that region.

8. Archeology and science students might investigate artifacts that tell us about the mythology of a country in which they are interested.

9. Topics for essays or oral reports:

   a. The stars in mythology
   b. Ancient inventors
   c. Music in the myths
   d. Words from the myths
   e. My favorite god or goddess
   f. Fire in mythology
   g. A letter to. . .(a mythical hero)
   h. Women in mythology
   i. Primitive mythical depictions in art
   j. Archeology and myth

Part 3.   Heroic Literature

The Classical Tradition

1. Read the myth of Psyche and compare the account to our account of the Golden Fleece. Retell the story to the class.

2. Write a book report on Robert Graves' book *Hercules, My Shipmate*. Be sure to relate the voyage of his Argo to the myth.

3. Make charts and diagrams to show the star clusters of Perseus and Andromeda and other related mythological figures such as the constellation of Argo.

4. Do a study of ancient Greek pottery that contains episodes or figures from the Jason and Perseus myths. Explain how pottery is dated and what it reveals about people as well as the art of the time. This information can be found in a museum or in art books.

5. Art students might copy, present slides, or show on an opaque projector the series of paintings on Jason painted by the followers of Pesellino. Herman I. Wechsler's *Gods and Goddesses in Art and Legend* (Washington Square Press) contains reproductions of these paintings.

6. Compare the dramatic presentation of Euripides' *Medea* with the Jason myth. What portrayals of women emerge? Write an essay or debate this issue from a Women's Lib point of view.

7. Two films worth viewing for an understanding of the Greek quest are *The Odyssey: The Central Themes* (Encyclopaedia Britannica Films) and *The Search for Ulysses* (Association Films, N.Y.). What aspect of truth are they examining?

The Medieval Tradition

1. Compare the myths of Siegfried to the King Arthur cycles. Explain their similarities and differences in mythological terms. For a good account of the Siegfried epic, read *The Niebelungenlied,* translated by A.T. Hatto (Penguin).

2. Very distinct similarities exist between Norse and Medieval values. Compare Arthur's Round Table with Odin's Valhalla. Be sure to examine the emphasis on and concept of valor.

3. Look up the legends of Robin Hood. Write a ballad based on your understanding of these stories. Be sure to bring in the mythological elements.

4. Lovers of parody would enjoy reading Stephen Leacock's "Guido the Gimlet of Ghent: A Romance of Chivalry." Turn this story into a puppet show.

5. Write a monologue for Launcelot in which he contemplates his divided loyalties between Arthur and Guinevere.

6. Many romantic tales come from the medieval period. The reader would not want to miss Tristan and Isolde in Bullfinch or Mallory as examples of the medieval hero.

7. Write a book report on Mary Stewart's *The Hollow Hills* (Morrow).
   Other related novels, written in another age but worth reading for their medieval slant, are *Ivanhoe* by Sir Walter Scott and *Don Quixote* by Cervantes.

8. Topics for discussion:
   a. Is the story of Guinevere and the apple mythologically familiar?
   b. Why is Launcelot never fully condemned?
   c. Is Merlin a witch figure on the order of Medea?

The Modern Tradition

1. Collect contemporary poems which reveal any aspect of the quest and write an essay about that facet of your study.
   The Hero's Way: Contemporary Poems in the Mythic Tradition (Prentice-Hall) is an excellent source for getting started, as well as a detailed and scholarly source upon which to base your discussion. Some of the chapter headings are: Versions of the Quest, The Call, The Journey, The Beast, The Double, The Lady, The Rescue, Atonement, The Return.

2. Make a checklist of heroic qualities, including heroes from all ages. Analyze the checklist and tell what insights it reveals.

236

3. Politically oriented students might be interested in comparing the slaying of the beast (St. George and the Dragon idea) as it appears in our modern world. What appearance do our modern knights present?

4. The epic is a literary form of the journey with a tradition stretching back through Milton, Spenser, and Dante to Homer and Vergil. Investigate what modern forms it takes in the novel, epic theatre, the film, and modern epic poetry and report back to the class. Paul Merchant's *The Epic* (Barnes and Noble) has a short but excellent chapter on this aspect.

5. Listen to old radio hero tapes (Superman, The Shadow, The Lone Ranger) or read about them in *The Great Radio Heroes* (Ace). Write a short radio play based on these heroes and their quests, and record it on tape, complete with sound track.

6. Collect newspaper and magazine clippings for a myth display which shows that we are still myth-makers. Supplement this with pictures as well, such as the space shots, new athletic records, etc.

7. Make a collection of comic book heroes and exchange them around the class. After reading these, compare them with the latest TV heroes.

8. Listen closely to the lyrics of many of our modern songs and report your findings as to what our modern heroes are like or what quests are now being undertaken.

9. Art students would enjoy showing society's modern cries for help and how the artist sees the rescue.

10. The "rite of passage" is one aspect of the quest: it is that moment when society declares a juvenile fit to pass as an adult. In some societies it involves actual rituals and tests; in others it occurs with just a celebration. Movies like *The Graduate* and *The Summer of '42* show how this often occurs in Western society. Form an open forum on this topic in which you discuss all facets of this rite in our society. Be sure to discuss both its mythical implications as well as future implications for us and our society. Arnold van Gennep's book *The Rites of Passage* (University of Chicago Press) or a good encyclopedia would be helpful.

Part 4.   Applications of Myth

1. Look through your local television guide and categorize all the programs that you know into their corresponding mythical counterparts. Explain the myths. Apply archetypal criticism to any one of these programs. Be thorough in that you classify each program into its proper genre and predict its necessary outcome each time. For some fun, try this first on some of the noon hour soap operas.

2. Carl Jung's book *Man and His Symbols* (Dell) gives a fascinating account of comparative symbology. Collect your own symbols from art, architecture, and advertising, and write a psychological critique of them.

3. Freud's dream theory came under much criticism in the 1960s. It was said to be too narrow an interpretation resulting from Freud's own Victorian past. As a result, some of his other psychological teachings have fallen into disfavor. Interview your Board or County psychologist (or social worker) to find out what psychological school he belongs to and to what extent Freud is coming back into favor.

4. Make a symbol T-shirt, poster, or display. Include symbols from mythology, astrology, modern highway and conveniences signs, or logos.

5. Investigate the symbols that hobos use to help other travelers-of-the-rail, and report back to the class. (See page 205).

6. The *Bible* is an important source of archetypes for much contemporary literature, especially in the use of names. Read the Book of Genesis and then write an exposé of your findings for one of the following:

    "The Door in the Wall," a short story by H. G. Wells
    "Noah," a poem by Roy Daniells
    "Wedding Procession, From a Window," a poem by James A. Emanuel

7. Authors who write consciously with mythical personages or archetypes in mind have a carefully worked out allegory that provides extra dimensions of meaning and pleasure. Review any of the following:

    Marshall Fishwick, *The Hero, American Style* (McKay)
    Bernard Malamud, *The Natural* (Pocket Books)
    William McIlwain, "Speed, Sex and Heroes" (*The Atlantic*, June 1973)

238

Thomas Tryon, *Harvest Home* (Knopf)
John Updike, *The Centaur* (Knopf)

8. Drama students might like to portray symbols and archetypes through this medium. Several scripts are available for dramatization:

   Eric Berne, *What Do You Say After You Say Hello* (Grove)
   Eugene O'Neill, *The Great God Brown* in *Nine Plays* (Random House)

9. Students interested in dream psychology might like to enact an instance of psychodrama. Use Frederick S. Perls' *Gestalt Therapy Verbatim* (People Press) for examples.

10. Music lovers might investigate the symbols used by musicians in either their lyrics or choice of instruments. For contemporary musicians, the Beatles or Jim Morrison will provide ample evidence. For classical musicians, Wagner's Ring Cycle is excellent. Hundreds of books have been written about the conscious use of symbols in symphonic form and motif.

11. Write a paper on any aspect of the following important mythographers and their books.

   Albert Camus, *Myth of Sisyphus & Other Essays* (Random House)
   John Collier, *All About Eve/Milton's Paradise Lost: Screenplay for the Cinema of the Mind* (Alfred A. Knopf)
   Mircea Eliade, *Patterns in Comparative Religion* (World Publishing)
   Sir James Frazer, *The Golden Bough* (Macmillan)
   Marshall McLuhan & Wilfred Watson, *From Cliché to Archetype* (Viking)

PRONUNCIATION GUIDE

Acheron   'Ak-uh-ron
Achilles   Uh-'kil-eez
Acrisius   Uh-'kris-yus
Adonis   Uh-'don-us
Aeetes, King   Ee-'ee-teez
Aegir   'Ay-jir
Aeolus   'Ee-uh-lus
Aesir   'Ay-sir
Aeson, King   'Ee-son
Agamemnon   Ag-uh-'mem-non
Agnar   'Ahg-nahr
Aiakos   Ay-'yah-kos
Akroteri   Ak-ruh-'tir-ee
Alcmene   Alk-'mee-nee
Alfheim   'Alf-haym
Andromeda   An-'drom-a-duh
Angakok   'Ahng-uh-kok
Angurboda   'Ahng-gur-boh-dah
Antigone   An-'tig-uh-nee
Aphrodite   Af-ruh-'die-tee
Apollo   Uh-'pol-oh
Apollodorus   Uh-pol-oh-'door-us
Apollonius   Ap-uh-'loh-nee-us
Apsyrtus   Ap-'sir-tus
Ares   'Ay-reez
Argonauts   'Ahr-guh-nots
Ariadne   Ar-ee-'ad-nee
Arion   Uh-'ry-un
Artemis   'Art-uh-mus
Athene   Uh-'thee-nee
Atlas   'At-lus

Atropos   'A-truh-pohs
Audhumla   Ow-'thum-la
Aurora Borealis   Uh-'rohr-uh Bohr-ee-'al-us
Balder   'Bahl-duhr
Barri   'Bah-ree
Bedivere, Sir   'Bed-uh-veer
Bellerophon   Buh-'ler-uh-fun
Bergelmir   Ber-'gel-mer
Boeotia   Bee-'oh-shuh
Boreas   'Boh-ree-us
Bragi   'Brah-jee
Breuer, Joseph   'Broi-er
Buddhism   'Boo-dizm
Buri   'Boo-ree
Cadiz   Kuh-'diz
Calais   Ka-'lay
Callisto   Kuh-'lis-toh
Calypso   Kuh-'lip-so
Cape Malea   Muh-'lay-uh
Cape Matapan   Mat-uh-'pan
Cassiopeia   Kas-ee-uh-'pee-yah
Celeus   'Se-li-us
Cepheus   'See-fyoos
Cerberus   'Sir-buh-rus
Ceto   'See-toh
Chaos   'Kay-ahs
Charon   'Kar-un
Charybdis   Kuh-'rib-dus
Cheiron   'Ky-run
Circe   'Ser-see
Cleito   'Kly-toh

Clotho   'Kloh-thoh
Clytemnestra   Kly-tuhm-'nes-truh
Cocytus   Koh-'sy-tus
Colchis   'Kahl-kis
Confucianism   Kun-'fyoo-shuh-niz-um
Crete   Kreet
Critias   'Kri-tee-us
Cronus   'Kroh-nus
Cyclops   'Sy-klops
Cyzicus, King   'Si-zi-kus
Daedalus   'Ded-ul-us
Danae   'Dan-uh-ee
Danaids   'Dan-uh-ids
Daphne   'Daf-nee
Darkalheim   'Dar-kal-haym
Deimus   'Dee-mahs
Demeter   Dih-'meet-ur
Deucalion   Dyoo-'kayl-yun
Dionysus   Die-uh-'nee-sus
Draupnir   'Drowp-ner
Echo   'Ek-oh
Eleusis   Ih-'loo-sus
Elli   'El-lee
Elysian Fields   Ih-'lizh-un
Epimetheus   Ep-ih-'mee-thee-us
Erebus   'Ehr-uh-bus
Eris   'Eh-ris
Eros   'Ehr-ahs
Eteocles   Ee-'tee-oh-kleez
Euripedes   Yuh-'rih-puh-deez

Europa Yuh-'roh-puh	**Hsi Wang-Mu** Shee Wang-Moo	**Menelaus** Men-eh-'lay-us
Eurydice Yuh-'rid-uh-see	**Hugi** 'Hoo-gee	**Midas** 'My-dus
Fenrir 'Fen-reer	**Hugin** 'Hoo-geen	**Mimir** 'Mee-mir
Forseti For-'seh-tee	**Hyperion** Hy-'peer-ee-un	**Minoans** Muh-'noh-uns
Freud, Sigmund Froid	**Icarus** 'Ik-uh-rus	**Minos** 'My-nus
Frey Fray	**Idun** Ee-'doon	**Mjolnir** 'Myol-neer
Freyja 'Fray-uh	**Io** 'Eye-oh	**Modred** 'Moh-dred
Frisians 'Frizh-uns	**Iolcus** 'Ee-ohl-kus	**Moirai** 'Moy-reye
Gades 'Gay-deez	**Ismene** Is-'mee-nee	**Munin** 'Moo-neen
Gadir 'Gah-deer	**Isolde** Ih-'zol-duh	**Muse Calliope** Myooz Ka-'lie-oh-pee
Gaea 'Jee-ah	**Ixion** Ik-'sy-un	
Galahad, Sir 'Gal-uh-had	**Jason** 'Jay-son	**Muspellheim** 'Moos-pel-haym
Galanopoulos Gal-ahn-'op-oh-lus	**Jocasta** Joh-'kas-ta	**Nanna** 'Nah-nah
	Jotars 'Joh-tars	**Narcissus** Nar-'sis-us
Gawaine, Sir Guh'-wayn	**Jotunheim** 'Yoht-uhn-haym	**Niflheim** 'Neefl-haym
Gilgamesh 'Gil-guh-mesh	**Jung, Carl** Yoong	**Od** Ahd
Ginnungagap Gin-'oong-gah-gahp	**Keats, John** Keets	**Odin** 'Oh-dun
	K'ung Fu-tse Koong Fuh-tsay	**Odysseus** Oh-'dis-ee-us
Gjallarhorn 'Yahl-lar-horn	**Kvasir** 'Kuh-vah-seer	**Oedipus** 'Ed-uh-pus
Glauce 'Glaw-see	**Lachesis** Lah-'kee-sis	**Osiris** Oh-'sy-rus
Gorgons 'Gor-guns	**Lao-tze** 'Loud-zuh	**Ovid** 'Ah-vid
Gorlois 'Gor-loh-is	**Larissa** Luh-'ris-uh	**Pandora** Pan-'doh-ra
Graeae 'Gray-yee	**Laius** 'Lay-us	**P'an Ku** Pahn Koo
Guinevere 'Gwin-uh-veer	**Launcelot** 'Lan-suh-lot	**Pegasus** 'Peg-uh-sus
Hades 'Hay-deez	**Leda** 'Leed-a	**Pelias** 'Pee-lee-as
Hecate 'Hek-uh-tee	**Lemnos** 'Lem-nos	**Pelles** 'Pel-leez
Heidrun 'Hayd-roon	**Leodegrance** Lee-'ah-duh-granz	**Peloponnesus** Pe-luh-puh-'nee-sus
Heimdall 'Haym-dahl		
Helle 'Hel-lee	**Lethe** 'Lee-thee	**Percivale, Sir** 'Pur-suh-vul
Hephaestus Hih-'fes-tus	**Leto** 'Lee-toh	**Persephone** Puf-'sef-uh-nee
Hera 'Hee-ra	**Lodur** 'Loh-dur	**Perseus** 'Pur-see-us
Heracles 'Her-uh-kleez	**Loki** 'Loh-kee	**Phegethon** 'Fay-uh-thon
Hermes 'Her-meez	**Lyly, John** 'Lil-ee	**Phineas, King** 'Fin-ee-us
Hermod 'Her-mud	**Mador, Sir** 'May-door	**Phobos** 'Foh-bahs
Hesiod 'Hee-see-ahd	**Maenads** 'Mee-nahds	**Phorcys** 'For-sis
Hodur 'Hoh-dur	**Manitou** 'Man-uh-too	**Phrixus** 'Friks-us
Hoenir 'Hoon-er	**Marmora** Mah-'mor-ah	**Pindar** Pin-dar
Hringhorni Ring-'or-nee	**Medea** Muh-'dee-a	**Plato** 'Play-toh
Hrungnir 'Roong-neer	**Medusa** Mih-'doo-sa	**Polybus** 'Pol-ih-bus

241

Polydectes Pol-uh-'dek-teez
Polyneices Pol-uh-'ny-seez
Polyphemus Pol-ah-'fee-mus
Poseidon Poh-'side-un
Priam 'Pree-um
Proetus Proh-'ee-tus
Prometheus Proh-'mee-thee-us
Pyrrah 'Pir-uh
Rhadamanthys Rad-uh-'man-thus
Ran Rahn
Rhea 'Ree-uh
Roskva 'Rohsk-vah
Satyr 'Sayt-ur
Schliemann, Heinrich Shlee-mahn, 'Hine-rik
Scylla 'Sil-uh
Sedna 'Sed-nuh
Semele 'Sem-uh-lee
Seriphos Sir-'if-us
Shaman 'Shah-mun
Sif Seef
Sig Seeg

Sigyn 'Sig-un
Sisyphus 'Sis-uh-fus
Skrymir Skree-meer
Skuld Skoold
Sleipnir 'Slayp-neer
Sturluson, Snorri 'Stur-loo-son, 'Snor-ree
Styx Stiks
Sun Hou-tzu Sun Hoh-tzoo
Surt Soort
Symplegades Sim-'pleg-uh-deez
Syrinx 'Sir-inx
Tantalus 'Tant-uhl-us
Taoism 'Dau-izm
Tartarus 'Tart-uh-rus
Themis 'Thee-mis
Theseus 'Thee-see-us
Thjaffi 'Thyah-fee
Thjazi 'Thyat-see
Timaeus Ty-'mee-us
Titans 'Tite-uns
Tityus Tit-y-us

Tiu (Tiw) Tee-yoo
Tristram 'Tris-trum
Trolls Trohls
Typhon 'Ty-fahn
Tyr Tuhr
Tyrns Turns
Uranus 'Yoor-uh-nus
Utgard 'Oot-gard
Utgard-Loki 'Oot-gard 'Loh-kee
Uther Pendragon 'Yoo-thur
Valhalla Val-'hal-uh
Valkyries Val-'kir-eez
Vanaheim 'Vahn-uh-haym
Vanir 'Vahn-uhr
Ve Vay
Verdandi Ver-'dahn-dee
Vili 'Vee-lee
Woden 'Woh-d'n
Ygerne Ih-'guhrn
Yggdrasil 'Ig-druh-sil
Ymir 'Ee-muhr
Zeus Zoos

INDEX

S

sacrifice, animal, 105
Saint Michael's Mount, 178
salmon, spirits of, 99
Sangreal, 167, 184–187
Santorini, 222
Satan, 79
satyrs, 18, 26
Schliemann, Heinrich, 36, 141, 165, 215
science myth, 29, 30, 97
Scylla, 23, 164
sea, god of, 60
   See also Poseidon
seasonal growth, in agriculture, 25–26
Sedna, 81, 82
self-determination, in Greek mythology, 33–34, 37
Semele, 11
Seneca Indian tribe, 110
Seriphos, 144, 148
Sha-Lana, 94
Shaman, 82–84, 91, 99, 103
Shen I, 131–132, 135–137
shepherd's pipe, 27
ship, as symbol, 60
"Ship of the Dwarfs," 67
shoes with wings, as symbol, 16
Shu King, The, 124
Siege and Fall of Troy, The, 36
Siege Perilous, 185
Sif, 60
Sig, 78
Sigyn, 59, 77
Sirens, 23, 164
Six Nations, 110–111
Skidbladnir, 61

Skirnir, 66
Skrymir, 69–71
Skuld, 52
Sky Beings, 108–109
Sky Father, 114–115, 122
sky, god of, 8
   See also Zeus
Sky World, 102
Sleipnir, 54–55, 59
snake, as archetype, 205, (literary example) 206–207, 208
"Snake, The," 206
society, Greek, 6
South Star, 120, 122
Sphinx, riddle of the, 218
Spinner, 34
spirits
   in Crow Indian mythology, 114
   in Eskimo mythology, 82–85, 86, 91
   in Haida Indian mythology, 96–97, 99
   in Iroquois Indian mythology, 103, 111
Spiritual Palace, 186
Spring Festival, 103
sprites, 26
star that never moves, the, 106–107
stars, in Indian myths, 120–122
Starvation, 63
Sturluson, Snorri, 46, 79
Styx, 38
suicide, among Eskimos, 92
sun
   in Chinese myths, 127, 129
   in Eskimo myths, 86

   in Haida Indian myths, 96, 118–119, 122
sun, god of. *See* Apollo
Sun Dance, 105, 115
sun shadow, 110–111
superhumans, 8
Superman, 189
Supreme Spirit, in Indian myths, 96, 99, 103, 108, 110
Surt, 79
Sutting, 67–68
sword, in the stone, 170–172
symbols, of Greek gods, 13, 15
sympathy, 124
Symplegades, 155
Syrinx, 26–27

T

taboos, 85
Tacitus, 46
Taoism, 124, 125
Tao-teh-king, 124
Tartarus, 39, 164
Taweskare, 102
Ten Kings, 131
Ten Suns, 131–132
Tennyson, Alfred Lord, (excerpt) 172
terror, god of, 17
Thebes, 216–218
Themis, 34
Theogeny, 141
Thera, (map) 3, 221, 222, 223–224
Theseus, 30, 141, 164
Thjalfi, 68–69
Thjazi, 74–75

ILLUSTRATION

Francesco del Cossa, detail of fresco, Schifanoia, Ferrara, Scala, cover; Courtesy, Museum of Fine Arts, Boston, H.L. Pierce Fund, ii; Giraudon, x-1; Hirmer Photo Archives, Munich, 10; Bruckmann K.G., Munich, 15; Hamlyn Group Picture Library, 24; Courtesy of the Swedish Information Service, 42–43; British Museum, 47 (left), 171, 201; Courtesy of the Norwegian Information Service, 47 (right); Arthur Rackham, 51; National Historical Museum, Stockholm, 55; From *A Book of Ogres and Trolls* by Ruth Manning-Sanders, Methuen Children's Books Ltd., Robin Jacques, artist, 62–63; The National Museum, Copenhagen, 69; Royal Ontario Museum, Toronto, 83, 84, 96, 106, 107; Kenojuak © 1960, Courtesy West Baffin Co-operative Association, 92; Courtesy of the British Columbia Provincial Museum, Victoria, 97, 98, 112; C.P. Picture Service, Toronto, 100; Courtesy of National Collection of Fine Arts, Smithsonian Institution, 114; The Denver Art Museum, 118; Smithsonian Institution National Anthropological Archives, 120; The Thomas Gilcrease Institute of American History and Art, Tulsa, Oklahoma, 123; The Cleveland Museum of Art, John L. Severance Fund, 125 (left); Spink and Son, Ltd., London, 125 (center); Museo D'Arte Orientale, Rome, 125 (right); Chinese Classic Art Publishing House, Peking, 126; Courtesy of the American Museum of Natural History, 127; Seattle Art Museum, 128; The Minneapolis Institute of Arts, 129; Nelson Gallery-Atkins Museum, Kansas City, Missouri, 133; Courtesy of the Smithsonian Institution, Freer Gallery of Art, Washington, D.C., 136–137; The Pierpont Morgan Library, 138–139; From Vol. III, *Troy: The Sixteenth Settlement,* Part 2, Plates by Carl W. Blegen et al (© 1953 by Princeton University Press). Reprinted by permission of Princeton University Press and the University of Cincinnati, 143; Uffizi Gallery, Florence, 147; Louvre, Paris, 159; Fellows' Library of Winchester College, 166; Radio Times Hulton Picture Library, London, 181; The Mansell Collection, London, 184–185; Pablo Picasso, *Study for Bull's Head,* 1937. On extended loan to The Museum of Modern Art, New York, from the artist, 195; Gianni Mattioli Foundation, Milan, Italy, 217.

ACKNOWLEDGMENTS

Faber & Faber, Ltd.: For "The Snake" from *Collected Poems 1927–57* by Emily Dickinson. Robert Graves: For "Escape" by Robert Graves. Harcourt Brace Jovanovich, Inc.: For "Advice to a Prophet" from *Advice to a Prophet and Other Poems* by Richard Wilbur; © 1959 by Richard Wilbur. Houghton Mifflin Company: For "The Minotaur" from *Birthdays from the Ocean* by Isabella Gardner; © 1955 by Isabella Gardner McCormick. McGraw-Hill Ryerson Ltd.: For "Filling Station" from *The Rocking Chair and Other Poems* by A. M. Klein. For "The Golden Ship" from *Selected Poems of Emile Nelligan,* trans. by P. F. Widdows. The Viking Press, Inc. and G. Duckworth and Co., Ltd.: For "One Perfect Rose" from *The Collected Dorothy Parker;* © 1973 by National Association for the Advancement of Colored People.